THE COMPLETE GUIDE TO
REMIXING

Produce Professional Dance-Floor Hits on Your Home Computer

Erik Hawkins

Berklee Media

Vice President: Dave Kusek
Dean of Continuing Education: Debbie Cavalier
Business Manager: Linda Chady Chase
Technology Manager: Mike Serio
Marketing Manager, Berkleemusic: Barry Kelly
Senior Designer: David Ehlers

Berklee Press

Sr. Writer/Editor: Jonathan Feist
Writer/Editor: Susan Gedutis
Production Manager: Shawn Girsberger
Marketing Manager, Berklee Press: Jennifer Rassler
Product Marketing Manager: David Goldberg

ISBN 0-87639-044-0

1140 Boylston Street
Boston, MA 02215-3693 USA
(617) 747-2146

Visit Berklee Press Online at
www.berkleepress.com

DISTRIBUTED BY

HAL•LEONARD®
CORPORATION
7777 W. BLUEMOUND RD. P.O. BOX 13819
MILWAUKEE, WISCONSIN 53213

Visit Hal Leonard Online at
www.halleonard.com

11 10 09 08 07 06 05 04   5 4 3 2 1

To Kai, my son.

You are my inspiration.

Contents

CD Tracks

1. ReCycled Drum Loop (chapter 3, chapter 8)

2. Micro-Edit on a Bass Performance (chapter 8)

3. Repairing Time-Compressed Lead Vocals (chapter 9)

4. Lyric Edit (chapter 9)

5. VocAlign (chapter 9)

6. Repairing Out-of-Tune Lead Vocals (chapter 9)

7. Open Hi-Hat on the Upbeats (chapter 10)

8. Typical Drum Patterns (chapter 10)

9. Rhythm Elements with Delays (chapter 10)

10. Groove Quantize (chapter 10)

11. Rearranging a Breakpoint-Edited Drum Loop (chapter 10)

12. MIDI Performance Double Time (chapter 10)

13. Triggered Hi-Hat Pattern (chapter 10)

14. Audio to MIDI Note Converter (chapter 11)

15. Standard Bass Lines (chapter 11)

16. Bass Line with Portamento (chapter 11)

17. Chords with Fast and Slow Attacks (chapter 11)

18. Arpeggiating Chords (chapter 11)

19. Filter Sweep (chapter 11)

20. Typical Chord Progressions (chapter 11)

21. Lead Line Examples (chapter 11)

22. Counterpoint Melodies and Odd Beat Counts (chapter 11)

23. Realistic Drum Fills (chapter 12)

24. Drum Machine Snare Rolls (chapter 12)

25. Crescendo and Decrescendo (chapter 12)

26. Dramatic Pause (chapter 12)

27. Synth Swells (chapter 12)

28. Backwards Reverb (chapter 12)

29. Changing Keys (chapter 13)

30. Tempo Changes (chapter 13)

31. From Straight to Funky (chapter 13)

32. Whole Mix Effects (chapter 13)

33. Effects Automation (chapter 13)

34. Keyed Gate Effects (chapter 13)

35. Graintable Effects (chapter 13)

36. Periodic MIDI Controller Curves (chapter 13)

37. Random Patch Changes (chapter 13)

38. Echoing Lead Lines (chapter 13)

39. Stutter Edits (chapter 13)

40. Tape-Style Edits (chapter 13)

41. Scratch Your Own Tracks (chapter 13)

42. Transforming with ReCycle (chapter 13)

43. Dirty Sounding (chapter 13)

44. Turntable Mimic (chapter 13)

45. Get on the Group Effects Bus (chapter 14)

46. Compression (chapter 14)

47. Hum Eliminator (chapter 14)

48. Panning and Stereo Effects (chapter 14)

49. Reverb for Near or Far (chapter 14)

50. Pre and Post Mastering (chapter 15)

51. Live Sequencing (chapter 17)

Acknowledgments

Contributions to this book came from so many different sources that it's a bit overwhelming to try to name them all. At the top of the list, I would especially like to thank all of the artists who contributed quotes. As a contributing writer for publications like *Mix* and *Remix* magazines, it has been my privilege to interview many great artists over the years. I feel like I've gotten the inside scoop on lots of killer production techniques thanks to the willingness of these artists to share their trade secrets during our conversations. I realize that to share a production trick is a conscious decision, not made lightly, and I applaud artists like BT, Deepsky, Thunderpuss, and Dave Audé for openly discussing techniques that have taken them years to develop. It's exciting to be given the permission to include their words in *The Complete Guide to Remixing*.

There is no way that I could have learned how to remix without the proper gear, so I must acknowledge all of the exceptionally creative and talented folks behind today's wonderful music applications and equipment. Companies that gave me support specifically regarding products featured in this book include, in no particular order: Digidesign, Korg, MOTU, Cakewalk, Steinberg, Emagic, Glyph Technologies, M-Audio, Mackie, TC Electronic, Antares, and Ina-GRM. Several artist/press relations representatives that have really come through for me in recent years are: Chandra Lynn (Digidesign), Jim Cooper (MOTU), Brian McConnon (Steinberg), Clint Ward (Emagic), Kyle Ritland (Mackie), Leslie Buttonow (Korg), Peter Glanville (Glyph Technologies), and Marsha Vdovin (Montara Creative Group representing M-Audio).

Then there's my back-line, that network of family and friends without whose support completing this book would have been impossible. My parents deserve extra special thanks for pulling out all the stops and coming to help baby-sit their grandson, as well as their son, for a couple of weeks while I completed the book's final draft. Jason Bowman, you're so much more than an intern, you're an assistant (albeit, working on an intern's wages) whose contributions to "the cause" are truly invaluable. Jeff Roberts and Jack Edward Sawyers of 2RS Entertainment Studios, thank you for the studio space, I really appreciate your support and trust. My friends Maxwellhouse and Seganti, the fact that you both offered to help me out during my many months of writing really touched me.

Writing this book has been a longstanding dream of mine, so I must thank Debbie Cavalier (Dean of Continuing Education) for the opportunity to publish *The Complete Guide to Remixing*. Jonathan Feist (Senior Writer/Editor at Berklee Press), your editing chops are tops, working with you has been a pleasure. The incredible indie artists, Artemis, Sakai, and Lygia Ferra; your music is amazing and deserves to be heard the world over. Thank you so much for allowing me to remix your tracks and include excerpts from these remixes on this book's audio CD.

Introduction

Before today's DJs began pioneering live remixing on stage, back in the glory days of disco, producers and engineers (Like Shep Pettibone and Tom Moulton, the father of the first continuous play "mix tape") worked in major studios splicing 2-track tape to create extended versions of songs and remixing multitrack tape recordings. This was often done at a high cost to the record label that commissioned the remix. However, there was little choice in the matter because the tape editing and multitrack remixing required large tape machines and mixing consoles that were the exclusive domain of expensive studios.

Despite all that recording equipment and those lavish budgets, only songs that were at, or near, a dance tempo were good candidates for a dance remix. You could change a tape machine's playback speed, but only conservative tempo changes could be made because the pitch of the material being played back would also change. Stand-alone time compression/expansion processors that could change a track's tempo without affecting its pitch (and vice versa) were available, but they were often prohibitively priced and didn't sound very good.

Today, thanks to recent advances in personal computer technology and music software programs, the tracks from practically any song, regardless of their original tempo, can be digitally altered to work over a huge range of tempos and keys. This technology is a driving force behind the popularity of remixing, because just about anybody with a powerful enough desktop (or laptop) computer and the proper software has the potential to produce a hit remix. Remixing is a lot of fun, it's creatively fulfilling, and your homespun remixes might land your name in lights and generate cash flow. Who knows, you might even make a career of it.

TOOLS OF THE TRADE

Computers and music software have emerged as indispensable tools for remixers. Digital audio sequencer programs combine multitrack audio recording and waveform editing, virtual instruments and effects, and MIDI sequencing into single cohesive applications. Examples of the best digital audio sequencers include: Emagic's *Logic Audio Platinum*, Digidesign's *Pro Tools*, MOTU's *Digital Performer*, Cakewalk's *Sonar XL*, and Steinberg's *Cubase SX*. Even a few programs lacking multitrack audio have proven their remixing metal, such as Propellerhead's *Reason*. Programs like these have been the breeding ground for new music: vessels where technology, culture, and traditional music principles come together.

Remixing is the wonderful union of today's incredible electronic music equipment with basic music theory. It's impossible to discuss one without the other. Talking about the music in a remix requires talking about the gear. Conversely, talking about how to engineer a great remix requires using some music theory terms.

IS THIS BOOK FOR YOU?

The Complete Guide to Remixing is intended for those who already own a digital audio sequencer and want to learn how to use the program to produce inspired remixes. Chances are you can still get something out of this book if you don't have the software, but it's crucial that you at least understand a digital audio sequencer's basic operations. For example, you should understand how to record a track, sequence a MIDI part, quantize a performance, automate an effect, instantiate a virtual instrument, and get around the software's Arrange window. Without this background, it will be very difficult to understand the technical portions of this book.

In terms of traditional music background, you don't need to read sheet music or be proficient at any particular instrument. However, you will find it very useful to at least know the names of the notes on a keyboard, have a general knowledge of scales and chords, have a clue about time signature, meter, the divisions of bars and beats, and be familiar with popular song structures. Most people who know the basics of a digital audio sequencer also know these basic music skills. If this rudimentary knowledge of music is over your head, begin by taking a few piano lessons, and read a book that outlines the basics of music theory and harmony.

It's true that great remixes have been done with far fewer skills. Talent and a clear sense of what people want to hear on the dance floor can overcome a lot. For when all is said and done, the principle requirement of a great remix is that it rocks the house.

THE BASIC STUDIO

All you really need to get started remixing is a current computer (no more than a couple of years old) with a sound card, and a digital audio sequencer. There are, of course, other peripheral components that can add substantially to your production arsenal, and I bring these products up throughout this book. However, integrating these products into your studio is not the focus, here. For more on that subject, I recommend my book, *Studio-in-a-Box* (published by ArtistPro and distributed by Hal Leonard), which is a fairly comprehensive guide to understanding and learning how to set up a computer-centered studio (like those used by top remixers).

Since different brands of digital audio sequencers have so many similarities, including similar windows, features, and many basic operating principles, most remixing production techniques are easily translated between all the programs. Though there may be a trick that one program can do that the others can't, the digital audio sequencer you choose isn't as important as knowing your way around your software in order to follow along with my examples. When I do discuss a production technique that is unique to a particular program, I'll try to make that clear.

USING THIS BOOK

Remixing requires specialized production skills and a good familiarity with the dance music genres. This book will guide you through both the fundamentals and advanced techniques of crafting hit remixes using your personal computer. Most aspects of the remixing process are covered: understanding the essential remixing tools, procuring artist tracks, learning the production tricks, creating dance-floor friendly arrangements, getting a good mix, releasing a single, and having your remix heard and played by DJs. Chapters are organized to follow the usual sequence of production steps during a remix. So work on your remix while you're reading along.

The included Audio CD features examples of production and arrangement techniques. Some of the examples are short excerpts of a solo track to illustrate a specific technique, while others are a combination of elements to show how different parts work together. A narrative

accompanies each track, explaining what you are hearing. Whenever there is a CD track that accompanies an example in the book, you'll see this icon:
While you'll want to listen to the audio examples as you're reading the book, feel free also to just casually listen to the CD simply for the sake of soaking up ideas. The CD's complete track listing can be found on page vi.

Throughout the book, you'll find tips from the industry's best remix artists and DJs. Contributors include: BT (Brian Transeau), Dave Audé, Deepsky (J. Scott G and Jason Blum), and Thunderpuss (Barry Harris and Chris Cox). To learn more about all of these remarkable artists, see Appendix D.

This book covers a lot of ground, and you probably won't use all of these techniques in a single remix. But keep in mind, these production and arrangement methods will remain more or less the same for years to come, regardless of new technology and the latest fads. These are tried and true techniques that have been pounding dance floors for years. So you can be sure this book will be handy to have in your studio for some time as a source of inspiration and fresh production ideas.

SECTION I
Getting Started

CHAPTER 1

History

Remixing live with a pair of turntables and a DJ mixer took off in the early 1980s with DJs (such as the late, great Jam Master Jay of Run DMC, see figure 1.1) adding their own musical elements to commercially available songs during their sets. (Jam Master Jay mixed rock guitar samples with hip-hop beats and came up with the hit remake of Aerosmith's "Walk This Way.") Rather than just playing the same old songs straight through, like everybody else, the most inventive DJs (such as Kool Herc, Francis Grasso, and Larry Levan) figured out how to control the duration and intensity of the songs they played. By using two copies of the same record, they could extend a song indefinitely, while at the same time dropping in extra beats, sound effects, and scratches to build crescendos and make musical changes.

Mixing several different elements together on stage has to be done in time. So as not to disturb the groove, every sound and segue must be perfectly synchronized to the original track's tempo. This skill is called "beat matching" and is done by manually adjusting the beats-per-minute (BPM) of one record to match the BPM of another record. DJ turntables have a pitch fader (see figure 1.2) that allows the platter's rotation speed to be easily and smoothly controlled to make tempo changes. (To learn more about such DJ tricks, read Stephen Webber's *Turntable Technique: The Art of the DJ*, published by Berklee Press.)

Before long, DJs were playing the *a cappella* (vocal only) versions from singles (such as Gloria Gaynor's "I Will Survive" or the Eurythmics "Sweet Dreams") and beat matching completely new backing music using several different records. The most skilled practitioners even added a third turntable and sometimes a drum machine to their setup. This type of remixing is called "live remixing," as opposed to "remix production," which is done in the studio. It's important to recognize that these two types of remixing require different, though related, skills. The best live remixers

FIGURE 1.1 Run DMC's Jam Master Jay (left). Jam Master Jay is one of the indisputable pioneers of turntablism and remixing.

are expert turntablists, while the top studio remixers are skilled producers, composers, and often, excellent musicians.

FIRST OFFICIAL IN-STUDIO REMIX

A version of remix production actually began before live remixing, with 2-track tape editing.

> *Perhaps the earliest and most influential remix was legendary New York disco DJ Walter Gibbons' eleven-minute remix of Double Exposure's "Ten Percent" in 1976, which laid out the foundation that most remixers adhere to today. Gibbons took an average-length song and extended it to full eleven-minute dance workout by repeating certain sections and by adding extended intros and outros with repetitive beats to make the record easier to mix with other records. He also applied a variety of effects such as delays and phasing to the mix to give the song those hypnotic effects that go over so well on the dance-floor.*

—Chris Gill (Gilla Monsta)
editor of *Remix* Magazine (1999–2002)

Photo: Jason Bowman

Figure 1.2 Technic's SL-1200 Turntable. This turntable, with its pitch fader (right) for smoothly changing a record's playback speed, is the forerunner of all of today's DJ turntables and the inspiration for many music remixing products.

Home Studio Revolution

The development of live remixing coincided with the start of the "home studio revolution." Some of the very first affordable MIDI (Musical Instrument Digital Interface, see figure 1.3) instruments also began to show up in the early 1980s. MIDI is a communication protocol that was developed by several top electronic musical instrument manufactures as a standard means for interfacing all of their products. For example, MIDI can be employed to make a drum machine and a synthesizer workstation perform parts in time with each other. With the advent of MIDI, just about anybody could get several electronic instruments to work together for a totally self-contained system—perfect for remix production.

By the early 1990s, the market was awash with reasonably priced studio gear—all the gizmos you needed to build your own home studio: mixing boards, effects units, samplers, microphones, preamps, and multitrack recorders. Musicians and producers jumped at the creative opportunities these new recording technologies and electronic instruments brought to their palettes. Technology was finally making the dream of the home studio an affordable reality. With the purchase of the right gear, we were free at last to follow the recording muse from start to finish, totally unfettered by the high hourly rates of major studios.

Hip-hop and house jockeys soon realized that this gear was not just for recording engineers and major studios; they could record beats and remixes of their own. Producing custom tracks in the home studio (like those of Frankie Knuckles and John "Jellybean" Benitez) and then pressing them to vinyl was a great way of creating ready-made material for their DJ sets. And so began a wonderful time of experimentation

(A)

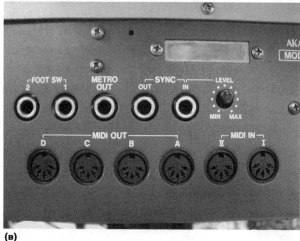

(B)

Figure 1.3 (A) Akai's MPC-60 II Sampling Drum Machine. The MPC-60 II was an early model in the popular MPC drum machine line, and **(B)** featured MIDI In and Out ports.

> *Home studio technology, especially the advances in computer technology, have led to an incredible increase in remixing activities. Thanks to computer software that lets you cut up, pitch shift and time stretch audio, almost anyone with a good idea can create a remix.*
>
> —Chris Gill (Gilla Monsta)
> editor of *Remix* Magazine (1999–2002)

Going Forward

As the technology for audio recording and composing continues to improve and become more affordable, the resources for remixing have never been better. The amazing advances in computers, music software, and audio peripherals have made this especially true. Opportunities for remixing have also grown, as independent artists and major labels alike have opened their doors to the wonderful creative and business possibilities that remixers bring to the table. With some basic gear, knowledge, and the production techniques discussed in the following chapters, anyone interested can get started remixing.

> *It's a great time to get into remixing.*
>
> —Pablo La Rosa, Tune Inn Records

and discovery, with home studios of every level acting as forums for the exchange of ideas between turntablists, musicians, producers, and equipment manufacturers. There are certainly other social, political, and economic forces that shaped remixing (as is the case with all art forms), but by and large, it's the phenomenon of "DJ meets home-studio enthusiast" that has cultivated so many of the production techniques used by today's remix producers.

CHAPTER 2

Finding Songs to Remix

The first step in creating a remix is to find song material to remix. Ideally, this will be either *a cappella* (a vocals only mix), or some type of multitrack recording of the original song. Of course, you could grab a stereo mix of a song, such as any track off a commercially released CD, then cut up and rearrange the song's sections, and even layer custom sounds on top of the new arrangement, but working this way is not ideal. It's much preferable to get your hands on a song's multitrack recording, for complete control over its individual tracks (like lead vocals, bass line, guitars, drum parts, and so on) before they are blended and set in the stereo mix. For example, if you like a song's lead vocals, strings, and conga tracks, but nothing else, just take those tracks from the multitrack recording for your remix.

Unfortunately, procuring a song's multitrack recording, especially of a major recording artist, is very difficult unless you are already a well-known remixer. Luckily, there are a couple of options, such as "breakout tracks," a batch of sampled loops taken from the original multitrack recording and made available to aspiring remixers. The other alternative is finding a single release with an *a cappella* version so that, at the very least, you can work with a stereo mix of just the vocals.

Breakout Tracks

A great resource for breakout tracks is remixing contests. Web sites sponsoring a remix contest will often post the breakout tracks for you to download. The audio file format is usually WAV (designated by the document extension, .wav), and the loops are generally between two and eight bars in length. Use a search engine such as Google (www.google.com) to find out about remixing contests on line.

Sonic Foundry, the makers of *Acid* (a popular multitrack loop program), maintains a Web site for its users,

ACIDplanet (www.acidplanet.com, see figure 2.1). There are regular remix contests with lots of breakout tracks, and even a free, limited features version of *Acid* for the PC. It's easiest to download the posted WAV files to a PC because their compression format is native to this computer platform. (You'll need a program like *WinZip* to unpack the .exe files.) There are programs for unpacking .exe files on a Mac running OS 9.2.2 (such as *ZipIt*), but nothing is available for OSX at the time of this writing. Magazines that routinely come bundled with a CD-ROM containing samples and software demos, such as Future Music (www.futuremusic.co.uk) and Computer Music (www.computermusic.co.uk), will sometimes publish breakout tracks too.

FIGURE 2.1 Sonic Foundry's ACIDplanet Web Site. A page at the ACIDplanet site where breakout tracks for a current contest are made available for downloading.

Mixman

There are tons of breakout tracks available for purchase and free download at Mixman's Web site (www.mixman.com). However, these samples (called Track files; their extension is .trk) can only be used with the company's remixing software, *Mixman Studio* and *Mixman StudioXPro* (see figure 2.2). (The Mixman applications are PC only.) But once loaded and sequenced in Mixman, they can be exported as standard WAV files for use in any digital audio sequencer. Having *StudioXPro* in your remixing arsenal is not only handy for converting Track files, but also because you can create unique performance effects with its real-time effect controller element, and use it to import and scratch your own samples and loops (see chapter 13).

A Cappella Singles

There are usually several different versions of a song on a single. Sometimes one of the versions will be *a cappella*. This version is almost always created during the same mixing session as the song's main mix. The music tracks are simply muted, leaving only the lead and backing vocals. An advantage of working with an *a cappella* mix is that the sound of the vocals, their levels and effects processing, are identical to the song's main mix. The disadvantage of working with

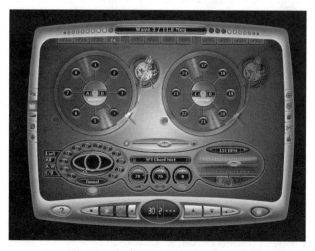

FIGURE 2.2 *Mixman StudioXPro.* Mixman is a company that offer's breakout tracks for remixing in their *Mixman StudioXPro* remixing program, for PC. However, it's possible to export these breakout tracks as standard audio files for playback in another program.

an *a cappella* mix is that the lead and backing vocals can not be separated, and effects such as delay and reverb can't be removed and might sound odd after a big tempo change.

Finding an *a cappella* version may be as simple as a visit to your local record store, but likely not. Most current singles do not include an *a cappella* version, and instead feature a variety of dance remixes. Singles of the mid to late '70s, '80s, and early '90s are more likely to include an *a cappella* version. But as remixing has become more and more popular, such singles are coveted and becoming increasingly difficult to find. Looking through used record and CD collections before they have been picked over by other remixers and DJs is probably your best bet for finding a real "gem." Performing a text search for "*a cappella* versions," using an online search engine, may also be helpful, giving you leads to MP3 files, specialty record dealers, and private parties selling rare 12″ singles.

VOCAL SEPARATION VOODOO

If you just can't seem to find an *a cappella* version, there is a method for separating the lead vocals from a stereo mix that occasionally works. For this trick, you will need to find a single that includes a radio mix and an instrumental version of the radio mix. By perfectly lining up both versions in your digital audio sequencer (all the hardware and software needed for this operation is discussed in chapters 4 and 5), it is sometimes possible to use the instrumental to phase cancel all the music of the radio mix, leaving only the vocals intact. This works because a waveform that is aligned to a 100-percent out-of-phase copy of itself, results in no signal. Be aware that if the instrumental was changed in any way (like it was mixed or mastered differently) from the radio version, this technique will not work, because the waveforms of the two versions are no longer identical.

STEP 1. Line up the instrumental with the radio mix. Make sure that the waveforms' peaks and valleys of the instrumental are perfectly aligned with those of the radio mix. You can check this alignment by comparing sections of the radio mix that has no vocals to its counterpart section in the instrumental. Zoom all the way in to make sure that the waveforms are lined up at the sample level.

STEP 2. Make both stereo files mono. The easiest way of doing this is to pan each side (a stereo file contains two channels, a Left and Right side) of each track to the center pan position (for more on panning, see chapter 14). Alternately, some programs have Stereo to Mono processing option among their file-based, offline effects.

STEP 3. Invert the phase of the instrumental mix. Most programs have a phase-invert processing option among their offline effects. Some plug-ins, such as Digidesign's stock EQ II plug-in, feature a phase-reverse button.

STEP 4. If your waveforms are perfectly lined up, and the output levels of both mixes are identical, playing back both mixes at the same time should phase cancel the music. If all or most of the music is successfully cancelled out, bounce the resulting lead vocal track to disk as a new file.

STEP 5. If there are still remnants of the backing music between words, these can sometimes be suppressed with a "noise gate" (explained in chapter 14).

Remixing Independents

There's no rule that says you must remix *Billboard* hits and name artists. Lots of unsigned artists and lesser-known independent labels have top-notch songs that could benefit from a remix. Artists and labels such as these are much easier to reach and more receptive about negotiating the use of a song's multi-track recording. Though a remix of a hit song has the advantage of familiarity to propel it into the dance charts, a stellar remix of a great indie song can be a dance-floor hit as well (for example, the big Dirty Vegas hit, "Days Gone By").

Web sites such as MP3 (www.mp3.com) and Garageband (www.garageband.com) are excellent resources for auditioning indie songs and making contacts. Getting out to see local artists perform in your neighborhood clubs is also a good way of finding talent. Don't worry too much about genre, when looking for material, as just about any song has the potential to be remixed. Do keep your ears peeled for catchy vocal hooks and memorable lead instrument lines, because these are key to any successful song—dance remix or otherwise.

When approaching an indie artist, be prepared to share some of your best and most recent work. When you're just getting started, it isn't important that you have a hit remix under your belt, but your work should be of a high caliber and sound ready for commercial release. Any artist you speak with will want to feel confident that if they give you permission to remix one of their songs, you will treat it with respect. They will also want to feel that the remix will not be released without their authorization and that the multitrack recording, breakout tracks, or *a cappella* mix will only be used by you, for this remix. Once you've completed the remix, be prepared that they may not like it and won't want it released. In that situation, you have little recourse; it is, after all, their song. But on the more optimistic side, if they love your remix, then working together, you may be able to pool your financial resources to release a single.

Major Labels

Major label artists are unlikely to grant permission to remix their work unless you have a few solid remixes under your belt. Before approaching labels, you will need a demo of your best material. Master three or four of your most successful remixes and burn excerpts of these to an audio CD. Put all of your contact information on the CD's label, then use this as your calling card for introducing your remixing talents.

Most major labels will not accept unsolicited demos because there's no way that their staff can listen to all of the material that comes pouring in each day. This means that you will need an introduction—somebody who is familiar with your skills and can put in the good word for you. If you don't know such a person, make some friends. The receptionist can be as good a place to start as any, and it's their job to know the names of everybody that works at the label.

If the label thinks you have a shot at nailing the style of remix they are looking for, you may be given the opportunity to submit a rough draft. This is standard practice, even for remixers who are reasonably well known. The label supplies a digital audio tape (DAT) or, preferably, a data CD containing the song's tracks, and then it's up to you to impress them with your remixing skills. Don't expect to get paid big bucks, in the beginning. However, if the label does not pay you good money up front, you should ask for a percentage of record sales so that you can at least make some money on the back end. It's reasonable to ask for a couple of thousand dollars as a flat fee after you've proven your remixing skills; below this, make sure to negotiate for points on units sold.

> When I first started remixing, in the early '90s, everything would come in on DAT; they were called "part DATs." The process has changed drastically since then. What's cool now is that most everybody is using Pro Tools, so often I'm just sent complete Pro Tools session on a couple of CDs. It's great, I don't have to convert anything, everything is right there. I can go through the parts and use some guitars or maybe the room mics from the drums. There are a lot more elements available now.
>
> —(BT) Brian Transeau

Copyright Notice

When you remix a song, you are likely using somebody's copyrighted material. The parts that you remix, whether from a multitrack recording or downloaded breakout tracks, are the property of the copyright holders, probably the artist and record label. It is illegal to distribute or profit from a remix that uses somebody else's material without their written consent. For the most part, remixes are for personal use only, until otherwise agreed upon between yourself and the original song's owner(s). (The legal implications of remixing are discussed further in chapter 16.)

Sound libraries (discussed at length in the next chapter) that contain audio samples and loops (a sample of a performance that when played back to back, loops seamlessly) are also a big part of remixing. For example, many remixes include a combination of breakout tracks and sound library elements. Though a sound library's samples and loops may sound similar to breakout tracks, they are subject to an entirely different set of copyright rules. When you purchase a sound library, you are buying the rights to use that library's samples and loops in your projects, personal or otherwise. Copying a sound library's files from a friend does not entitle you to use those sounds, because the license is nontransferable. Sound designers, just like songwriters, work hard to create quality products, and this needs to be respected by purchasing the libraries that you intend to use.

CHAPTER 3

Sound Library

It's nearly impossible to create a professional sounding remix unless you have a good library of sounds at your fingertips. Samples and loops are essential building blocks for remixing, so having plenty of sounds saved on your computer's hard drive, and intelligently organized to make finding files a snap, will make producing a remix that much more enjoyable. Subsequently, developing your own custom library plays an important role in defining your sound.

There are three basic file types around which to build your sound library: audio samples, MIDI samples, and sound module presets. *Audio samples* are standard sound files (WAV, AIFF, and Digidesign's SDII), including loops and single-shot sounds (samples that are not looped). *MIDI samples* are sequences that have been played or programmed and saved as a Standard MIDI File (SMF). Hardware and software sound modules generally ship with their own set of stock *presets* (factory-programmed sounds for use by the module), and additional *presets* are usually for sale through third party sound developers, and sometimes free for downloading through Internet user groups.

Sample Formats

A *sample* is a recorded sound. The two most common types of samples are hits and loops. A *hit* is a short, single-shot, percussive sound, such as a kick drum, cymbal, or the clank of a pipe. Hits that are related, or simply sound good together, are often organized into a *kit*, like the samples of a tuned drum set. A *loop* is a sample of a performance that has been edited to repeat seemlessly when the audio file is played end to end. Drum beats are the most common loops, but chord progressions, melodies, and even sound effects are all possible candidates for looping. Kits and loops are an important part of a sound library. Kits are essential for adding extra percussion parts, fills, and playing your own beats, while loops are a cornerstone for building up beat-matched grooves.

Different platforms used to prefer different audio file formats. WAV files (having the file extension .wav) are native to the PC, and AIFF files (with the extension .aif) are native to Apple computers. SDII files (designated by .sd2) are the original file type of Digidesign's *Pro Tools* software. Most applications today, no matter the platform, will read all three types, even if the program itself only works with one. As a result, there's no need to worry much about your samples' formats. However, if you are buying a sample CD-ROM and you have a choice of file formats, select the type that is native to your system. That's usually a safe bet.

AUDIO CD FILES

The music tracks contained on audio CDs are not any of the three standard, computer sound-file formats. Even though your computer can play back an audio CD, your digital audio sequencer cannot use an audio CD track until it has been converted to one of the standard sound file types. To do this, you will likely need a stand-alone application like *QuickTime Pro*, or a waveform editing application like Peak by Berkeley Integrated Audio Software (Bias). Some digital audio sequencers (such as *Digital Performer* and *Cubase SX*) include a feature for importing audio CD tracks. Stay away from programs that convert audio CD Tracks specifically to MP3 files, because this will degrade the audio; MP3 files are inferior to standard sound files (WAV, AIFF, and SDII), and since most digital audio sequencers will not play MP3 files without first converting them, the result is a lesser quality standard sound-file.

Loops for Sale

There's a wealth of great loop libraries available covering just about every instrument and musical style you can imagine. A company that offers several titles developed by dance music pioneers (such as Fatboy Slim, Coldcut, and Vince Clark) is AMG. Another manufacturer with titles by well-known music figures (BT and Public Enemy) is EastWest. Both of these companies are also good candidates for titles that are not specifically dance; you never know when Brit Horns (AMG) or Deepest India (EastWest) might come in handy for a remix.

Acidized Loops

A variation on WAV files are "acidized" loops. For the most part, they act just like normal sound files, and even have the .wav file extension. What makes them different is that a loop's tempo is written into the metadata portion of these files. Originally conceived for use with Sonic Foundry's hit loop-sequencing program, *Acid*, there are now several programs that can take advantage of acidized loops. For example, *Digital Performer* (starting with Version 3.1) can use an acidized loop's tempo as a starting point for automatically time stretching (or compressing) the loop to match your project's tempo.

There are many great acidized loop libraries available. A lot of good titles can be found at Sonic Foundry's

Web site. Luminary contributors include Mick Fleetwood, David Torn of Splattercell, and Meat Beat Manifesto's Mark Pistel. Many titles target a specific dance music genre, such as Futurist Drum 'n' Bass or Downtempo Beats. For drums, funky guitar chords, and extra percussion parts (such as congas, bongos, and tablas), check out Smart Loops' line of acidized loops.

Recycled Loops

CD 1

Loops that have been chopped up into their component hits, making each hit one sample, are called *recycled* or *beat-mapped* loops (see figure 3.1). (The process of chopping up a loop is called breakpoint-editing.) Each sample is automatically assigned to a MIDI note. Then, an associated MIDI performance file is used to play the individual samples in time to recreate the original loop (see figure 3.2). Beat-mapped loops give you a high degree of tempo control over a loop without using time compression/expansion, letting you avoid the artifacts sometimes associated with this type of audio processing. Via the MIDI performance, you also get complete control over how the loop is played back. Individual hits can be quantized, re-grooved, and even rearranged (a favorite trick of Drum-and-Bass producers, explained in chapter 10).

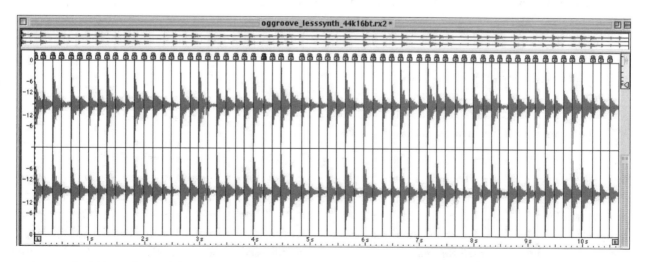

FIGURE 3.1 Beat-Mapped Loop. A beat-mapped loop as it appears in Propellerhead's ReCycle. The vertical lines dissecting the loop's waveform mark each sample's in and out points.

You can recycle any loop with the right software, and it's important to know how to do this for serious remixing (see chapter 8). However, having several beat-mapped libraries handy is also recommended. Because these loops are so flexible, they can be inspiring to work with and end up becoming very important elements in your remixes. There are two main types of beat-mapped loops on the market: *REX* and *Ilio's Groove Control.*

Two file types are referred to as REX: the original mono-type *REX* (having the file extension .rex), and the updated stereo version, *REX2* (with the extension .rx2). There are lots of REX and REX2 libraries available. (Check out www.reasonrefills.com, for starters.) In order to take advantage of a REX library, you must have software that recognizes REX files. (Applications that support .rx2 files also support .rex files, but the opposite is not the case.) Depending on your software, REX files can be played in several ways: they can be imported to an audio track (as with *CubaseSX* and *Digital Performer* Version 3.1), they can be loaded into a REX file player (such as Reason's Dr. REX Loop Player), and some software samplers can import REX files and extract their MIDI performances (such as Emagic's *EXS24* software sampler).

Ilio's Groove Control libraries are an extensive collection of chopped up loops and their companion MIDI performances. Titles are available in Roland and Akai (which works for Emu too) sampler formats, and MIDI performances are Standard MIDI Files (SMF) documents (see "Standard MIDI File Explained," on page 13). Using a conversion program such as Propellerheads' *Reload* (see figure 3.3), or a software sampler that can import Akai instruments, converting the Akai samples into standard audio files is a snap. Since all digital audio sequencers support SMF, the MIDI performances are easily imported.

Ilio's beat-mapped loops aren't as intuitive to use as the self-contained REX files. There are more elements to coordinate; samples must be lined up with the proper MIDI performance, or else nothing will sound right. However, the quality of Ilio's libraries are top notch. For example, the *Stark Raving Beats* title features drums by Chris O'Brien, who has worked with

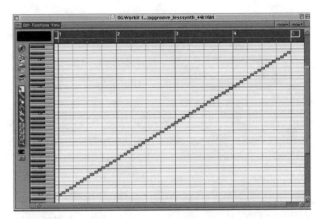

FIGURE 3.2 MIDI Performance Map. The MIDI performance of the loop in figure 3.1 appears like this in *Logic Audio's* Matrix Edit window.

Michael Jackson, Amy Grant, and Lionel Richie. *Ethno Techno* offers a wealth of percussion performances by Bashiri Johnson, who has played with Whitney Houston, Madonna, Celine Dion, and Boys II Men. Both are multitrack titles that give you what are essentially beat-mapped breakout tracks of all the grooves. (Loops are broken into their individual multitrack elements, such as kick, snare, hi hat, room mics, percussion, and so on).

MIDI Samples

The great thing about MIDI performances is that they can be assigned to play just about any MIDI instrument. There's no rule that says an r&b MIDI drum loop must play an r&b kit at a tempo of 80 BPM. Try assigning this same MIDI sample an electronic dance kit and turning up the tempo to 130 BPM. Separate out the hi-hat notes, and use their pattern to drive an analog synth sound. Make a groove template of the kick drum pattern, and use it to quantize your bass instrument, or vice versa. The flexibility is wonderful, the possibilities endless.

The downside to MIDI samples is that because they are not audio recordings, they lack the ambience and sonic subtleties that make an actual recording sound "real." A common complaint about MIDI samples is that they sound sterile. Fortunately, this problem can be addressed on several levels. Using a MIDI instrument with lots of velocity-layered samples (see

FIGURE 3.3 Propellerhead's *Reload*. *Reload* software is handy for converting Akai samples into WAV files, and Akai instruments into patches that can be loaded into *Reason's* NN-XT Advanced Sampler.

"Velocity Layers," page 14) adds more realistic sounding dynamics to the MIDI performance. Tastefully applied reverb can impart a cohesive ambience, creating the illusion that the instrument was recorded in a real space. Mixing and matching REX loops with the MIDI samples can hide the fact that you're even using a MIDI instrument at all.

The *Twiddly Bits* MIDI sample series, by Keyfax, includes lots of useful titles. For example, the Bill Bruford CD-ROM, featuring performances by this legendary progressive rock drummer (who has worked with Yes and King Crimson) or Dangerous Drums by Paul Kodish (the drummer behind Prodigy's "Firestarter" and "Breathe"). Several decent MIDI drum sample titles are also available from BeatBoy.

STANDARD MIDI FILE EXPLAINED

A Standard MIDI File, or SMF, is a generic MIDI document that can be read by just about every digital audio sequencer on the market. There are two SMF formats: Type 0 and Type 1. Both formats have the file extension .mid, so it's impossible to determine a file's type just by looking at its extension. Type 0 saves all performances sequentially, one after the other, to a single track; Type 1 is multitrack, saving each performance to its own track (see figure 3.4). Most good MIDI sample libraries employ SMF documents and offer both formats. Getting a SMF document into your digital audio sequencer is always a simple "import file" command, and often a straightforward drag-and-drop operation.

Kits and Hits

Sounds for hardware samplers have been available on CD-ROM for some time. There is an especially large selection of Akai sampler-formatted CD-ROM titles. (Check out the Ilio Web site, for starters.) Most titles feature instruments that contain lots of samples, mapped across the keyboard and on different velocity layers. Hits from different drum and percussion instruments can be used to create your own custom drum kits. Many of the best virtual samplers (such as Emagic's *EXS24*, Steinberg's *Halion*, and MOTU's *Machfive*) can import instruments and samples directly from an Akai CD-ROM.

Virtual drum machines, such as Steinberg's *LM-4 Mark II* (see figure 3.5) and Native Instruments' *Battery*, offer a great way to jump-start your collection of kits. Both of these instruments come with a set of good stock sounds. If you want more presets, aftermarket CD-ROM titles with lots of huge, multi-sampled kits are available (such as Wizoo's Kit Connection for the *LM-4 Mark II* and Native Instrument's *Studio Drums* for *Battery*). Both virtual drum machines can import WAV, AIFF, and SDII sound files, so you can easily assemble your own custom kits. *Battery* can also import instruments and samples right from an Akai CD-ROM.

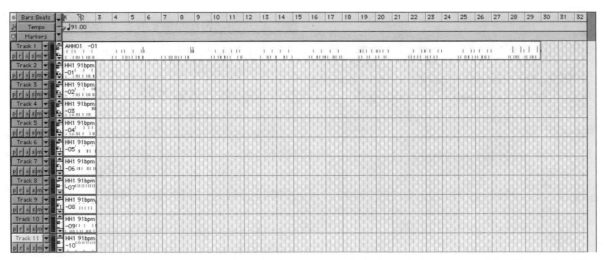

FIGURE 3.4 SMF File Types Compared. A SMF Type 0 performance has been imported to Track 1, while a Type 1 file of the same performance fills up the remaining tracks.

VELOCITY LAYERS

Wizoo's *Kit Connection* for the LM-4 Mark II and Native Instruments' *Studio Drums for Battery* feature velocity-layered sounds. Several samples of a single drum, hit at different velocities, are mapped to a range of velocities (0 to 127) on individual drum pads (see figure 3.6). When a pad's assigned MIDI note is played at different velocities, different samples get triggered, making for a very realistic-sounding instrument. Grooves and fills are more interesting and dynamic with kits that contain well-made, velocity-layered sounds.

FIGURE 3.5 Steinberg's LM-4 Mark II. LM-4 Mark II is a great virtual drum machine that comes stocked with solid sounding, multisampled kits.

Keeping Samples Organized

One CD-ROM can have hundreds of samples, so it's crucial to keep them all organized. There are few things more frustrating than knowing you have the perfect sample to top off your remix, and not being able to locate it. Keeping all of your samples in neatly arranged folders, in one location, so that you can quickly find a sample, or browse samples by category, will make your entire remixing process more efficient, and subsequently more enjoyable.

Start by picking up an extra hard drive and dedicating it just to sample-library storage. External FireWire drives are great because they have fast access times and a lot of storage space in small packages. LaCie's PocketDrive hard drive is particularly nice. It's small enough to fit in your pocket (as its name implies) and can draw its power directly from the FireWire bus. Having your sample library on a portable drive makes bringing your arsenal of sounds to a remixing session at another studio a snap. Just be sure to back up your precious library regularly, either to a partition on your main computer's system drive or CDRs.

A good way of keeping samples organized is by instrument: drums, bass, guitars, vocals, and so on. Make these categories your root folders, then create sub-categories. For example, in the Guitars folder, you might have the folders Heavy Metal, Funk, Acoustic, and Ambient. Don't mix up file types; instead, keep each

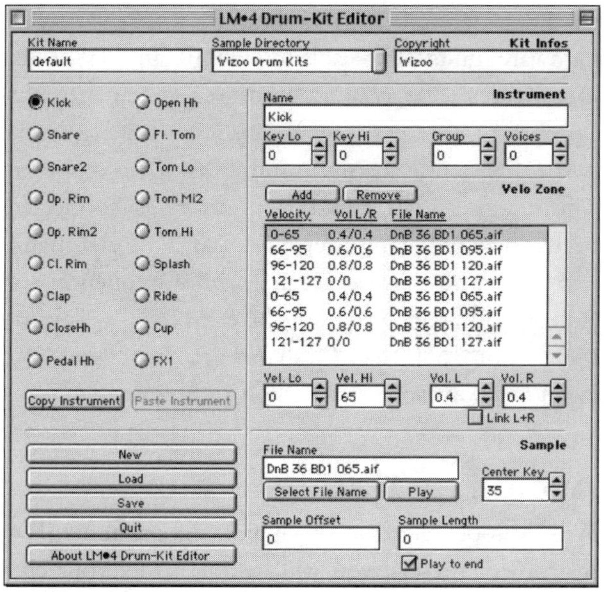

FIGURE 3.6 Velocity Layered Drum Sound. The LM-4 Drumkit Editor by Wizoo displays the samples used to create a velocity-layered kick drum in a Wizoo preset. Each sample's name is shown under File Name and its velocity range under Velocity.

file type in its own folder. In the Funk Guitars folder, you might have the folders REX, Acidized, AIFF, and Groove Control (along with the appropriate companion MIDI files). Figure 3.7 shows the folder hierarchy of a well-organized, typical sample library.

Over the course of a remix, you will probably end up modifying some of your samples, either by effects processing or simply converting a sound file from one type to another. If you warp a sample into a fantastic new creation that you're sure you will want to use in many more remixes, store it in your sample library. Otherwise, if it's a creation that's only going to be useful in your current remix, just save it in that project's Session folder. When you import a sound file that needs to be converted to a supported format, many programs will ask you where you want to save the converted file. If it's a regularly used file type, save it to an appropriate folder in your sample library. Program's that don't ask where you want to save the converted file generally put it in the current project's Audio Files folder. Remember, in order to open and play a session that draws on sounds in your sample library, if your library is on an external drive, it must be connected.

PROFESSIONAL FIREWIRE DRIVES

Recording tracks on consumer FireWire drives is not recommended. Though these drives are fine for straight storage tasks (like holding your sample library), actual audio recording should be done only on professional grade FireWire systems, like Glyph Technologies' GT-103 and GT-051 Tabletop units. These units have been optimized for audio recording (with Oxford-911–based bridge boards in every drive), highly reducing the risk of data corruption occurring during demanding recording sessions and transfers between computers.

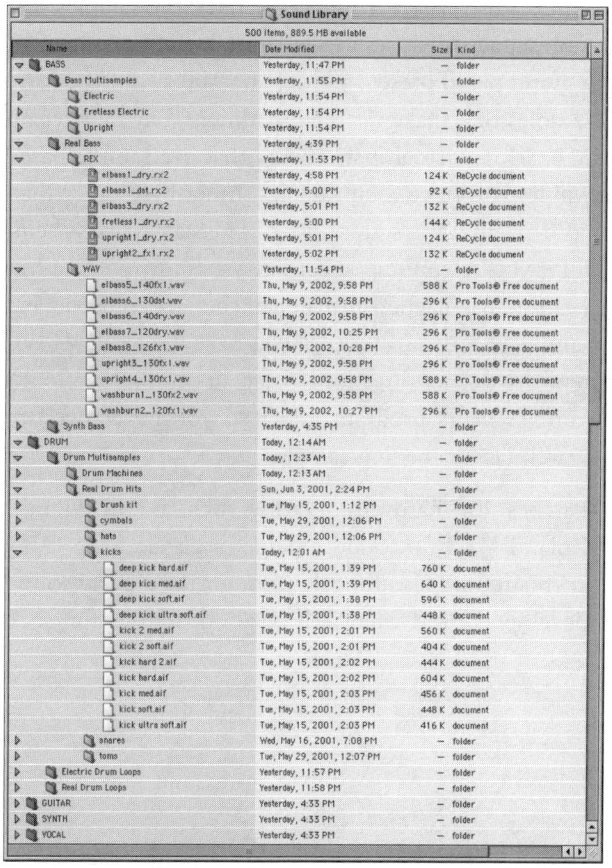

FIGURE 3.7 Good Folder Hierarchy. A well organized folder hierarchy for a typical sample library.

Instrument Presets

Most software synths come with several banks of stock presets. More presets are usually for sale through third-party sound developers (such as Kid Nepro), or available as free downloads through user groups. (Check out the sound archives posted by *Reason* users at the Propellerheads Web site.) Preset documents have very small file sizes because they are simply a set of synthesizer parameter values. Since they take up so little space, always keep all of a software synth's presets in its default preset folder on your system drive (not in your sample library).

Software samplers and sample-based virtual drum machines are a bit different. Though their preset documents also have very small file sizes, the samples that a preset actually uses can be quite large. For example, a grand piano preset may only be 100 k, but the forty samples that make up the instrument may be over 50 MB. Most virtual instruments that are sample-based will let you store their samples somewhere other than your computer's system drive. This can be very helpful if you're running short on system drive space but want to install a new instrument that depends on a big sample library. However, if you have the available system-drive space, it's nice to keep all of an instrument's samples in its program folder so you never need to search far for missing samples.

Patches for hardware synths, such as the vintage Roland MKS-50 sound module or classic Korg O1W keyboard, are also for sale through third party sound developers. Kid Nepro is a good source for such patches, offering banks of sounds for a wide variety of hardware units (like Roland's D-50 and JV-1080, Oberheim's Matrix1000, and Sequential Circuits Prophet-5). Patches can be loaded to a synth via a MIDI System Exclusive dump from your computer. This requires that a MIDI interface is connected between your computer and MIDI instrument, and that you have a digital audio sequencer or Editor/Librarian program, like MOTU's *Unisyn* (Mac) or MIDI-OX shareware for the PC (www.midiox.com), installed on your computer.

Avoid Frustration

With a good selection of samples, loops, and MIDI instrument presets, you will be able to let your creative ideas run wild when you begin a remix. The ability to throw lots of ideas down quickly is an important part of creative inspiration, and spending time looking for sounds can put a real damper on the process.

The next section (chapters 4, 5, and 6) explains the technical details of setting up your computer, software, and key peripheral gear necessary for remixing. If your system is already operational, you understand computers and digital audio sequencer programs, and you can't wait to jump right into a remix, then you may want to skip ahead to section 3. However, don't completely ignore section 2 because there may be a piece of hardware or software discussed that you're missing—something that may solve a problem or simply make your remixing experience a lot more fun.

System Setup

CHAPTER 4

Setting Up Your Computer

Having the right computer setup for remixing is crucial. If your computer does not meet the minimum system requirements necessary to run remixing applications, like digital audio sequencers, effects, waveform editors, and virtual instruments, your productions will hit a brick wall. It is better to surpass these specs. A complex remix, with lots of audio tracks, edits, automation, effects, and virtual instrument tracks, will require a whole lot of processing power and storage space. A system that is constantly overtaxed will lead to crashes, and will force you to work within its limitations, hampering your creativity. Your system should be translucent in the creative process—something you don't have to think about, as it works in the background to enable and underpin your remixing.

Choose Your Platform

The two most popular computer platforms to choose from for remixing are Apple Macintosh (Mac) and PC (any Windows-compatible computer). Each platform has its pros and cons, its own operating system, and its own reputation for dependability. The opinions regarding which platform is better are largely subjective, but they should be explored, as there is usually some truth to them.

Apple has a longstanding reputation as the computer to get for audio and music production. With fast, standardized central processor units (CPUs) across many models, Macs offer a straightforward solution. Pick up a G4 1.2 GHz single or dual processor, or faster, and you've got a good machine to start building a system around. Be wary of brand new Apple computers, as they are usually way ahead of available software (often making them unstable), are quite pricey, and devalue quickly. Used Macs that are a year or two old generally offer very good value, at roughly half the price of the newest models. Often their original owners have added enhancements (like more System RAM and expansion cards), and software programs have had their kinks ironed out using these models.

While PC computers have enjoyed large-scale commercial success in business and the consumer electronics industry, the wide variety of CPUs across competing brands has made choosing the right model confusing. Make sure to stick with a Pentium III or better, and stay away from less expensive CPUs (such as Intel's Celeron). The only other central processor that has proven its mettle is AMD (like the AMD AthlonXP 2100+). If you're set on a PC but don't want to worry about choosing the right model, companies such as Carilon Audio Systems sell pre-configured and tested systems.

For a long time, tower computers with lots of PCI slots were the way to go for professional digital audio. The PCI slots where essential for sound and processing cards, and the ample case space necessary for extra, high-speed internal hard drives. Today, these features aren't crucial because of FireWire-based audio I/O (like MOTU's 896 and 828mkII, see figure 4.5), control surface combinations with audio and MIDI I/O (such as Digidesign's Digi002, see page 51), and external storage devices. TC Electronic has even announced a single-rack-space FireWire version of their PowerCore DSP card, succinctly dubbed, PowerCore FireWire (see page 42). A fast laptop (such as a 1 GHz Mac G4 Titanium PowerBook) with the right FireWire peripherals can now approach the power of a tower computer, and is much more flexible in terms of portability.

Operating Systems

The *operating system* (OS) dictates how a computer will run, and subsequently, whether it will be prone to crashes or rock solid. The graphical user interface (GUI) portion of an OS plays an important role in how a computer feels, whether using the computer (actions such as finding folders, opening programs, moving items, etc.) is intuitive or a real headache. An operating system that you feel uncomfortable with will cause you problems at all levels. Though MacOS and Windows are similar in appearance these days, there are a few big differences. Furthermore, both operating systems have gone through major changes in the past several years, and it's important to understand how this has affected digital audio applications.

OS 9.x was the standard for Apple computers running digital audio sequencers for some time. There were many programs that grew up with 9.x and had become very stable running under this OS. The transition to OS X turned out to be a pretty rough road for digital audio and music software developers; an enormous number of revisions were required in order to address OS X's new Core Audio and MIDI features. Initially, many of these updates where anything but stable. But by the time you will be reading this book, most programs and hardware drivers should be working okay with OS X. If you buy a new Mac, since they are all being sold exclusively with OS X, just double-check to be sure the software and hardware you want to use are supported.

There are several PC OS versions that are all referred to as Windows. Windows 98 was the OS of choice for running digital audio sequencers on PC for many years. However, like the MacOS, Windows 98 went through a major retooling to become Windows 2000. There are now three versions of Windows 2000: Professional (usually just called Windows 2000), ME (the "home" version), and XP (the Windows NT update). Most Windows 98 programs have made the transition to Windows 2000 and XP. Of the two operating systems, Windows 2000 is the closer in appearance to Windows 98, but Windows XP has proved to be a real workhorse. (For example, with some MIDI interfaces, XP allows more MIDI ports than 2000.) If you have a choice between operating systems, Windows XP is a good bet.

Apple computers have a reputation for being easier to navigate and configure, and this reputation is not entirely unfounded. PC systems can be trickier to set up, Window's GUI is a little less intuitive, and system peripherals management a bit more involved. For example, moving or deleting a program folder in Windows can lead to serious system problems. (On a Mac, moving a folder is always a simple drag-and-drop operation.)

Keep in mind that having friends who do music on the same platform can also be a wonderful resource; the ability to call a friend for a little help rather than comb through the manual for answers is invaluable. But be wary of advice from friends who lack experience with music applications. Setting up a music production system with MIDI, audio, and internally routed software instruments is very different than installing a word processing program.

Cross Platform

Not all digital audio sequencers are cross-platform, so you'll want to consider this when selecting a program (see figure 4.1). If you favor a digital audio sequencer that's only available for one platform, than there's little choice in the type of computer you need. For example, if you want to use *Logic Audio*, Version 6 and higher, then you must have a Mac. (Emagic halted development of *Logic Audio* for PC when the company was acquired by Apple.) On the other hand, if your top choice is *Pro Tools*, since it's available for both Mac and PC, your platform of choice is less important.

When choosing your software and platform, keep in mind what system any potential co-writer might be using. Exchanging song files is easiest between like programs, and even easier between the same brand of computer.

APPLICATION	MANUFACTURER	MAC	PC
Acid	Sonic Foundry	No	Yes
Cubase SX	Steinberg	Yes	Yes
Digital Performer	MOTU	Yes	No
Live	Ableton	Yes	Yes
Logic Audio Platinum	Emagic	Yes	No
Project5	Cakewalk	No	Yes
Pro Tools	Digidesign	Yes	Yes
Reason	Propellerhead	Yes	Yes
ReCycle	Propellerhead	Yes	Yes
Sonar XL	Cakewalk	No	Yes

FIGURE 4.1 Applications and their Computer Platforms. Computer platform requirements for the top digital audio sequencers and a few other popular remixing programs.

Extension Sets

Small software applications that help your computer communicate with programs and external peripheral devices (such as sound cards and MIDI interfaces) are called *extensions*. Most programs and all peripheral devices require system extensions for proper operation. With several system extensions running at the same time (typical for a digital-audio sequencer setup), "extension conflicts" are bound to happen, where one extension's operation interferes with another. Digital audio and MIDI programs are particularly vulnerable to such conflicts because they demand high amounts of processing power while performing time-sensitive tasks. Even the slightest pause in a groove can cause a train wreck. Extensions that force your system to time out, stealing resources from the CPU for tasks like automated virus scans, software updates, and even extension conflict catching, can wreak havoc with your music programs.

In order to keep your computer running smoothly, operate your digital audio sequencer and other remixing software with a very basic system extensions set. Turn off all unnecessary extensions—the ones that are not directly related to your music applications and the OS. In Mac's OS 9.x, this is done using the Control Panel's *Extension Manager* application. From here, you can turn extensions on and off, and even create separate extensions sets for different tasks (such as a Virus Protection Set versus a Remixing Set). Mac OSX does not operate in quite the same way; there are no longer system extensions in the System folder. Instead, an application's crucial extensions are stored in the Application Support folder (inside the Library folder), in the folder for that program, so there's no direct way to manage extensions in OS X; just do your best to avoid installing conflicting applications.

Windows doesn't have a built-in extension set manager. It's simply a matter of turning devices off that you don't need. This is done in the Device Manager of the System Control Panel. (In XP, the path is: Control Panel/Administrative Tools/Computer Management/Device Manager.)

VIRUS VIA E-MAIL

Minimize the chances of your music computer catching a virus by not downloading e-mails to your hard drives. Either keep a separate computer for all your e-mail business, or use a Web-based e-mail account (like Yahoo or Hotmail) that allows you to read, respond to, and compose e-mails online without having to download anything. These tactics are especially important when the system extensions that enable virus protection software are turned off.

FIGURE 4.2 Aliases in Mac OSX. A control bar called the Dock acts as a handy place for storing shortcuts in Mac OSX.

Organized Computer

When you sit down at your computer to remix, there's no reason to waste time searching for applications and documents. You should be able to jump right to your digital audio sequencer program and open a project with very little digging. Keep your files and folders organized. Store applications in the Programs folder and data files in your Documents folder. Session files go in their perspective project folder on your audio drive, as do the project's audio files. Don't store endless numbers of files on your desktop. This will lead to a very cluttered desktop, you will lose files, and your system will eventually become unstable.

Create *shortcuts* (also called "aliases") to access your most often opened programs, folders, or documents. In Mac's OSX, you simply drag an application's icon on top of the Dock bar to add a shortcut (see figure 4.2). In Mac OS 9.x, select a program's icon, then press [Command-M] to create an alias. Drag the alias to one corner of your desktop. On the PC, right-click on the program's icon and choose the command Create Shortcut. Then drag the alias to a free corner of your desktop or other convenient location. Keeping a few aliases on your desktop will not cause system problems. Aliases give you the absolute fastest way to open a program. For quick access to your session documents, most programs have a list of recently opened projects in their File menu.

System Memory

Hard drive storage space and system RAM (Random Access Memory) are often confused. Hard drives are for long-term storage (such as for audio files and session documents); system RAM is for short-term, working memory (such as for a program's undo/redo list, or a virtual instrument's samples). RAM chips come on small, rectangular circuit boards (sometimes called, "sticks") that fit into slots on a computer's motherboard. Because different computers require different types of RAM, sticks come in a variety of memory sizes, with different chip types and bus speeds. Vendor Web sites that have RAM compatibility charts include www.macwarehouse.com (for Mac) or www.microwarehouse.com (for PC).

Current computers come with enough system RAM to run most digital audio programs at a basic level, but it never hurts to have extra memory. Computers have a maximum amount of system RAM that can be installed (such as 1 or 2 GB). It's user installable and the proper type of RAM for your computer is often available at the same retail outlet where you purchased the computer. If you feel uncomfortable about installing the RAM yourself, most dealers will install it for a small fee.

Having more than enough system memory for your digital audio sequencer is very important. This will help it run smoother and faster, with fewer crashes. For example, screen redraw times will be quicker, and you will be able to operate more RAM-based virtual samplers (like the EXS24) with patches that employ larger samples.

Mac OS 9.x lets you designate how much RAM will be reserved for a program when it's running. Select the application's icon, press [Command-I] for information, then go to Show: Memory and increase the Preferred Size value (see figure 4.3). If you have the available memory, reserve at least 200 MB for your OS and any other programs that might be running at the same time as your digital audio sequencer. (For example, with 512 MB installed, your digital audio sequencer's Preferred Size should be no more than 300 MB.) In OS X and Windows, RAM allocation is done automatically, so there's nothing to worry about. Just make sure to have plenty of system RAM installed.

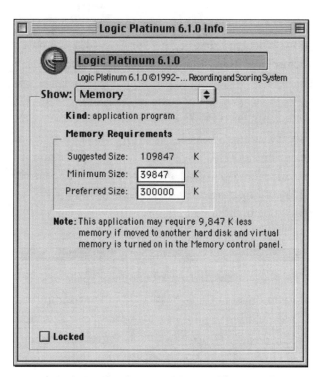

FIGURE 4.3 Increasing Program Memory. The Mac OS 9.2.2 Preferred Size memory setting for *Logic Audio* increased to 300 MB.

> **THE INVISIBLE RAM**
>
> Virtual memory is a method of causing unused hard drive space to act like system RAM. Most digital audio sequencers don't use virtual memory, and instead depend entirely on actual installed RAM. In Mac OS 9.x, virtual memory should be disabled (in the Memory, Control Panel) before booting a digital audio sequencer. Most digital audio sequencers that run on OS X and Windows will ignore virtual memory settings, so these systems take care of themselves.

Dedicated Audio Drives

Recording audio can require a lot of storage space, so it's important to have a big hard drive connected that is dedicated to audio. Having a drive that's separate from your system and sample library drives will help you avoid *file fragmentation* (what happens when a file is stored across multiple sectors of a disk). An audio track that is scattered among system documents or samples requires a lot more processing power to play back than one that has been stored as an unbroken file. Multitrack sessions with lots of highly fragmented files is bad news and may even lead to system crashes and lost data. To maintain the health of your audio drive, defragment it between projects using a program such as Norton *SpeedDisk* (an application that comes bundled with Symantec's *Norton Utilities)*.

Ultra-fast, ultra-wide SCSI drives (like Seagate's Cheetah drives) used to be the standard drive type for audio applications, but they are pricey and require a dedicated PCI SCSI expansion card to operate. Today, there are alternatives: both IDE Type II and FireWire drives can now get the job done. Most computers come stock with an internal IDE Type II system drive. Towers generally have enough space and connections to mount a second internal IDE drive dedicated to audio. Drives rated better than 7,500 rpm (rotations per minute) generally work the best.

FireWire drives are generally IDE Type II drives adapted to a FireWire connection. They are very convenient because FireWire drives are hot-swappable (you can disconnect them without turning the computer off), and practically all computers now come standard with FireWire ports. Though some towers have an internal FireWire bus for mounting a FireWire drive inside the computer, the majority of FireWire drives in use are external. However, there have been stability issues reported with consumer FireWire drives used for heavy recording duties. Glyph Technologies has addressed these problems with their GT-103 and GT-051 Tabletop units (see figure 4.4). These units have been optimized for audio recording with Oxford-911 based bridge boards in every drive tray, highly reducing the risk of data corruption occurring during demanding recording sessions and transfers between computers.

An alternative to installing a second internal hard drive is to *partition* your system drive. This is an elegant solution for a laptop because it saves you the hassle of carrying around an extra external device. And if you're tight on cash, partition your tower computer's system drive and save money by not buying another drive. The drive should be at least 40 GB: 20 GB for the OS and applications, and 20 GB for the audio drive. Partitioning the system drive should be done when you first begin setting up your computer, before you install the OS or any programs. In most cases, this means that you will need to erase and re-format your computer's system drive. The OS installer CD-ROM that came with your computer usually contains a disk-formatting application. Boot from this CD-ROM, then use the application to reformat and partition the system drive. Remember that reformatting a drive erases all of it contents, so back up anything that you want to keep.

CDR BACKUPS

For backing up and endless archival space of your audio drive, nothing beats CDR. If your computer doesn't have a built-in CDR burner, pick one up. CDR drives are user installable, or an authorized service center can perform the installation for a fee. Easier still, just go with an external FireWire unit, and there's no installation required. CDR burners are also essential for creating audio CDs of you remixes.

FIGURE 4.4 GT-103 FireWire Drive Systems. Glyph Technologies' GT-103 and GT-051 Tabletop FireWire drive systems are highly recommended for professional audio recording.

Audio I/O

For gaming and hearing alert sounds, stock sound cards are fine; they may even be okay for rudimentary music production. However, if you are serious about remixing, you will want a hi-fidelity, professional sound card. This will ensure that you hear all the sonic details of your remix, and that the tracks you record are being captured through quality A/D (analog-to-digital) converters.

FireWire audio interfaces are wonderful because they don't require any installation: just plug-and-play. For example, MOTU's 828mkII (see figure 4.5) and the larger, more full featured 896 both pack microphone preamps, ADAT digital I/O, no latency headphone monitoring (for recording), and eight simultaneous analog ins and outs. They work with both Mac and PC, and with most digital audio sequencers via ASIO (a common audio-interface system extension). USB audio interfaces such as Emagic's emi 2|6 or Tascam's US-224 are also convenient. These units are also plug-and-play, though they offer fewer channels of audio because of the data throughput limitations of USB. For more audiophile soundcard alternatives, check out the book, *Studio-in-a-Box* (ArtistPro/Hal Leonard).

Quality, powered studio monitors can be connected directly to any audio interface that features a monitor section with a discrete level control (like the 828mkII, 896, and Digi002). If your sound card doesn't have such a feature, you will need to use a small sub-mixer, such as Mackie's 1402 VLZ. Run the main outputs of the sound card into the mixer, then plug the powered speakers into the mixer's monitor section (see figure 4.6). This will give you control over the output level of your sound card before it reaches the speakers.

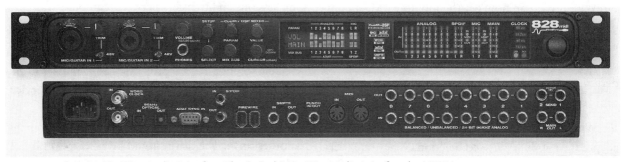

FIGURE 4.5 Popular FireWire Audio Interface. The 828mkII FireWire audio interface by MOTU.

Though some manufacturers recommend plugging their sound card's outputs directly into powered speakers, this is not recommended. (See the sidebar, One Good Monitor Section.)

A good pair of powered monitor speakers is just as important as a good sound card. Without good speakers, you won't be able to hear all the sonic details of your remix. A speaker with an 8″ woofer will provide adequate low-end frequency response for composing dance music. There are lots of wonderful powered monitors on the market that fit the bill, including the modestly priced Event 20/20bas, or the very popular Mackie HR824. For more bottom end, you can always add a powered sub-woofer. (A 12″ woofer is good, but 15″ is even better—keeping the low end of your mix sounding tight in the studio and at dance clubs is discussed in chapter 14.) Try Event's 20/20/15, or Mackie's HRS120 or HRS150. High-quality headphones are also an essential ingredient of any good monitoring setup, such as Sony's venerable MDR-V6 or the more expensive and very comfortable, Sennheiser HD280.

ONE GOOD MONITOR SECTION

Controlling speaker levels from your virtual mixer's master fader is not a good idea. For example, if you encounter feedback, it's difficult to go searching through your virtual channels for the master fader (especially if your fingers are stuck in your ears). If you turn down your master fader, the feedback problem will go away, but without a visible signal on your master meters, you will have no way of tracking down the feedback loop.

Monitor and master-fader controls are supposed to be separate so that you can turn down your speakers without changing your main output level. Other reasons for a dedicated monitor setup include running copies (whether to an internal bus or an external DAT deck) without having to listen to the program material, and the ability to switch between different sets of reference speakers during mixing. Furman Sound offers a dedicated, single rack space monitor solution, the SRM-80A.

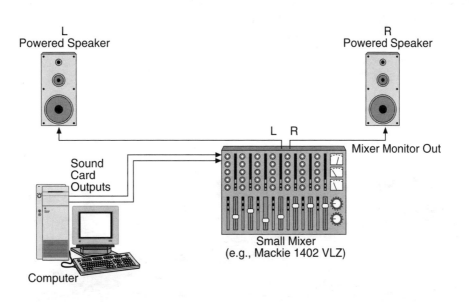

FIGURE 4.6 Sub-Mixer Between Sound Card and Speakers. Powered monitors can be plugged directly into any sound card with a dedicated monitor section. However, if your sound card lacks a monitor section, you should use a sub-mixer's monitor section.

MIDI I/O

For your computer to communicate with external hardware (such as sound modules and effects units) you'll need a MIDI interface. If you plan on using virtual instruments and effects exclusively, you can get along without a MIDI interface. With today's incredible software, there's certainly no rule that says you must use outside sound sources. Many controller keyboards (like M-Audio's Oxygen and Radium, see figure 4.7), and some control surfaces (such as Tascam's US-428 and US-224), can interface directly via USB, reducing the need for a MIDI interface as well. However, over time, you will likely acquire a few select MIDI modules, or want to synchronize your digital audio sequencer to external time code, so understanding your MIDI interface options is important.

There are a variety of MIDI interfaces available, ranging in features and number of ports. Practically all the interfaces today support both Mac and PC, and work with all the top digital audio sequencers. For complex setups, few MIDI interfaces beat the tried and true MTP AV by MOTU. It has eight Ins and Outs, is networkable for daisy chaining multiple units, can store up to 128 user presets, reads and generates a variety of time code formats, and has several nice controller features (such as programmable knobs and footswitch jacks). However, if all you need are a couple of MIDI Outs, a small 2x2 box such a M-Audio's MIDIsport 2x2 will get the job done. Some USB controller keyboards (such as Oxygen 8 and Radium) and a few audio I/O units (such as the US-428 and the Digi002) include MIDI I/O.

Ergonomics

Having a comfortable workspace is very important. It will enhance your creativity by easing the stress of staring at a computer screen for hours on end. Pick up an ergonomically designed computer desk (like those sold at office supply stores), or if you have the money, a dedicated music workstation (such as those by Omnirax). The furniture should have ear-level space for your speakers, a spot for your computer screen at eye level, and plenty of desk space for controllers (see figure 4.8). Invest in a comfortable chair too. This may seem expensive and unnecessary, but if it spares you the agony of upper neck and shoulder pain, it's priceless. A staple in professional studios worldwide are Herman Miller's Aeron Chairs, starting around $500 used.

Digital audio sequencers can present a lot of information at the same time, so having a 17″ computer screen or larger is a must. Better yet, use two monitors. If your computer is not equipped with dual monitor outputs, you will need a dual-monitor-output expansion card. They can be found at most computer stores with prices starting around $100. Make sure that the card you get is compatible with your monitors. There are several connection types to choose from, including standard VGA and DVI digital flat panels.

FIGURE 4.7 Radium. M-Audio's Radium controller keyboard communicates with the computer via USB. It features eight faders and knobs that are ideal for controlling virtual instrument parameters, and a 1x1 MIDI interface.

Figure 4.8 The Ideal Setup. An ideal music workstation setup, where the speakers are on a plane equal to the listener's head. The computer screen is on this same plane and close enough to see without eye strain, and there is plenty of desk space for controllers of all types.

CHAPTER 5

Essential Software

The software cornerstone of your remixing system is a digital audio sequencer. This program is the focal point for a remix, where you assemble all of your remix's elements: multitrack audio, loops, MIDI performances, virtual effects and instruments, track automation, and the synchronization of external equipment. For a program to qualify as a digital audio sequencer, it must be able to perform all of these functions. While it's possible to connect several hardware and software components (such as a digital tape recorder, automated mixing console, hardware sequencer sound module, and a software waveform editor) to create a pretty good remixing system, a digital audio sequencer offers the ease, convenience, and power of integrating all these components into a single application.

There are five top digital audio sequencers in today's market: Cakewalk's *Sonar XL*, Digidesign's *Pro Tools*, Emagic's *Logic Audio Platinum*, MOTU's *Digital Performer*, and Steinberg's *Cubase SX*. Each has its own set of strengths and weaknesses, despite the fact that they are all strikingly similar in features and appearance. The application you prefer is largely a matter of personal taste. Some remix producers use more than one, switching between programs to take advantage of each software's special features. For example, Emagic's *Logic Audio* has features that make it particularly suited for composing MIDI tracks, while Digidesign's *Pro Tools TDM* is renowned for its excellent audio quality and powerful plug-ins, making it ideal for recording and mixing.

Whether you have decided on a digital audio sequencer or not, familiarity with all the top programs will give you a clear picture of how a digital audio sequencer should operate and the features it ought to include. When you buy an application, you're not just buying the current version; you're investing in the development of the software (and by default, the software company itself). You will want to be able to

envision and communicate your suggestions for improvements, and the software company needs to be open to user feedback, be prompt with technical support, and repair software bugs in a timely manner.

SPECIAL POWERS

A few programs, such as Propellerheads' *Reason* (see figure 5.8), Ableton's *Live*, Cakewalk's *Project5*, and Sonic Foundry's *Acid*, while they don't qualify as digital audio sequencers, are important remixing tools. Programs like these are often synchronized with a digital audio sequencer in order to take advantage of their unique programming and loop sequencing capabilities, which are especially suited for remixing.

Cubase SX

The most recent incarnation of Steinberg's veteran Cubase application is *Cubase SX* (see figure 5.1). The company claims that SX is not simply an updated version of *Cubase*, but a complete redesign. For those of you keeping track of Steinberg's product line, *Cubase SX* takes over where *Cubase VST/32* and *Cubase Score* left off, and *Cubase SL* (the "light" version of SX) replaces *Cubase VST*. The simple fact that *Cubase* has continued to evolve over the years speaks volumes for both the application and the company behind it. *Cubase SX* also continues to be only one of a couple digital audio sequencers that is available for both Mac and PC.

Steinberg pioneered virtual studio technology with their integration of plug-in effects, and later, virtual instruments in *Cubase VST*. They were also the first to support the REX file format (explained in chapter 3) and ReWire protocol (see the sidebar, ReWire in a Nutshell). Continuing in the legacy, *Cubase SX* works with a wealth of Steinberg co-developed virtual instru-

FIGURE 5.1 *Cubase SX.* The *Cubase SX* Arrange and Mixer windows.

ments. Communication with these instruments is simply the best in the business. REX file support has grown to include REX2, and there is now a built-in break-point editor (similar to *ReCycle*) called *Hitpoint*. ReWire support now includes ReWire2, for excellent communication with programs like *Reason* and *Live*.

Though there were gripes about the program's automation features in previous versions, these rough spots have been largely ironed out. However, the program's redesign adds so many new automation controls, its interface can get confusing. How *Cubase* handles quantizing and groove templates bothers a select few who are particularly sensitive to a program's "feel"—its swing factor. Nevertheless, *Cubase* has long been popular among dance and electronic music producers, and this is not likely to change anytime soon. Many of the program's features are ideal for creating these types of music. Steinberg's reputation for customer support is pretty good, and the company always offers reasonably priced upgrades, not only between versions (such as *Cubase SL* Version 2.1 to *Cubase SX* Version 4.0) but from competitors' digital audio sequencers as well.

> Cubase *makes remixing easy. VST works seamlessly from the software synths to the software samplers. Steinberg has nailed it.*
>
> —Robbie Rivera

REWIRE IN A NUTSHELL

Originally developed by Propellerheads as a way for *ReBirth* to communicate with a digital audio sequencer running on the same computer, ReWire is now an integral part of *Reason* and Ableton's *Live*. The latest generation of ReWire (ReWire2) lets you synchronize the transport of *Reason* and *Live* with your digital audio sequencer, send individual outputs from these applications into the host program's virtual mixer for processing and mixing, and you can even control *Reason's* instruments via the sequencer's MIDI tracks.

Digital Performer

From the beginning, *Digital Performer* (see figure 5.2), by MOTU, has been exclusively Mac. The program began as a straight-ahead MIDI sequencer (called simply, *Performer*) in the late 1980s, running on such seminal Apple computers as the Mac Plus and SE. It has since grown into a full-fledged digital audio sequencer whose development has paralleled Apple's quest to produce faster and more powerful computers. *Digital Performer* was one of the first programs to take complete advantage of dual G4 processors.

The program has a wonderfully intuitive interface, commands are generally easy to find, and most features are well documented in an excellent manual. *Digital Performer* uses its own plug-in format called MAS (MOTU Audio System), which does not support VST plug-ins directly. Instead, a VST adapter must be employed (like *VST Wrapper* by Audioease) in order to instantiate VST plug-ins. However, there are plenty of wonderful native MAS plug-ins available (check out Native Instruments' selection). Though *Digital Performer's* initial integration of third party virtual instruments seemed klugey and strangely processor heavy, these issues are being addressed. ReWire support is included, and REX file support has been recently added.

The program has a well-deserved reputation for having a great "feel." Its groove template features are very comprehensive. Automation features are well designed and a snap to use. An innovative RAM-based loop recorder feature, called Polar, is an outstanding tool for creating live, multitracked loops. However, even though a selling point of *Digital Performer* is that it can work with Digidesign's TDM audio systems, Polar only works with native interfaces (like MOTU's FireWire 896 and PCI-324 systems). Since MOTU manufacturers a selection of great audio and MIDI interfaces as well, *Digital Performer* users that employ these units are assured of solid software and hardware communications. The company has a decent reputation for customer support, and always offers reasonably priced upgrades, including trade-ins on competing digital audio sequencer programs.

> *We've used* Digital Performer *for years. It's really great, plus the built-in plug-ins are so strong.*
>
> —Chris Cox, Thunderpuss

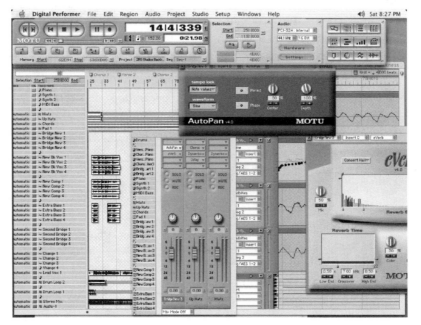

FIGURE 5.2 *Digital Performer.* The *Digital Performer* Arrange and Mixer windows.

Logic Audio Platinum

For years now, Emagic's *Logic Audio Platinum* (see figure 5.3) has garnered the reputation as the top choice for serious remix production on either Mac or PC. With version 5, a batch of great new automation features and impressive, built-in virtual instruments were introduced that looked to secure the program's reputation well into the future. But then, very unexpectedly, in February of 2002, Emagic was sold to Apple. When the announcement came, shortly after the sale, that development for the PC would be halted at version 5.x, an enormous number of PC users were left out in the cold. Though Emagic continues its groundbreaking work, starting at Version 6 for the Mac only, a company that turns its back on nearly half of its user base as part of a business decision doesn't earn high marks for support and long-term commitment.

Logic Audio's powerful features are legendary (like its simultaneous audio driver, multi-engine support, letting you run TDM and ASIO virtual mixer channels side by side), but so too is its confusing and unintuitive interface. Basic commands are too often hidden, essential functions poorly titled, and special features barely explained. That said, with a little patience (or at the very least, a good tutorial from an experienced friend), the program can do just about anything you can imagine (like translating an audio recording into a MIDI performance). Its groove-control functions are some of the best around, with non-destructive, easily interchanged groove-quantize templates that sound and feel perfect.

Emagic's suite of virtual instruments, sold separately, but designed to be used exclusively with *Logic Audio*, are amazing. Among these instruments are the invaluable EXS24 mk II sampler and the superb ES2 synthesizer. The built-in synths, like the ES M and ESP, sound good as well. If you want to use Emagic's software instruments, you must use *Logic Audio*. REX files are supported, and can be imported to either an audio track or as an EXS24 mk II sample instrument (a great trick, discussed further in chapter 10). ReWire support has been sketchy in some versions, but it is part of the program. Beginning with version 6 for OS X (a version 6 for OS 9.2.2 is also available), VST plug-ins are no longer directly supported, but can be used with the VST to AudioUnit Adapter (VST-AU Adapter) from FXpansion Audio. Also introduced in version 6 is "Freeze," a very handy feature for managing the strain on your computer's processing power caused by demanding plug-ins.

FIGURE 5.3 *Logic Audio Platinum.* The *Logic Audio Platinum* Arrange and Environment windows.

> *I mostly compose in* Logic Audio. *Its stock synths are great, and I use the ES2 a lot.*
>
> —(BT) Brian Transeau

Pro Tools

A top program in the world of high-end, professional audio recording is Digidesign's *Pro Tools TDM* (see figure 5.4). The *Pro Tools* application, combined with a TDM audio processing and interface system (like a Mix|24 or HD setup) excels in audio fidelity, plug-in quality, and mixing features. However, as much as the TDM architecture has been applauded for its handling of audio, the MIDI sequencing features in *Pro Tools* have lacked the sophistication of competing digital audio sequencers.

However, with the release of version 6, Digidesign's diligent efforts to add more, better MIDI sequencing features started bearing fruit. MIDI updates in Version 6 included groove templates (the ability to extract a groove from one MIDI performance and apply it to another MIDI performance) and several MIDI note-editing enhancements (such as an improved Pencil tool). Though Pro Tools does not read REX files, a built-in breakpoint editor called

Beat Detective is the *Pro Tools TDM* equivalent to *ReCycle*. As an alternative to the expensive hardware dependent TDM plug-ins, a native plug-in format called RTAS is supported (TDM and LE systems). There is a rapidly growing collection of third party RTAS effects and virtual instrument plug-ins (check out Native Instruments' selection), so the fact that *Pro Tools* does not support VST plug-ins is not such a big deal.

If you can't afford a *Pro Tools TDM* setup right now, not to worry, as Digidesign offers a complete selection of systems (for both Mac and PC) to suit every level. *Pro Tools FREE* is a complete working version of the program, free for the downloading. The catch is, there's no communication with an audio interface other than the computer's own built-in sound card, and there are only eight tracks of audio. *Pro Tools LE* is for the mid-level native systems, bundled with an appropriate interface (either the Digi001, Digi002, or Mbox). Note that, to use TDM plug-ins and take advantage of 96 kHz and higher recording rates, you'll need a minimum of an HD Core card paired with a 96 I/O or 192 I/O interface. At the time of this writing, *Beat Detective* was only available in TDM systems.

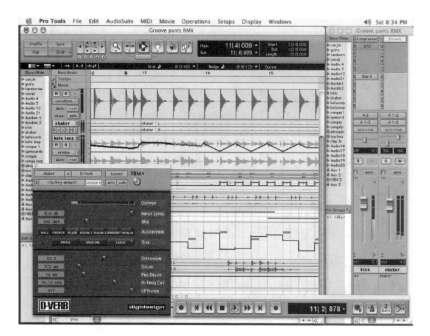

FIGURE 5.4 *Pro Tools.* The *Pro Tools* Edit and Mix windows.

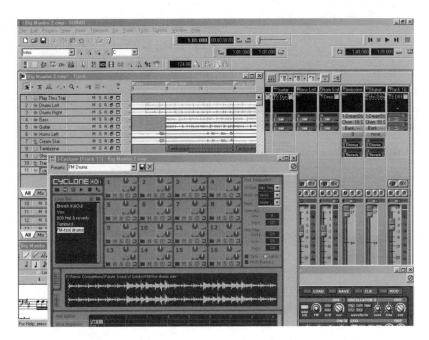

FIGURE 5.5 *Sonar XL*. The *Sonar XL* Track and Console windows.

Digidesign used to have a nasty reputation as a company that didn't care about its end users, but with a new management team in place and their efforts to meet the needs of customers at every level (from complete novices to top hitmakers), this old reputation has been fast fading into history.

> *In my world, I use* Pro Tools *for everything. The reasons are obvious: total recall, great plug-ins, convenience, and it's very easy to use.*
>
> —Dave Audé

Sonar XL

Cakewalk surprised the industry when they released, from what seemed like left field, a new and comprehensive digital audio sequencer exclusively for PC, *Sonar* (see figure 5.5). Actually, the program was a major overhaul of their early digital audio sequencer, also just for PC, *Pro Audio 9*. That program was not taken very seriously by professionals, but *Sonar XL* is quickly garnering a reputation as a dependable workhorse with all the right features to compete with the best digital audio sequencers on the market.

Sonar's interface is much improved over its predecessors. PC style controls abound, making navigation a breeze, and most features are fairly intuitive (and should you need help figuring something out, the manual is good). VST plug-ins are not supported directly, as the program prefers the native PC plug-in format, DirectX. However, a VST to DirectX plug-in adapter (like VST Adapter by FXpansion) can be employed to take advantage of the wealth of VST plug-ins available. The DirectX virtual instrument format is called DXi. There are a burgeoning number of DXi instruments hitting the market. (Again, check out Native Instruments' offerings.)

ReWire is well supported, but REX files are not. Though Sonar does offer an extensive collection of built-in MIDI drum patterns and supports SoundFont samples (a popular sample format for consumer sound cards, such as Creative Technology's SoundBlaster cards). A stock DXi instrument called *Cyclone* even lets you build grooves by automatically tempo-matching acidized WAV files. Quantize and groove controls are fine, and the automation features, while not extraordinary, get the job done. Cakewalk's reputation for releasing updates in a timely manner is not the best, but they do offer free unlimited technical support (though they can be hard to reach).

Plug-Ins

All top digital audio sequencers come with their own set of stock plug-ins. These usually range from purely utilitarian, like compressors and EQ, to essential effects, such as delay and reverb. Many programs also toss in a couple of special effects plug-ins, such as modulators, filters, and distortion. The purpose behind these plug-ins is to provide a comprehensive recording and mixing software bundle, without the need to buy any third party plug-ins. However, despite the fact that many stock plug-ins are pretty amazing (like the classic AutoFilter and Tape Delay found in *Logic Audio*), adding third party plug-ins can really spice up your sonic palette, giving you not only a professional edge but an individual sound as well.

There are a ton of third party effects plug-ins available, from a variety of companies. Distinguishing which company's reverb sounds better, or who has the most radical sound mangler, is easy: read the reviews and get a demo copy to try yourself. (Many companies offer downloadable demos at their Web sites.) What is not so easy is wading through all of the different plug-in formats on the market, and the number of formats seems to be constantly growing. Every digital audio sequencer supports its own unique set of formats (see figure 5.6). This usually includes not only the program's own proprietary format, but a couple third party formats as well. The first thing to do, before shopping for extra effects, is to know the plug-in formats your digital audio sequencer supports.

Of all the third party plug-ins, Waves' plug-ins seem to be the most universally popular. Their Renaissance series (see figure 5.7), in particular, can add a warm, vintage-analog sound, and a degree of frequency and dynamics control that is hard to beat. It's tough to find a remix producer that doesn't depend heavily on Waves' plug-ins. (The plug-in pack of choice is usually the Gold Bundle; all standard native plug-in formats are included.) Other third party plug-in manufacturers worthy of note include: GRM Tools, Bomb Factory, TC Electronic, Universal Audio, and Wave Mechanics (not to be confused with Waves). Digidesign and Steinberg also distribute many great third party plug-ins. For a more in-depth discussion of plug-in formats, and lots of examples, check out the book, *Studio-in-a-Box* (ArtistPro/Hal Leonard).

MIDI EFFECT PLUG-INS

Another type of effect plug-ins, which have nothing to do with audio, are MIDI plug-ins. These plug-ins are inserted on MIDI tracks to process MIDI performance data. Common MIDI effects include delays, arpeggio, transpose, quantize, voice double, and so on. Not all digital audio sequencers support MIDI plug-ins. *Cubase SX, Digital Performer,* and *Sonar XL* all come with a set of stock MIDI plug-ins. The MIDI mixer channels of these programs operate similarly to audio virtual mixer channels, with insert points for plugging in the effects.

	DIRECTX	LOGIC	MAS	RTAS	TDM	VST	AU
Cubase SX	Yes	–	–	–	–	Yes	No
Digital Performer	–	–	Yes	–	Yes (in DAE Mode)	Yes (with adapter)	Yes
Logic Audio Platinum	–	Yes	–	–	Yes (in DAE Mode)	Yes (with adapter)	Yes
Pro Tools	–	–	–	Yes (LE and TDM systems)	Yes (TDM systems only)	Yes (with adapter)	No
Sonar XL	Yes	–	–	–	–	Yes (with adapter)	No

FIGURE 5.6 Supported Real-Time Plug-in Formats. Real-time plug-in formats supported by the top five digital audio sequencers.

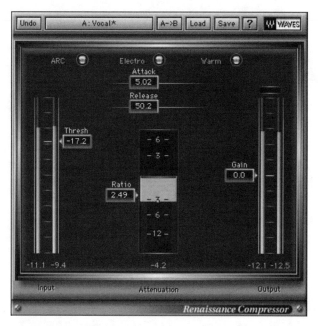

FIGURE 5.7 Renaissance. To add an analog flavor to your digital recordings, try Waves' Renaissance series of plug-ins. The compressor is particularly popular.

Virtual Instruments

There are basically two types of virtual instruments: stand-alone and plug-ins. Stand-alone instruments operate in the background of your digital audio sequencer, and plug-ins work within the host program. Plug-ins are definitely easier to use than stand-alone instruments because they are designed to integrate seamlessly with your digital audio sequencer. Stand-alone instruments require additional setup, including system extensions and other peripheral programs for MIDI communications and audio routing. You can make all the necessary audio and MIDI connections for a plug-in instrument right in the host program, after a few menu selections.

There are so many plug-in type virtual instruments available that you shouldn't need to bother with a stand-alone type. The main exception to this rule is *Reason* (see figure 5.8). Because of its powerful remixing tools and virtual rack of great sounding instruments, it's definitely worth the extra setup hassle. Luckily, all the best digital audio sequencers include the ReWire communications protocol, and this makes connecting MIDI and audio between programs on

the same computer just a bit easier. With a host program that supports ReWire, installing *Reason* will automatically set that program up for ReWire communications. Boot your digital audio sequencer, then *Reason*, and the ReWire connection will be made automatically. (Sometimes you must also enable the ReWire audio input in the host program.)

Virtual instrument plug-ins follow the same format rules as effect plug-ins. Only those virtual instruments that are of a plug-in format supported by the digital audio sequencer will work. Fortunately, virtual instrument plug-in formats exactly parallel effect plug-in formats. There are DirectX (called DXi), MAS, RTAS, AU, and VST instruments. Many third party instruments (such as those by Native Instruments) are available in all the most popular formats, so there is sure to be a version that will function in your program. Only Emagic's amazing set of native instruments (such as the ES2 and the EXS24 mk II) are exclusive to *Logic Audio* and can not be used in any other program (a convincing reason alone to remix in *Logic*). Some plug-in adapters support virtual instruments (such as Audioease's *VST Wrapper*), but an instrument's stability and functionality are sometimes compromised when using an adapter.

AUDIO AND MIDI REQUIRED

Virtual instruments require MIDI and audio connections, just like a MIDI keyboard or sound module do. There must be a MIDI sequence track telling the virtual instrument what to play, and its output must be plugged into an audio mixer channel for sound. It's easy to forget these basic rules because software connections are less tangible; they run in the background and aren't made by plugging in physical cables.

Some digital audio sequencer's integrate MIDI and audio functionality into a single mixer channel, called an *instrument channel*. It acts like an audio channel in your virtual mixer, and a MIDI track in your arrange window. Other programs take a more traditional approach and require that the instrument is inserted on an aux mixer channel for sound, and that you create a separate MIDI track for performance control. No matter the system your digital audio sequencer employs, remember, both audio and MIDI connections are required for an instrument to function properly. Keep this in mind and you should be able to troubleshoot most problems.

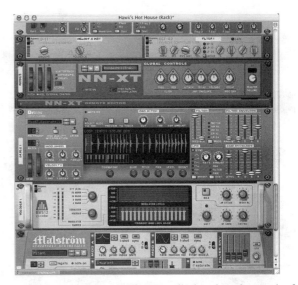

FIGURE 5.8 *Reason. Reason*, by Propellerhead, and its rack of many virtual instruments and effects.

Virtual Instrument Categories

There are many different categories of virtual instruments. Some emulate hardware units, others are thoroughly original with no counterpart in the real world. Many instruments are multi-timbral (can respond to more than one MIDI channel at a time with a different sound for each MIDI channel), some are not. However, the fact that plug-ins, and some stand-alone programs (such as *Reason*) let you run more than one copy of an instrument at the same time means that being multi-timbral is not so important. As with hardware units, it's nice to have several different types of instruments at your disposal: synths, drum machines, and samplers. Since the price of virtual instruments is a fraction of what comparable hardware units cost, a small budget is no longer a big roadblock to these ends.

SYNTHESIZERS

There are so many soft synths on the market, certainly there will be more than a few that strike your fancy. Popular software copies of vintage gear include Native Instruments' *Pro53* and *FM7* (see figure 5.9), emulations of Sequential Circuits' Prophet 5 and Yamaha's DX7 II units, respectively. Popular instruments that don't copy any particular hardware unit include Native Instruments' *Absynth* and Steinberg's *Plex*.

SAMPLERS

Hardware samplers get broken into two categories: those that can record and those that can't, the later being for sample playback only. Software samplers, especially plug-ins, usually don't have recording

capabilities. They have no need for this feature because all soft samplers can import and play back standard audio files. Recording samples can be done in your digital audio sequencer, then these samples can be bounced to disk and imported to the sampler. This is a common technique in remixing used for creating a wide range of effects (like taking advantage of a soft sampler's filter envelope, see chapter 13).

Most soft samplers read WAV files, and many also recognize AIFF and SDII. The best samplers can even import the CD-ROM instrument disks of hardware samplers, like Akai and Emu, giving them access to years of sound library development. Popular soft samplers among remix producers include Emagic's *EXS24 mk II* (see figure 5.10), MOTU's *Machfive*, and Steinberg's *Halion*. Reason also has two easy-to-use samplers—the NN-19 Digital Sampler and NN-XT Advanced Sampler—which can import WAV and AIFF audio files.

DRUM MACHINES

Synths and samplers are often used to create and play drum sounds. However, well designed virtual drum machines offer features that are specifically tailored to drum programming. For example, drum pads, preset amplitude and filter percussion envelopes, mute

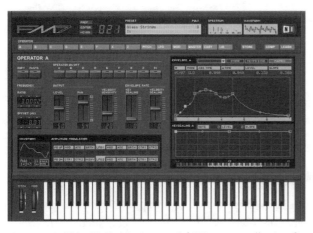

FIGURE 5.9 FM7. Native Instruments' FM7, an excellent software emulation of Yamaha's popular, vintage DX7 II hardware unit.

FIGURE 5.10 EXS24 mk II. Emagic's EXS24 mk II sampler is a favorite among remix producers, despite the fact that it is exclusive to Logic Audio.

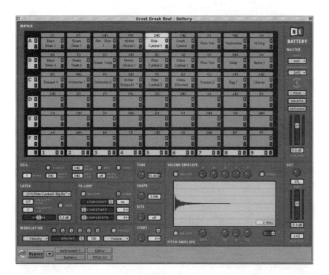

FIGURE 5.11 *Battery.* Native Instruments' *Battery* is a virtual drum machine with huge, multi-sampled preset kits that sound great.

groups (for multi-sampled instruments like hi-hats and triangles), and even built-in pattern sequencers (such as those found on vintage Roland drum machines).

Native Instruments' *Battery* (see figure 5.11) is a wonderful virtual drum machine, as is Steinberg's *LM-4 MarkII*. Both instruments allow you to drag and drop audio files from your computer's desktop to their drum pads, making the creation of custom kits very fast. *Reason's* Redrum Drum Computer module is also a particularly nice instrument for remixing projects because of its onboard pattern sequencer, classic swing settings, and large selection of electronic and dance drum sounds.

Key Peripheral Programs

For the most part, with a digital audio sequencer and a few choice virtual instruments, you're ready to remix. But there are a few other programs that can come in handy, and really help to round out your remixing arsenal.

AUDIO CD AUTHORING

By far, the most important peripheral program is an audio CD authoring application. When your remix is complete, you'll want to burn an audio CD of your mix for listening, getting feedback, and promotional purposes (such as handing out to club DJs). You might already own the CDR burner, but without a good authoring program, it doesn't do you much good.

Often, CDR burners come bundled with very basic authoring software. It's usually fine for simple jobs, such as backing up computer files or burning one song to disk. However, if you need more control, such as track level adjustment, custom pause times, track crossfades, and disk-at-once (a recording feature necessary to ensure error free copies should you want to mass duplicate from your CDR), then you'll need a more professional program. Roxio's *Toast Titanium* and *Jam* are good choices for the Mac. For the PC, *WaveLab* by Steinberg boasts comprehensive CD burning capabilities. (For a less expensive application, try *Easy CD Creator* by Roxio.)

WAVE EDITORS

All the top digital audio sequencers have fairly well developed wave editing functions built-in. However, there are still times when a separate wave editor program comes in handy, offering a feature or a way of doing something that isn't available in your digital audio sequencer. For example, you'll need them for tasks such as batch processing a group of files, converting one file type to another type, importing a CD audio track, viewing a waveform with better resolution, or just auditioning and fine tuning a stereo audio file (such as a mixdown) without opening your digital audio sequencer and creating a whole new project simply to hear that track.

Bias' *Peak* for the Mac is an excellent program for most of these tasks. *Sparks*, by TC Electronic, also for Mac, is perfect for radical effects processing using the programs' FX Machine (a powerful effects matrix), and for batch converting (especially standard audio files to MP3 files). Steinberg's *WaveLab* has long been a popular wave editor program on the PC, featuring a good arsenal of editing tools, built-in effects, batch processing, and support for hardware samplers.

MISCELLANEOUS

There are a few very important programs that are widely used by remix producers, in conjunction with their favorite digital audio sequencer, to open up new and interesting creative avenues. *Reason's* Matrix Pattern Sequencer module is wonderful for concocting a wide range of rhythmic gated effects, in addition to its more traditional use as a neat step sequencer. *ReCycle* (see figure 5.12), also by Propellerheads, not only lets you create your own custom REX files (for more on this subject, see chapter 8), but can also produce its own set of unique effects (such as rhythmic gated effects, something like a DJ would do using a crossfader, see chapter 13). For building grooves using loops, nothing beats Ableton's *Live* and Sonic Foundry's *Acid*. *Live* also features some stunning built-in effects, such as Grain delay (for more about this effect, see chapter 13).

> *We use* ReCycle *for time correcting rhythmic parts. We've also been using* Reason *a lot more, incorporating it for sound design and instant inspiration stuff.*
>
> —Chris Cox, Thunderpuss

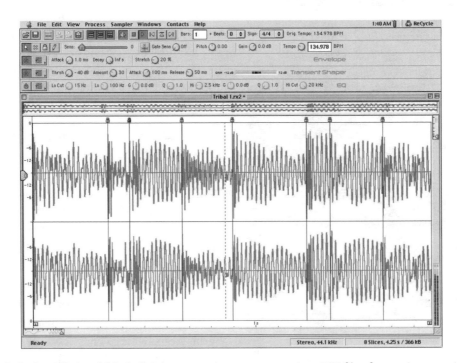

FIGURE 5.12 ReCycle. Propellerheads' ReCycle lets you create your own custom REX files for use in compatible digital audio sequencers and *Reason's* Dr. REX Loop Player module.

Additional Hardware

In addition to all the wonderful, essential hardware discussed in chapter 4, there are several pieces of gear that, though they are not absolutely necessary, can add significantly to your remixing setup. These are luxury items: extra hardware for more sounds, better effects options, and increased control of your remixing programs. Don't worry about getting all this gear immediately, but you should know about these tools so that when you're ready to take your remixing system to the next level, you can do it right.

TOO MUCH EQUIPMENT

Adding new gear should be done slowly—one, maybe two units at a time. Every piece of equipment has its own learning curve, and introducing too many units simultaneously will mire your remixing in the technical details of learning that new gear. When you are comfortable with your digital audio sequencer and the basics of remix production, adding new equipment to your setup will feel perfectly natural—an extension of your skills and desire to push your creative limits. Despite what a sales person might tell you, there is never a rush to buy a piece of gear. Prices on equipment are always falling, and new and improved units are always right around the corner. Remember, your computer, a good digital audio sequencer, and a basic sample library are all you really need to be remixing.

Controllers

There are two basic types of controllers available: MIDI controllers and control surfaces. Traditional MIDI controllers (such as MIDI keyboards) are for sending MIDI performance data to your sound modules and digital audio sequencer. A *control surface* looks like a traditional recording mixer, but its controls are designed instead to give you real-world controls over your digital audio sequencer's tracks and virtual mixer.

MIDI CONTROLLERS

Besides standard MIDI keyboard controllers, there are many other types of MIDI controllers too. Most mimic traditional instruments, like Roland's HandSonic HPD-15 hand drum (see figure 6.1), Yamaha's WX-5 wind instrument, and Blue Chip's Axon AX-100 guitar controller.

A fun and important part of dance and electronic music is turning knobs and pressing buttons to tweak synth parameters. Nothing compares to the physical knobs and buttons of a vintage sound module. When you're working with a software instrument, using a mouse and computer keyboard to dial in a parameter or press a button just doesn't feel right. Fortunately, MIDI controller boxes (such as the Pocket Dial by Doepfer Musikelektronik, see figure 6.2) can give you real-world control of a software instrument's virtual knobs and buttons. These units have a set of controls (usually some combination of knobs, buttons, or faders) that send MIDI Continuous Controller (CC) messages to your software instruments, letting you change, and automate their parameters in real-time. Some controller keyboards also feature onboard MIDI control sections, like M-Audio's Oxygen8 and Radium (see figure 4.7).

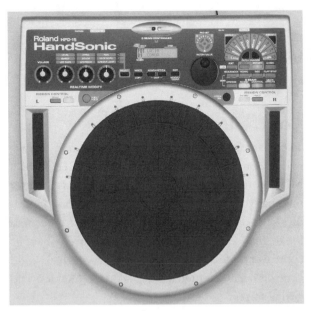

FIGURE 6.1 HandSonic. If the idea of a hand drum style MIDI controller sounds like a dream come true, than you must check out the HandSonic HPD-15 by Roland.

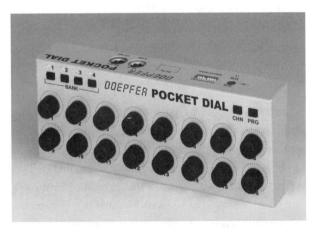

FIGURE 6.2 Pocket Dial. Pocket Dial, by Doepfer Musikelektronik, features sixteen rotary encoder knobs that are perfect for controlling the parameters of virtual instruments.

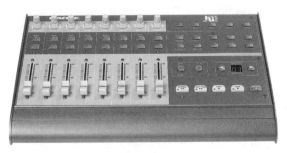

FIGURE 6.3 Baby HUI. For its quality motorized faders, compact size, and reasonable price, it's hard to beat Mackie's Baby HUI for controlling a digital audio sequencer's virtual mixer.

CONTROL SURFACES

There are a variety of control surfaces available. Some feature moving (also called dynamic or motorized) faders while others are static. Some have built-in audio interfaces and speaker-monitor control sections while others are pure control surfaces with no audio circuitry at all. Some control surfaces are designed to work exclusively with one digital audio sequencer, others take a more open-ended approach and can function with a variety of programs. When choosing a control surface for your setup, you need to take all of these features under consideration.

Moving faders are superior to static faders because they always perfectly mirror your virtual mixer's onscreen faders, providing constant visual and tactile feedback of your mix. Though control surfaces with moving faders have had a reputation as being pricey (especially when compared to their static fader counterparts), Mackie's Baby HUI (see figure 6.3), with an initial retail price of $799, sets a new standard. Control surfaces with a built-in speaker monitor control section (such as Mackie's HUI) are wonderful, but the importance of such a feature has not been so widely recognized (see One Good Monitor Section, page 25). Control surfaces that double as your digital audio sequencer's audio I/O, and can also serve as a stand-alone mixer (such as Digidesign's Digi002, see figure 6.4), are very convenient and can be an excellent value.

A control surface that works exclusively with one digital audio sequencer will provide the best interface for that application. The downside is that it will become a large, and useless appendage, should you decide to work in another program. If you work regularly with more than one application, units that can function with a variety of digital audio sequencers (such as Mackie's Mackie Control, see figure 6.5) provide the most flexibility. However, such surfaces may not include all of the really deep, application-specific controls of a dedicated surface. For these functions, you will likely need to keep your mouse and computer keyboard close at hand.

Most control surfaces use some combination of MIDI Control Change (see Appendix B) and SysEx messages to communicate with a digital audio sequencer. Consequently, each control surface that employs standard MIDI connections (such as Mackie's Mackie Control and its sidecar expander options, the Mackie Control Expander and C4) requires its own dedicated MIDI interface ports, In and Out. You will need a multi-port MIDI interface (such as MOTU's MTP AV) if you want to connect several control surfaces and sidecar expanders for an extended control surface setup (for example, one Mackie Control and three Expanders for 24 faders). The exceptions to this rule are control surfaces that employ FireWire, USB, or RS-232 ports to communicate data with the computer.

FIGURE 6.4 Digi002. Digidesign's Digi002 is an exclusive control surface for *Pro Tools LE*, featuring moving faders and a dedicated speaker monitor control section. It conveniently connects to the computer via FireWire, and doubles as a stand-alone 8x4x2 digital mixing board.

DSP Expansion Systems

The idea behind having a system that enhances the audio processing power of your computer is not new. For years, *Pro Tools* systems were entirely dependent on DSP expansion cards to provide the raw horsepower for Digidesign's TDM audio processing technology. Today, despite more powerful computers than ever, extra processing power for audio related tasks is especially important because plug-ins (both effects and instruments) require more and more processing power as their algorithms become increasingly complex. The amount of DSP power necessary to run a host of high-quality plug-ins is outpacing current computers. DSP expansion systems solve the problem of not having enough processing power to add that one last virtual instrument or effect plug-in, for that perfect remix.

FIGURE 6.5 Mackie Control. Mackie's Mackie Control is a control surface that can interface with a variety of digital audio sequencers, and features moving faders and several sidecar expander options.

There aren't too many expansion systems to choose from, yet. Digidesign's venerable PCI card TDM systems are expensive and only work with *Pro Tools* software and the company's high-end interfaces (like the 192 I/O). TC Electronic and Universal Audio (UA) both offer alternatives, PowerCore and the UAD-1 Powered Plug-ins card, respectively. These PCI expansion cards provide extra DSP power to many

FIGURE 6.6 Magma Chassis. A single slot CardBus chassis by Magma, the CB1F (left), houses the Digidesign Digi001 interface's PCI card, and is connected to an Apple Titanium laptop.

Figure 6.7 PowerCore FireWire. TC Electronic's groundbreaking PowerCore FireWire, delivers extra DSP and audio I/O in a single rack space, via FireWire.

of the top, VST-compatible (and MAS-compatible, in the case of PowerCore) digital audio sequencers. The catch is that they only work with their own proprietary plug-ins. However, this is only a minor problem since both cards come bundled with lots of great plug-ins, and using these plug-ins frees up the computers DSP resources for your native plug-ins.

Most DSP expansion systems are PCI-card based. However, if you have a laptop that features a Type II PC Card slot, you can employ a PCI expansion card using a PCI expansion chassis, like the CardBus PCI Expansion systems by Magma (see figure 6.6). Another alternative is TC Electronic's PowerCore FireWire unit (see figure 6.7), providing twice the processing power of its PCI card counterpart in a single rack space. This is a groundbreaking unit, the very first FireWire DSP system. It's likely to be the forerunner of many more similar units in the coming years.

BOUNCING TO DISK

Remember, if you don't have enough DSP power for a particular task, whether you own a DSP expansion system or not, you can always bounce a few tracks to disk as a means of freeing up processing power. Select a track that employs a lot of DSP intensive plug-ins, and that you are fairly certain won't need anymore changes. Solo and record that track to disk. (Some programs have a bounce-to-disk feature specifically designed to streamline this task.) Save your session with a different name, so you can go back to it later if you need to make changes. Then import the bounced file to a new track, and delete the old track with all of its associated plug-ins. Repeat this procedure until you have enough DSP power to complete your task.

Sound Modules

MIDI has been around for over two decades, and needless to say, there is a lot of MIDI gear floating about, from vintage keyboards to spanking new workstations. Any MIDI sound source can potentially add a unique edge to your remixes. Simply connect a MIDI sound module or keyboard to your digital audio sequencer to gain complete performance control, and possibly automation control over many of its parameters. Just mixing in a couple of choice MIDI sound modules with your virtual instruments can make a big difference in a track's quality and distinctiveness.

Dance and electronic music producers covet vintage gear, like Roland drum machines and synthesizers (such as the TR-808 and 909, or the Juno series of analog synths). However, units like these are hard to find and often overpriced when they do turn up. Fortunately, there are many great musical instrument makers like Korg, Yamaha, Roland, Access, and Clavia who have all taken cues from the popularity of these vintage products and created many new dance and electronic music instruments. These new instruments are characterized by modeled analog sounds, analog style interfaces (lots of knobs and buttons), and some even have pattern sequencers in the style of Roland's old drum machines.

Roland's SH-32 is a mean-sounding recreation of the company's old SH-101 synth with added analog drum sounds, and lots of extra features thrown in for good measure (like a multi-effects engine and an advanced pattern sequencer). Korg manufactures the Electribe series of tabletop sound modules that are designed specifically for dance and electronic music production, and sound great. They also make the Karma workstation (pictured on page 161), which is packed full of sounds that can be morphed and twist-

FIGURE 6.8 Nord Lead 2X. The Nord Lead 2X by Clavia is a wonderful analog-style synth that has become quite popular among producers of dance and pop music.

ed to fit just about any remix. Its unique style of synthesis allows you to synchronize practically all of its parameters to incoming MIDI Beat Clock for some really interesting effects. Access and Clavia both manufacture popular analog-sounding synths—the Virus c and the Nord Lead 2X (see figure 6.8), respectively—that are loaded with knobs and buttons for excellent analog-style sound tweaking.

For years now, we've pretty much used the Nord Lead on every Thunderpuss mix somehow or some way.

—Barry Harris, Thunderpuss

External Effects

Effect plug-ins cover an enormous amount of ground, and for the most part, will satisfy all of your processing needs. However, there are several DJ-inspired effects units on the market that offer a level of real-time control missing in software effects. These units give you the ability to continuously morph effect algorithms using distinctive physical controls. They are hands-on, dynamic effects designed to be used live by DJs, but work great for remixing in the studio as

well. (See chapter 13 for more on using effects to create dramatic builds and changes.)

One of the best examples is Korg's Kaoss Pad 2 (pictured on page 160), featuring a touch-sensitive pad that can be tapped and stroked to change several effect parameters simultaneously. Another such unit is the Alesis AirFX (see figure 6.9); with its unique light-beam controller, parameters can be manipulated in three dimensions. Having less radical controllers, but equally useful effects, the Electix Filter Factory (which has been unfortunately discontinued, so you'll need to find it on the used market), and the superior sounding TC Electronic's FireworX have big, easy-to-grab knobs for adjusting parameters on-the-fly. An effect unit with a MIDI input is generally more desirable than one without MIDI because its parameters can be automated by your digital audio sequencer, and its effect algorithms can often be synchronized to your remix's tempo.

We still haven't come across a plug-in that comes anywhere near the clarity and brilliance of outboard units like Lexicon and TC Electronic.

—J. Scott G., Deepsky

BRINGING IN EXTERNAL EFFECTS

The best way to connect an external effects unit to your digital audio sequencer is to set up a send-and-return effects loop (see figure 6.10).

STEP 1. Connect the output—one for mono or two for a stereo effects send (generally a mono send is fine)—of your audio interface to the input of the effects unit.

STEP 2. Connect both outputs (the return should always be in stereo) from the effects unit to a pair of inputs on the audio interface.

STEP 3. In your digital audio sequencer's mixer, assign a bus-to-send signal to the appropriate outputs of the interface. Most programs will let you name the bus for easy visibility; give that bus the name of your external effect unit.

STEP 4. Create an aux-return channel in your virtual mixer, and assign it the effect inputs. Most programs will let you name the interface's inputs as well; give these inputs the name of your effect unit. Now, using a channel's effect send, you can bus signal to the external effects unit. The return is heard at the aux channel.

If both your external effects unit and your audio interface feature compatible digital I/O (such as S/PDIF or ADAT Optical), you may want to create the effects loop using these connections. This will keep your interface's analog connections available for other tasks.

Microphones and Preamps

If you plan on recording quality vocals, or any acoustic instruments, you will need a decent microphone and microphone preamp. Low quality microphones produce poor sounding recordings, so try not to cut corners when selecting a mic. A condenser mic is preferable to a dynamic mic, and the ability to select pickup patterns (like cardioid, hyper-cardioid, omni, and figure-8) is always a nice option. Cad and Blue are two companies that make very good, mid-priced microphones. In particular, check out Cad's VSM and the Baby Bottle by Blue.

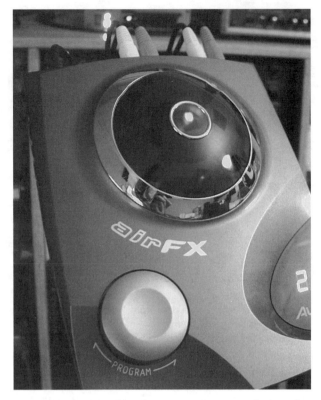

FIGURE 6.9 AirFX. The Alesis AirFX is centered around a unique lightbeam controller that allows you to manipulate its effects, by passing your hands over the controller, in fun and interesting ways.

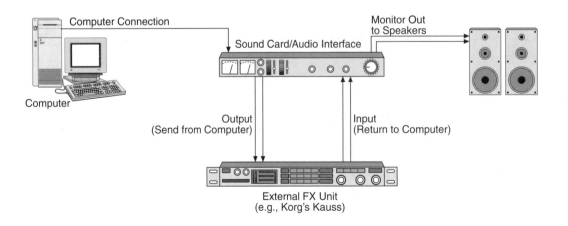

FIGURE 6.10 External Effects Loop. The connections for setting up an external effects loop directly through your audio interface without using a traditional mixing board.

FIGURE 6.11 6176 Channel Strip. Universal Audio's high-end 6176 Channel Strip isn't cheap ($2,500 retail), but if you want to record master quality vocals, it's a worthwhile investment.

Some audio interfaces include onboard microphone preamps (such as MOTU's 828mkII and 896), and these are fine for most tasks—especially when paired with a quality mic. If your interface doesn't have pre-amps, and you just need one good mic input, Mindprint makes an excellent sounding, single-rack-space tube unit for under a grand, the EnVoice. If you're really serious about recording master quality vocal tracks, look into investing in a high-end mic pre-amp, like Universal Audio's 6176 Channel Strip (see figure 6.11). Going this route isn't cheap, but a pre-amp of this ilk paired with a great microphone can take your recordings to the next level.

DJ Gear

Some might consider a DJ mixer and a pair of turnta-bles essential hardware, but the fact is you don't need to be a DJ to be a great remix producer. Many good DJs are also good remix producers because they know what dance-music audiences like—not because of their turntable skills, but because they are out playing the music and watching how people respond. Learning what's going on in the dance music scene is about having your ear to the ground, whether this is through DJing regularly or just being a fan is not important.

That said, since remixes are, for the most part, made to be played in a club by a DJ, having a basic DJ setup in your studio is a good idea. A simple, 2-channel DJ mixer (such as one by Stanton or Numark) will let you practice your DJ mix skills and give you the ability to compare other tracks to your own in the course of mixing a mock set. Since your final reference mixdown will be to CDR, a pair of inexpensive DJ CD decks (such as one by Pioneer or Numark) are more crucial than a pair of turntables. However, you should have at least one turntable (preferably an industry standard Technics SL-1200, pictured on page 4) for listening to vinyl-only releases, and eventually, checking the vinyl test pressings for your own releases.

SECTION III

First Moves

CHAPTER 7

Target a Style

Dance and electronic music is constantly evolving. Just when you think you have all the current styles identified, a new one crops up to confuse the categories. Nevertheless, there are many good reasons for labeling styles, despite the fact that doing so might initially seem narrow-minded. Without labels, record stores would have no means for creating sections, and customers would be unable to browse through records by music style. Everything would need to be organized alphabetically, and finding a particular recording would be an exercise in cross-referencing song titles and the names of artists. Categorizing make releases easy to find; this helps sell music, and that's a good thing for all of us.

When promoting your remix, or simply passing it out to potential fans, knowing what category your remix falls under will help you target an audience. Using industry-accepted labels to describe your remix will help people know what to expect before they hear that track, and this can help you focus your promotional efforts. For example, giving a drum-and-bass track to somebody who listens to smooth jazz probably isn't a great idea, and most likely just a waste of your product. Club DJs, in particular, tend to play very specific styles of music, and they like to know ahead of time if your remix will go with their sets. Do your best to match the style of a remix with that of the DJ you're pitching it to.

DESCRIBING YOUR SOUND

It's okay to combine a few different categories when describing a remix's sound, as long as the categories you use are well known (like drum-and-bass meets ambient, or tribal-progressive-house). Try not to get carried away with long, flowery descriptions; keep your prose short and sweet. DJs, A&R (Artist and Repertoire—the people at labels who are in charge of scouting new talent), and press people who are constantly swamped with promotional releases, will appreciate concise and to-the-point labels.

Style and Tempo

Before you begin a remix, it's a good idea to determine what dance music style you're going for. A key deciding factor is the original song's tempo. Most every style of dance music inhabits a select range of tempos, and it's impossible to make a song conform to the entire range of every style. The less you change a track's tempo, the better it will sound, in the end. Extreme time compression or expansion, no matter how it's done, and regardless of the algorithm that's employed, always results in reduced-quality audio. By first identifying the tempo of the original song, then comparing it to the tempos of popular dance music styles (see figure 7.1), you'll be able to narrow the field of possible target styles for the remix.

Tempo changes that are less than +/–25 BPM are usually safe. However, this figure may be significantly less if the track you are trying to tempo-change contains material that doesn't stretch or compress well (such as a vocal track with lots of effects or a bass line with long sustained notes). In general, speeding a track up sounds better than slowing a track down. When you slow a track down, attacks become mushy and lose their punch because transients get smeared. Speeding a track up has the opposite effect, compressing transients to create punchy, crisp attacks.

MUSIC STYLE	TEMPO (BPM)
Drum-and-Bass	150–170
Trance	130–150
House	100–130
Hip-Hop	85–110
Down Tempo	65–95
Ambient	85 and below

FIGURE 7.1 Style and Typical Tempo Ranges.

Recognizing Styles

There are several primary dance and electronic music styles that have evolved over the years (listed in figure 7.1). Many sub-categories have flowered, combining these styles in unique ways and with different world music influences (such as Brazilian or East Indian). However, at the root of every new style, there continues to be some component of these main styles. Recognizing these elements will help you to understand current trends and styles, and give you direction when targeting a style (or creating your own style) for a remix.

Know that even between dance and electronic music experts, labeling different styles is a heavily debated topic. Defining where one style ends and another begins is, at best, an imperfect science. The following are brief descriptions of several of the most popular styles today to help you distinguish one genre of dance music from the next. However, the best way to really understand the differences between the styles, is to listen to songs in those styles. Magazines such as

Urb are a great way to get the scoop on hot new releases by genre.

> It seems that new dance music styles are emerging every day.

—Chris Gill (Gilla Monsta),
editor of *Remix* Magazine (1999–2002)

DRUM-AND-BASS

Jungle is the slower paced forerunner of today's drum-and-bass. Drum-and-bass has probably succeeded in the popular spotlight, where jungle did not, because it adds melodic elements and sometimes vocals to the purely drum-driven rhythms of jungle. It is often portrayed as the thinking man's electronica because of its complex rhythms and jazz chord voicings. Tempos are always frenetic, between 150 and 170 BPM. However, the bass and melody lines are usually performed half-time, actually following tempos of 75 to 85 BPM. Bass lines are usually characterized by very low frequency, sub-bass sounds, and the drums generally have an acoustic, real-drum sound about them. In fact, the drums are often samples of an r&b or jazz drummer, either sampled from an old record, or made to sound that way, then cut up, sped up, and the individual beats rearranged to create unique sounding drum beats.

The complex technique of recycling and rearranging a live drummer's original beat has given rise to a popular style called breaks (also sometimes called *breakbeat*, though this term better describes the drum loop centered style that predates jungle). This style takes the production techniques of drum-and-bass and fuses them with the electronic sounds of trance, usually at less frenzied tempos of 135 to 140 BPM. *Tribal* is a return to the austere arrangements of jungle, but at house tempos and with acoustic percussion elements.

TRANCE

Starting around the same time as house, but originally dubbed "electro" (or "techno") because of its heavy electronic sound, trance has become hugely popular in dance clubs worldwide. It has really become the poster child of music for the pop rave scene. It's characterized by faster tempos than house, 135 to 145 BPM, combined with electronic drums, synthesizer pads, arpeggios, and hook-driven lead lines. Because of its tempos and lush synth arrangements, the bass lines are usually pretty simple, such as two alternating notes, or even a single note played on the up-beats. Vocals are usually simple, short, and catchy melodies, or ethereal female leads floating amongst the synths.

Trance has given rise to several other styles, characterized by fusing elements of drum-and-bass and house with the musical elements of trance. Today's *techno* is a sort of raw, stripped-down version of trance, with much simpler musical ideas and hints of breaks style programming. *Hardcore* is faster, with many more breakbeat influences and the sped up melodic elements of house. Trance has also turned inward, towards its darker emotional elements, to spawn *progressive trance* (such as *goa* or *psychedelic* and *acid*)—harder, deeper, grittier versions of the comparatively happy sounding, popular trance music.

HOUSE

Growing straight out of the '70s and early '80s disco music, that evolved into the Chicago "warehouse" dance-music scene of the mid-to-late '80s, house music's roots are still very prevalent in contemporary tracks. It's characterized by a conservative dance tempo (around 120 BPM), an open hi-hat on the up-beats driving the rhythm track, with a keyboard playing a simple, alternating major to minor (or vice versa) chord progression, and a plucked guitar (or similar sounding instrument) adding extra elements of funk. Often, the track will have a standard song structure (such as intro, verse, chorus, verse, chorus, break, and so on). The melodic hook is usually carried by gospel-tinged vocals, and sometimes a lead instrument, like a horn. Bass lines can sound like they would work equally well over an up-tempo r&b tune, and are usually performed by a real bass, or a synth patch with real-bass overtones.

Over the years, many harder-edged versions of house have emerged. They are generally characterized by faster tempos, more driving sounds, and less soulful lead lines. However, many of the distinctive drum elements remain intact, like the cliché open hi-hats or conga-like percussion parts. Garage (also called UK garage and two-step), progressive house, and acid house, are all styles that have evolved from house.

HIP-HOP

Not generally heralded as a form of electronic dance music, hip-hop does fit the mold. There are dance clubs that play hip-hop, the production of hip-hop depends heavily on electronic music equipment, and production teams like the Neptunes even do hip-hop remixes. In fact, to give credit where credit is due, many of the production techniques (such as loops and dirty drum samples) used in the more traditionally accepted forms of electronic dance music (like house, drum-and-bass, and breaks) were pioneered by hip-hop producers.

Hip-hop production techniques grew from kids making music in the streets, working with what they had available (old record players and drum machines) to create tracks for rappers. The musical influences behind hip-hop, its "feel," stems from r&b and soul, and to a lesser degree (depending on the song) funk, jazz, and disco. Most hip-hop songs are characterized by a lively groove, driven by a bouncy kick pattern, a laid back snare, and a swung hi-hat (often attributed to the MPC drum machine's quantize set to a swing value of 64%). Bass lines play a similar rhythmic pattern to the kick, and dirty vinyl samples and sound effects are usually employed to spice up the groove. Chords are played by a variety of instruments, from Rhodes keys, to analog sounding synths and funk guitars, while leads are almost universally performed by singers and rappers.

The most prevalent sub-genres on the electronic music scene, which have been heavily influenced by hip-hop, are acid jazz and trip-hop. From the conscious decision to merge the rhythms of hip-hop and the musical complexities of jazz comes *acid jazz*. At faster tempos and with a heavy jazz direction, acid jazz becomes a modern day bebop, while its less jazzed tinged and slower songs can melt into brainless lounge music (ideal "chill out" music). The combination of hip-hop and dancehall reggae forms the backbone of *trip-hop*. Less musically high brow than acid jazz, but striving for more enlightened lyrical sensibilities than gangster rap, trip-hop is characterized by ethereal sounding loops and effects, glued together by mid-tempo, funky grooves. Spoken word often delivers the song's lyrics, and may be underpinned by the soulful crooning of a female singer.

DOWN TEMPO

Lounge music and jazz ballads are the main progenitors of down tempo. With electronic sounds, noisy samples, and funkier grooves, these classic genres are given a musical facelift without losing that relaxed, cool vibe. Rare drum grooves culled from old records often form the down-tempo song's basic rhythm track. Bass, strings, pianos, and acoustic guitars sound real, and if they aren't sampled loops of real performances, they are probably live musicians. If there are vocals, they are likely sung by a female with a sultry and mysterious voice. Down tempo often follows traditional song structures, and its arrangements can be fairly complex, bordering on a pop music production.

AMBIENT

Not every electronica song must have a big, driving beat. At some point during an evening of dancing, you'll want to take a breather, and an ambient track may be just the ticket. A good DJ can mix an ambient track into their set without upsetting the evening's flow, using it to take the audience excitement level down for a spell. Warehouse raves have traditionally had at least one dedicated "chill-out" room where nothing but ambient is played.

The ambient style is characterized by lots of ethereal synth pads, mixed with a variety of world instruments (like East Indian sitar and Australian didjeridu), occasional light percussion (such as hand drums), unique sound effects, and everything is awash in lush reverbs and delays. Bass lines may be droning, extremely simple, or nonexistent altogether. Drum machine patterns are sometimes woven into the aural tapestry, usually with a lot of effects.

Tempo Figuring Tactics

Before you can decide on the dance music style you should target for your remix, you need to figure out the original song's tempo. The more precisely you can determine its tempo (preferably to at least two decimal places), the more precisely you will be able to change that tempo. For example, some time compression/expansion programs require that you enter the track's original tempo, then your target tempo. If your original tempo calculation is off, the program's output tempo will also be off.

There are only a couple of ways to calculate a song's tempo accurately. Both methods require carefully extracting a 2- to 4-bar loop from the song to use in calculating its tempo. Figuring out the tempo from a perfectly cut loop will give you the best estimate of the song's overall tempo, allowing you to focus on a specific section and ignore possible tempo variations over the course of the song as a whole (see the sidebar, Accounting for Human Feel). Tapping out the tempo while timing yourself with a stopwatch, no matter how good your timing is, will not give you a completely accurate reading, nor do most automatic BPM counters (such as those found on some DJ mixers).

ACCOUNTING FOR HUMAN FEEL

The tempo of a song that is arranged with a drum machine is easy to figure out because the drum machine's timing is constant and unwavering. By contrast, the tempo of a song played by a real drummer, live, without the benefit of a headphone click-track, will speed up and slow down over the course of the song. Many remixes just focus on short loops, extracted from key sections of a song (such as the first four bars of the chorus), so tempo variations aren't a big cause for concern. However, if your objective is to remix an entire song, using all of its verse, chorus, and bridge melodies (as is usually the case when remixing a name artist for a major record label), tempo variations can be a pain.

You should still follow the steps for calculating the song's basic tempo in order to decide on a remix target style. However, making an entire track that has lots of tempo variations conform to a new tempo requires time-consuming and painstaking editing, often at a microscopic level (a process called *micro-editing*). Though it's possible to create a tempo map of the entire song (in the top digital audio sequencers), and sequence parts to this map, this does nothing to straighten out its tempo. Dance music is best written with steady, repetitive beats, so using such a tempo map is not recommended for a dance remix. Micro-editing is really the only sure way to adjust an entire track with tempo fluctuations to match one straight tempo all the way through. Conforming all of a song's vocals to a new tempo, accounting for tempo variations, tuning, and fixing time-stretching artifacts is discussed in chapter 9.

EXTRACTING AN 8-BAR LOOP

Find a section of the original song that has a good solid beat, then cut out a 2- or 4-bar loop. This loop will be used for calculating the song's tempo.

STEP 1. Open the original song in either a waveform editing program or your digital audio sequencer's waveform editing window. You will need to zoom all the way into the waveform to find your edit points, zero crossing points (where the waveform crosses the X-axis), so make sure your waveform editor has good zoom controls.

STEP 2. Find a 2- or 4-bar section of the song with a clear, defined beat.

STEP 3. Set your program to play back your selection in a continuous-loop mode.

STEP 4. Find the first downbeat of the loop and make a cut, or "separation," at the very start of its waveform (see figure 7.2). This is the stage when you will need to zoom all the way into the waveform to find its zero crossing point, where the cut will be made.

STEP 5. Find the beginning of the first downbeat immediately following your looped section, and make a cut directly in front of its waveform. (What you should see will look very similar to figure 7.2, only that downbeat represents the end of your loop rather than its beginning.)

STEP 6. Check your loop to make sure that it loops in perfect time, that there is no delay or jump in the beats when the section loops around. This may take a couple of tries. Play with your loop end point, by moving it forward or backward slightly in time, until you get it right.

A CAPPELLA IS MISSING BEATS

If you are working with an *a cappella* version of a song, since there are no beats, it's pretty tough to extract a perfect loop. Instead, use a version of the song with beats, preferably the version that the vocal track matches, probably the radio version. (You can line up the *a cappella* version with the radio version in your digital audio sequencer to hear if they match, see figure 7.3.) Cut a 2- or 4-bar loop out of that version, and use it for calculating the song's tempo, and by default, the tempo of the *a cappella* version.

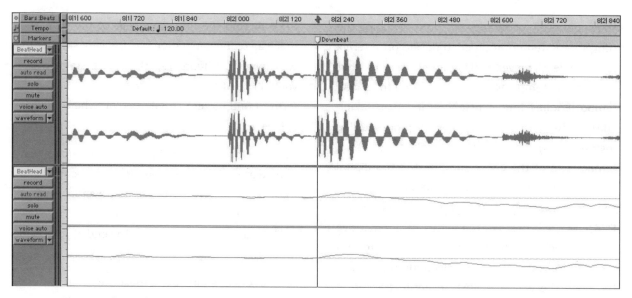

FIGURE 7.2 The Downbeat. The waveform of your downbeat will look something like this zoomed out (top), and zoomed in to make the separation at its zero crossing point, where the playbar sits (bottom).

I always start by determining the original tempo of the song. If all you have to work with is the vocals, the best way to figure out the tempo is by putting them on an audio track, then writing a very basic drum loop; kick on every quarter note, hi-hats on the eighths, and a clap on the backbeats. Adjust the loop's tempo until the vocals are in time with the drums. You may need to slide the vocal track around a bit to get its first downbeat to line up with the drums' first downbeat. When everything sounds good at the very beginning, check the very end of the song to hear if things are really on. If the vocals have drifted, you know that your tempo is a little off. A lot of times you can't just make whole number BPM changes to line things up, you have do hundredths of a BPM to get everything exact.

—Pablo La Rosa, Tune Inn Records

DO THE MATH

Here is the equation for figuring out the BPM of a loop, in 4/4 meter:

$$(60/\text{loop s length in seconds}) \times$$
$$(\text{number of bars} \times \text{number of beats per bar})$$
$$= \text{BPM}$$

Figure out what the BPM is for a 6.86 second loop that's four bars long.

STEP 1. $(60/6.86) \times (4 \times 4) = \text{BPM}$

STEP 2. $8.75 \times 16 = \text{BPM}$

STEP 3. The answer is 140 BPM.

LOOP CALCULATOR

A handy Loop Calculator to help you figure out tempo changes is available at AcidFanatic (www.acidfanatic.com), and it's freeware.

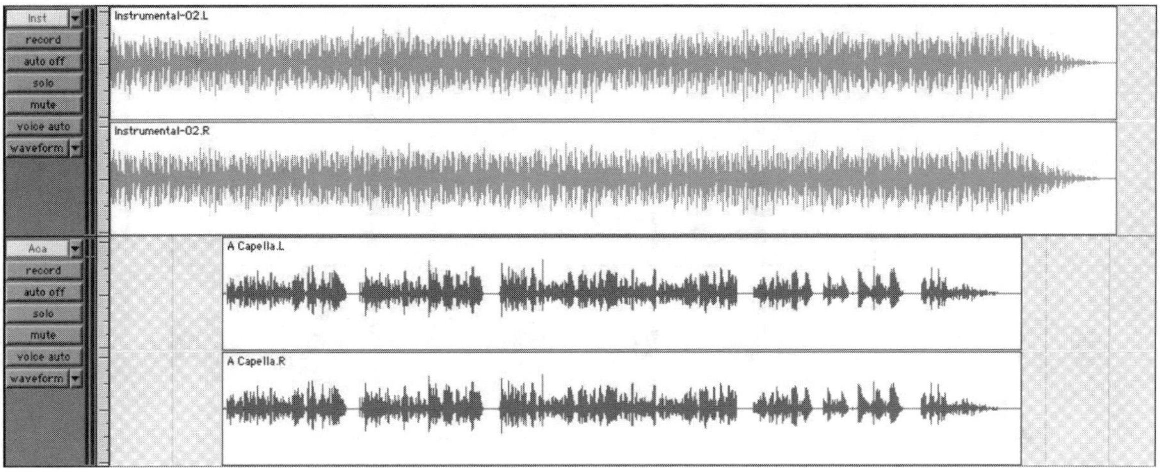

Figure 7.3 The Instrumental and *A Cappella*. An *a cappella* version of a song lined up with its radio version in *Pro Tools*. Since the vocals of the *a capella* version line up with the vocals of the radio version, we know that their tempos are identical and that it's okay to figure out the song's tempo using a loop from the radio version.

RECYCLE FOR TEMPO

Propellerheads' *ReCycle* program is excellent for figuring out the tempo of a loop. It can also expedite the entire operation, you don't need to crop a perfect loop in a waveform editor because *ReCycle's* breakpoint editing is excellent for designing loops.

STEP 1. Separate out a rough 2- or 4-bar loop from the original song. Make sure it's a section with a clear, well-defined beat, and that there is plenty of overhanging waveform on either side of the loop (see figure 7.4).

STEP 2. Save the rough loop as its own separate WAV audio file on your hard drive.

STEP 3. Open this WAV file in *ReCycle*.

STEP 4. Move the Sensitivity Amount slider forward until you see breakpoints on most of the beats (see figure 7.5).

STEP 5. Snap the L marker to the breakpoint at the beginning of the loop, and snap the R marker to the breakpoint at the end of the loop. Press Play to hear if the loop plays back seamlessly. If not, readjust the L and R markers until loop playback is correct.

STEP 6. Enter the loop's bars in the Bars field. Make sure that the effect Preview button and all of the Effect buttons are off. The loop's tempo will automatically appear in the Orig. Tempo field.

Speed Up or Slow Down

Now that you know the original song's tempo, you can make a wise decision about a style you want to target. If the song's tempo is 120 BPM, a trance style is within easy reach of the original tempo. At 104 BPM, you could keep this tempo and do a down-tempo remix, or speed the song up for a house remix. With an original tempo of 80 BPM, you could speed the song up for a down-tempo remix, or keep the tempo the same and do a double time, 160 BPM drum-and-bass remix.

Remember that slowing down a song doesn't usually sound as good as speeding it up. And double timing a song that you slowed down can lead to a train wreck. So if you have a 70 BPM song, slowing it down to a 60 BPM in order to make a house remix may not work. Ultimately, it depends on the material.

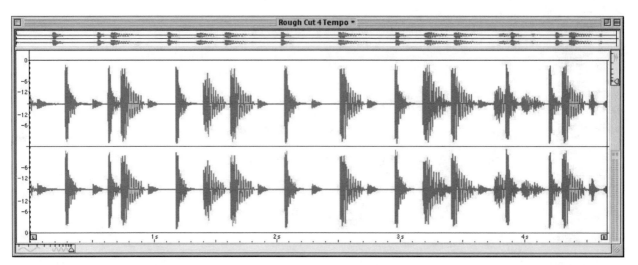

Figure 7.4 Extra Overhang. With lots of overhanging waveform on either side of this 2-bar loop, there is plenty of room to adjust the loop start and end points.

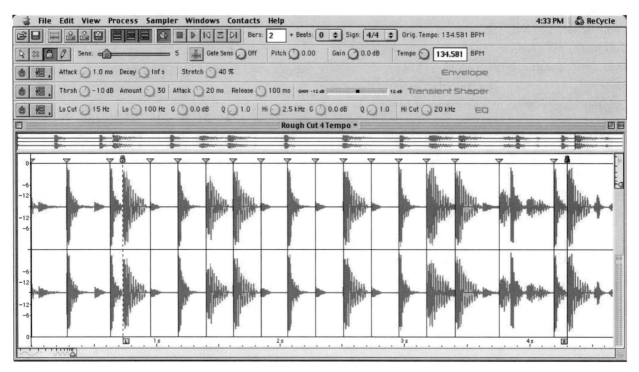

Figure 7.5 Working in *ReCycle*. The Sensitivity Slider in *ReCycle* lets you set breakpoints that follow the waveform's peaks.

CHAPTER 8

Project Preparation

Before you begin the creative phase of remixing, it's best to get all the technical grunt work out of the way. Create a project file, import tracks from the original song, make tempo and pitch corrections, breakpoint-edit key performances, bring in loops and samples, instantiate virtual instruments, and set up a custom mixer with effect sends. Take care of all these preparatory tasks at the start of your remix. Then, when it's time to write, arrange, and produce, you can concentrate on these more creative tasks, uninterrupted.

> *We get started on a remix by finding unique parts to work with in the original song. For example, there were a couple of things that came out of the Emilio Estefan camp, and of course, the percussion was just amazing. We pulled out those elements—recycled the percussion parts so we could utilize them.*
>
> —Chris Cox, Thunderpuss

TECHNICAL VS. CREATIVE

When you are working in the studio by yourself, it's easy to get mired in the details of the recording process and not get any real music done. One way to avoid this situation is to set aside separate, distinct times for the technical tasks and the creative tasks (just as if you were two people, an engineer and a producer). For example, if you know that you want to turn several loops from the original song into REX files, go ahead and recycle them all at the same time, getting all the breakpoint editing and file conversion tasks out of the way. Then import all of the REX files into your session and start having fun (rearranging beats, changing grooves, trying different effects, and so on).

Project Setup

The first thing to do is create a project file at the BPM and meter (usually 4/4 time for dance music) that you've decided will work best for your remix. Name and save the project to its own dedicated folder on your audio drive. Every audio file and document for this project should be stored in this folder. This will help you avoid lost audio files, should the project folder be moved (like if you back it up to a CDR), ensuring that the project's file directory remains unchanged.

If you have a song's breakout tracks or multitrack files to remix, import all of them (you never know which tracks you'll want to use for your remix) into your digital audio sequencer, and set them up in its Arrange window (see figure 8.1). Put the same instruments on the same tracks, one after the other, such as all the drum loops on the Drums track, the wah guitar on the Wah Gtr track, and so on. Line the first loop of each track up to bar 1, making sure that mono tracks are panned center, and that stereo tracks have their panning controls set to hard left and hard right. If everything is lined up properly, you should hear all of the elements of the song playing in time with each other. Don't worry right now about time-correcting the loops to match the project's tempo. We'll do that in a minute.

For reference, import a complete mix of the original song. It's always good to have a full mix handy to check key changes and chord progressions, or hear how the vocals sit with the original groove. Line up the track to bar 1, and nudge it into place (10 to 100 milliseconds at a time usually works well) so that its beats match up roughly with the loops' beats. The match doesn't have to be perfect—just good enough so that when you listen to the full mix, it isn't totally conflicting with the loops. Then mute that track so that you don't have to hear it until it's needed.

Set up your digital audio sequencer's mixer (see figure 8.2) with a few virtual instruments: something for drums, bass, and chords. These aren't your final instruments, just sounds to use for laying down a basic beat and beginning musical ideas. Create two aux return channels: one for reverb (a medium hall) and one for delay (a medium multi-tap delay line that can sync to tempo). These are essential effects that you will use on lots of instruments in every remix. Name the buses that you use to send signal to the aux channels, Reverb and Delay, and make sure that these buses are assigned as the inputs to the respective aux channels (where the effect plug-ins are inserted).

SACRED TEMPLATES

Most digital audio sequencers allow you to create a new project template that contains your preferred mixer setup, including virtual instruments and effects. The template can be made to automatically open when you boot the program or start a new project, saving you the hassle of recreating your favorite setup each time you start a new remix.

Choosing the Right Time-Correction Tool

There are two ways to adjust a track's tempo: time compression/expansion or *ReCycle*-style breakpoint editing. Each works very differently, and consequently, each should be used on different types of source material. Time compression/expansion quality is dependent on your digital audio sequencer's time stretching algorithm. Though third-party time-stretching programs are available (such as Serato's Pitch'n Time, available for all versions of *Pro Tools*), all the top digital audio sequencers have very good, built-in time compression/expansion algorithms, so a separate program is not generally necessary. By contrast, *ReCycle*-style breakpoint editing is not signal processing but a straightforward waveform editing operation. Whether you perform the edits in *ReCycle* or use a digital audio sequencer's built-in breakpoint editing system (like *Pro Tools'* BeatDetective or *Cubase SX's* Hitpoints), the results generally always sound about the same.

Time stretching works best on legato performances—material with medium length, slurred notes. It may cause tracks with rhythmic, percussive note, or drum performances to lose their integrity, especially when

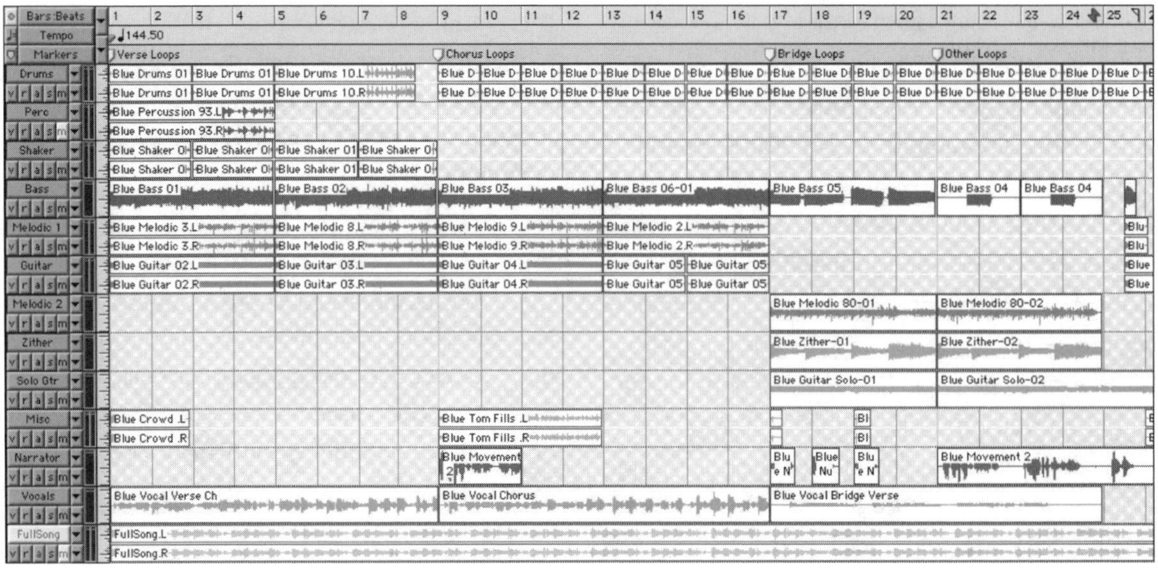

FIGURE 8.1 Lining Up the Breakout Tracks. All the break-out tracks of a song have been imported to audio tracks in *Pro Tools'* Edit window in preparation for remixing. (The radio version of the song has also been imported as a convenient reference.)

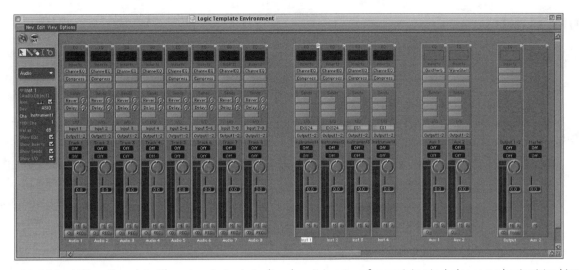

Figure 8.2 Virtual Mixer Template. The mixer in *Logic Audio* when it is set up for remixing includes some basic virtual instruments and effect sends with reverb and delay.

slowing down a tempo. When you slow material down, attacks become mushy and lose their punch because transients get smeared. Better results are usually achieved when speeding up material, having the opposite effect of shortening transients to create punchy, crisp attacks. Time stretching may also cause nasty artifacts when processing long sustained notes (like a held bass or vocal note), creating odd-sounding digital blips and gurgles in the background. The only way to correct such digital artifacts is to carefully cut out the problem notes and replace them with the unprocessed versions of those same notes from the original track, a process called *micro-editing* (discussed in detail in chapter 9).

The best way to tempo-change rhythmic, staccato performances is to recycle them. By cutting up a loop into its component beats, and locking those samples to their relative bar, beat, and tick positions (for example, the snare on the upbeat of bar 3, tick 242, always stays locked to that beat), you can change a project's tempo and the loop's tempo will follow along. Slowing the project's tempo down simply spreads the beats apart, while speeding the tempo up pushes them together (see figure 8.3). Since the individual beats are just being moved in time, not processed, audio quality is not affected and transients stay intact.

When changing a session's tempo, keeping audio regions locked to their relative positions is sometimes a function of the digital audio sequencer that may need to be enabled. Loading the individual beats into a sampler and then triggering them from a MIDI sequence gives you this type of performance by default, since MIDI events are always bar:beat:tick specific. (Having MIDI control over the individual beats, during the later stages of production, can also make rearranging the beats a blast.)

> A very important tool for me is Pitch'n Time by Serato, I've found it to be the best time compression/expansion plug available. I can't even count how many times in a day I use this software. It's one of the most valuable tools I have. You can tempo change everything perfectly, make every drum loop match the exact BPM without changing its key. It's pretty amazing.
>
> —Dave Audé

> We don't usually time compress rhythmic stuff, like percussion parts. If it's something musical, like a bass line, we'll time compress that. But generally, we'll ReCycle anything that's rhythmic.
>
> —Chris Cox, Thunderpuss

Time Stretching

Different digital audio sequencers handle time stretching differently. Some have a separate window where you enter a target BPM (such as *Logic Audio's* Time and Pitch Machine window, see figure 8.4), while others allow you to perform the time correction directly on an audio track in the arrange window (*Pro Tools* operates this way). This second method is extremely convenient.

CD 1

PRO TOOLS' TIME CORRECTION TOOL

The Trimmer Tool's Time mode, used for affecting time correction changes directly in the *Pro Tools* Mix window, has been available in *Pro Tools TDM* for quite awhile, and beginning with version 6, it is also available for *Pro Tools LE*.

STEP 1. Be sure that all of your loops are trimmed to whole bars. If you aren't sure, select them one at a time and listen to them with *Pro Tools* set to Loop Playback. Should you find a sample that is not properly looped, trim it so that it loops correctly. (Looping is explained in chapter 7.)

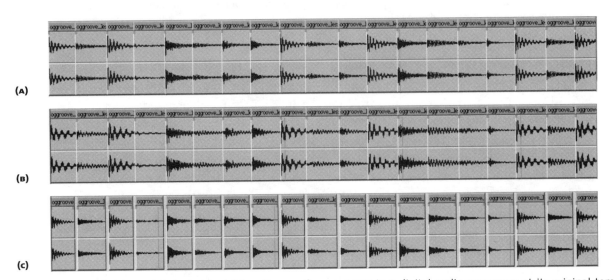

(A)

(B)

(C)

FIGURE 8.3 ReCycled Beat. A ReCycled beat **(A)** as its waveform appears in a digital audio sequencer, at its original tempo, **(B)** sped up, and **(c)** slowed down.

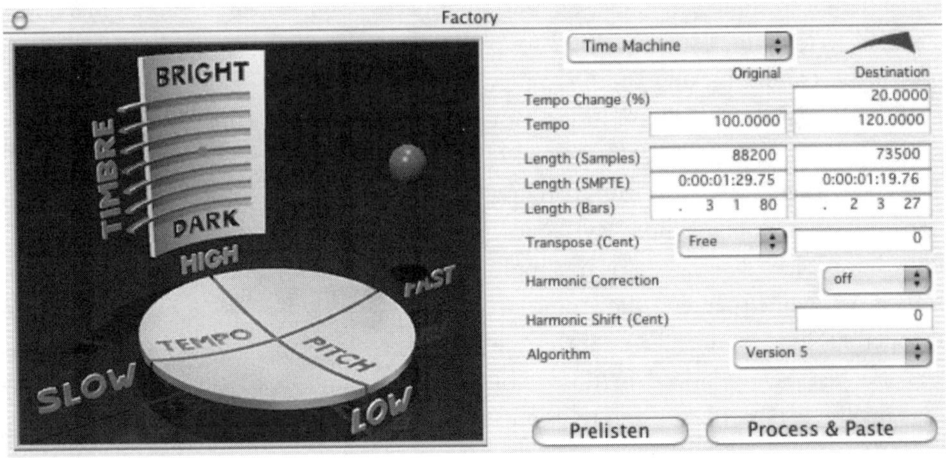

FIGURE 8.4 *Logic's* Time and Pitch Machine. The Time and Pitch Machine feature in *Logic Audio* automatically determines the BPM of your selection. Enter your target BPM in the Destination Tempo field, and click Enter to time compress or expand.

STEP 2. Set the Edit window to Grid and the Grid setting to "1 bar." Make sure that the project's master tempo is set properly for your remix. Then choose the Trimmer Tool, and select its mode as Time, indicated by the little clock (see figure 8.5).

STEP 3. With the Time Trimmer Tool, you can simply grab the end of a loop, drag it, and snap it to the bar where you want the loop to end. For example, if the loop is eight bars, 120 BPM, and begins at bar 1, but your remix is 130 BPM, then drag the loop's ending edge to the start of bar 9. *Pro Tools* automatically scales the audio to match the new bar figure. Repeat this for each loop that needs to be time corrected.

FIGURE 8.5 *Pro Tools'* Time Trimmer. The Time Trimmer Tool in *Pro Tools'* is very convenient for stretching or compressing loops to match your project's tempo, directly in the Edit window.

SMALL CHUNKS

Sometimes you can time correct an entire song file at once. However, processing such a long track doesn't always produce clean results. Time correcting short sections, like 8- to 16-bar lengths, often produces much better sounding audio. So to time correct a really long track with fewer artifacts, cut it up into a series of more bite sized loops first, then perform the time correction, one loop at a time.

A long time ago, when people first started remixing, they didn't have tools like time stretching. Maybe some pitch shifting, but that was it. You couldn't really use an entire vocal phrase unless you were at the same tempo as the original track. If you wanted to speed up the song and still use the vocals, all you could get was a word or two, that was it. So, a lot of things being remixed were club songs. You weren't remixing Bare Naked Ladies, you were remixing Faith No More, songs that were already at a dance tempo. What's cool nowadays is that just about any song can be remixed.

—(BT) Brian Transeau

LIVE'S ELASTIC AUDIO

Ableton's *Live* can be employed as a convenient time-correction tool. It can also do double duty, helping you find loops and build grooves that will work with the original song's time-corrected breakout tracks.

STEP 1. Make sure that all of the original song's breakout samples are perfect loops, and that they are trimmed to whole bars. Also, be sure to know the exact BPM of the breakout loops as this is important information to know as a point of reference. (Remember, you can load the breakout loops into *ReCycle* for a super-quick way of verifying tempos.)

STEP 2. Open *Live* and drag the breakout loops into the Session mixer for playback. It's important that each loop's original tempo is recognized correctly (check this in the Orig. BPM field under Warp, in the Clip window), or *Live's* automatic time correction will be off. If the tempo is off by half or doubled, use the Warp field's "2" and "+2" keys to proportionately double or half the BPM.

STEP 3. Make sure that *Live* is set to the tempo of your remix, then start the loops playing to hear how they sound.

STEP 4. If *Live's* time correction sounds good, the object is to bounce the affected loops to disk in order to import them into your digital audio sequencer, for the purposes of arranging. With *Live* synchronized to your digital audio sequencer via ReWire, you may not need to perform this operation immediately—indeed, you could just keep Live running in the background and arrange the loops right in *Live.* However, in the long run, having all of the remix's elements (loops, audio and MIDI tracks) in a single application really makes arranging, production, and mixing far easier.

Before you can bounce anything to disk, you must have something recorded in *Live* to bounce down. A quick way to accomplish this is to set *Live's* quantization to Bar and simply record a performance, starting the playback of each loop on every track. Then go to the Arranger window and line the loops up so that they all start at bar 1. If the breakout loops are 4- and 8-bar loops, then adjust their loop

end points to stop at bar 9 (or proportionately later if the loops are longer). (The final arrangement is shown in figure 8.6.)

STEP 5. Set the project's Loop to an appropriate setting (for example, bar 1 to bar 9). Still in the Arranger, mute (using a track's speaker icon button) all the tracks but the one you want to save as a time-corrected breakout loop, then from the file menu, choose Render to Disk (see figure 8.7). Make sure that the Render as Loop is set to On, then click OK. Perform this same operation for each time-corrected breakout loop, unmuting the track you want bounced to disk, muting the tracks you don't want to hear.

STEP 6: Import the time-corrected breakout loops into your digital audio sequencer. Save the *Live* project because you will be able to use it later for auditioning and time-correcting other loops in your remix.

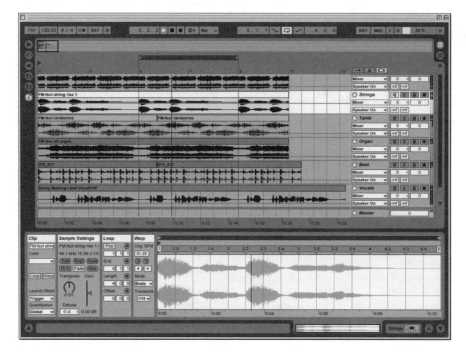

FIGURE 8.6 Breakout Tracks in *Live.* Load a song's breakout tracks into Ableton's *Live* to take advantage of its automatic time-correction and groove-building functions. Shown here, the breakout tracks have been arranged in preparation for bouncing the time-corrected files to disk.

Micro-Editing

Employ micro-editing to correct the digital artifacts sometimes caused by time compression/expansion. Carefully cut out the problem notes and replace them with the unprocessed versions of those same notes from the original track in order to create one flawless composite track.

CD 2

MAKING MICRO-EDITS

To perform micro-edits efficiently, you will need to be able to zoom in and out of tracks quickly (up to the sample level and out to a global view, respectively). Most top digital audio sequencers have key commands for performing these operations, and some even have user-definable zoom-level buttons that are very convenient.

STEP 1. Line up the original, unprocessed track's note on a separate track next to the processed note that needs repair (see figure 8.8).

STEP 2. Carefully cut the unprocessed note's waveform at zero crossings (where the waveform crosses zero), and slide it on top of the processed note. Be sure that the start of the unprocessed note lines up perfectly with the start of the processed note.

STEP 3. Zoom in about 75 percent to view each edit point, and crossfade the waveforms so that they blend together smoothly. Repeat this entire process for each note that needs to be replaced.

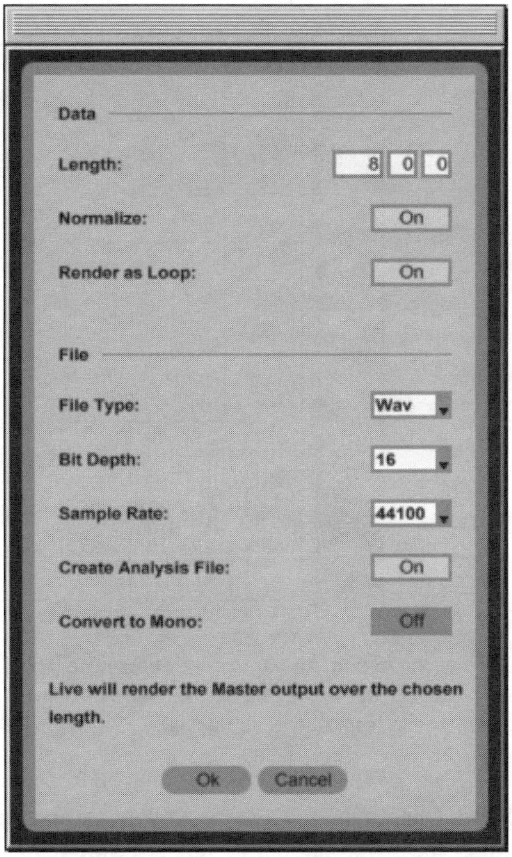

FIGURE 8.7 *Live's* Render to Disk Dialog. Under the File menu, you will find *Live's* Render to Disk options.

Cut Up and ReCycle

While Propellerheads' *ReCycle* software popularized the process of breakpoint editing, several digital audio sequencers now have built-in breakpoint editors. Nevertheless, *ReCycle* still works great and has the distinct advantage of being able to save edited loops as REX2 files for playback in a variety of other programs (such as *Reason* and *Logic Audio*).

SLICE-AND-DICE IN RECYCLE

Though the program is pretty straightforward, there are several tricks to breakpoint editing in *ReCycle* that will help you create perfect REX files. (Incidentally, most of the breakpoint editing techniques applied in *ReCycle* also work in other breakpoint editors.)

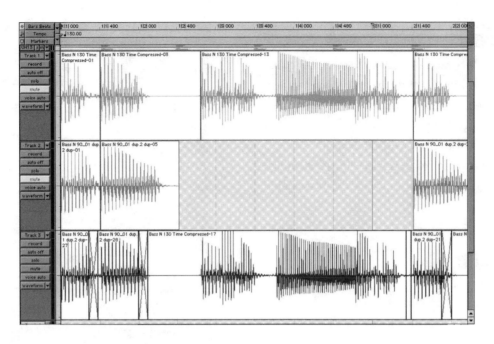

Figure 8.8 Micro-Edit. An unprocessed bass note (track 2) has been carefully lined up to the processed bass note (track 1) that needs replacing. Paste the unprocessed bass note over the processed bass note, carefully crossfading between the two takes to create a seamless transition (track 3).

STEP 1. Open a loop in *ReCycle*. (If your sample isn't looped perfectly already, follow the directions for creating a loop in *ReCycle*, on page 55, before you begin breakpoint editing)

STEP 2. Move the Sensitivity slider forward until you have a series of breakpoints that line up with the waveform's peaks. Don't worry if you don't get every peak, right off the bat. Just focus on getting breakpoints for all the obvious peaks. Select All (the key command for the Mac is Command-A, and for the PC Control-A), and use the Lock tool to lock these main breakpoints in place.

STEP 3. Starting from the beginning of the loop, use the Play Slice and Move to Next buttons to step through your slices one at a time. When you encounter a slice that contains more than one beat, move the Sensitivity slider all the way up until a breakpoint appears at that beat. Sometimes, more than one breakpoint will appear. Use the Lock tool to select and lock just the breakpoint you want to keep. If there are too many breakpoints clustered

together, zoom into the waveform to find the breakpoint at the exact beginning of the beat. Then move the Sensitivity back down to zero. (Because all of your breakpoints are locked, they will not be affected by the Sensitivity slider's setting.)

STEP 4. Occasionally, you will run into a beat that the Sensitivity slider does not catch. Use the Pencil tool to draw in the breakpoint manually, making sure to place the breakpoint at the zero crossing point directly in front of the beat. You can use the Play Current Slice button to audition the beat and make sure the breakpoint is in the right place.

STEP 5. Enter the loop's number of bar's in Bars field.

STEP 6. Turn on the Preview Toggle button and decide if you want to apply any effects. In general, if you are simply speeding up a performance to use in a remix, you don't need any effects, so make sure that they are all off. On the other hand, if you plan to slow the loop's tempo down by a significant amount, an Envelope Stretch setting of at least 20 percent is a good idea. For more creative sound warping, try out some of the Transient Shaper and EQ effect presets.

STEP 7. Save the edited loop (see figure 8.9) to your hard disk. (The *Recycle*, version 2 and higher, native file format is REX2, so there's no need to perform an export operation as there was in earlier versions of the program.) If the REX file is a loop that you plan on using in other projects, save it to a folder in your sound library for easy access. Otherwise, just save it in the remix's dedicated project folder. If you're using a sampler to playback the recycled loop, export all of the sample slices to your sampler, and save the loop's MIDI performance file (an SMF) to your project's folder.

STEP 8. Import the REX file to an audio track in your remix. Or import the MIDI performance to a MIDI track if the loop's samples are being played back from a sampler. Make sure to assign the MIDI track to your sampler. Recycle each breakout loop that will benefit from this type of time correction, and bring those breakpoint edited loops into your remix session.

Dealing with Tempo Fluctuations

A full-length song with many slight tempo variations because of live players is difficult to tempo-change smoothly. Performing time compression/expansion on the entire song often amplifies the tempo fluctuations and can sound like a real train wreck, as the beats drift back and forth over a straight, four-on-the-floor dance beat. If extracting short breakout loops from tracks of the song won't work because you're trying to use the entire song, there is a solution.

The trick to fixing tempo fluctuations over the course of a song is to cut the track into a series of 8-bar loops (see figure 8.10). Starting at the song's beginning, work your way through, separating each 8-bar section, one at a time. Then tempo-change each of the loops individually to your remix tempo. For example, if one 8-bar loop is 112.43 BPM, the next is 111.79 BPM, and the next is 112.04 BPM, time-stretch (or recycle, if the track is mostly percussive) every one to the remix's tempo. Snap the beginning of each loop to a downbeat so that all of the loops are sequentially butt spliced. It's okay if there are slight tempo variations over each loop, because the beat will always lock back up every eight bars, on the downbeat. (If you use the *ReCycle* method, you could apply quantization to get rid of the tempo fluctuations.)

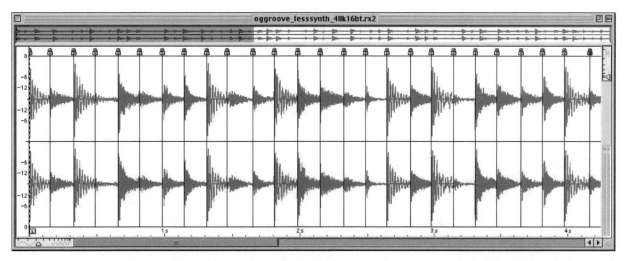

FIGURE 8.9 ReCycled Loop. Zoomed in on the breakpoint-edited loop in *ReCycle*, you can see the position of each locked breakpoint. (The entire loop can be seen in Figure 3.1).

Handling tempo fluctuations with time compression/expansion in this manner, instead of simply looping a couple of breakout loops produces a more human feel—less drum machine sounding and more varied. However, keep in mind that modern dance music actually benefits from looped, repetitive arrangements. It's this very type of production that creates the driving, hypnotic nature of today's club dance music. If you go to the trouble of tempo correcting an entire song, keep in mind that your remix will likely have a very unique groove—which may or may not sound great.

> With dance music, repetition is good.
>
> —Dave Audé

First Step In Arranging

Don't worry about creating an arrangement with the tempo-adjusted loops just yet. Simply copy them through the project until you have about five to six minutes worth of continuous material. All the loops should be placed back-to-back, and you can mute everything except the essential beats for now (see figure 8.11). This sets the framework for the next phase of your remix: building up the groove. Arranging the loops will follow.

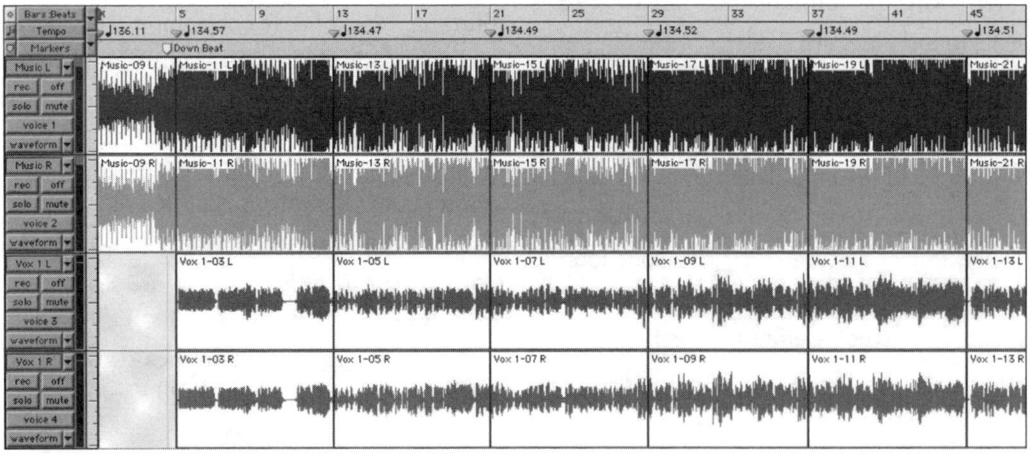

FIGURE 8.10 Eight Bars at a Time. The vocal and instrumental tracks from a song have been cut into a series of 8-bar loops in preparation for time correction.

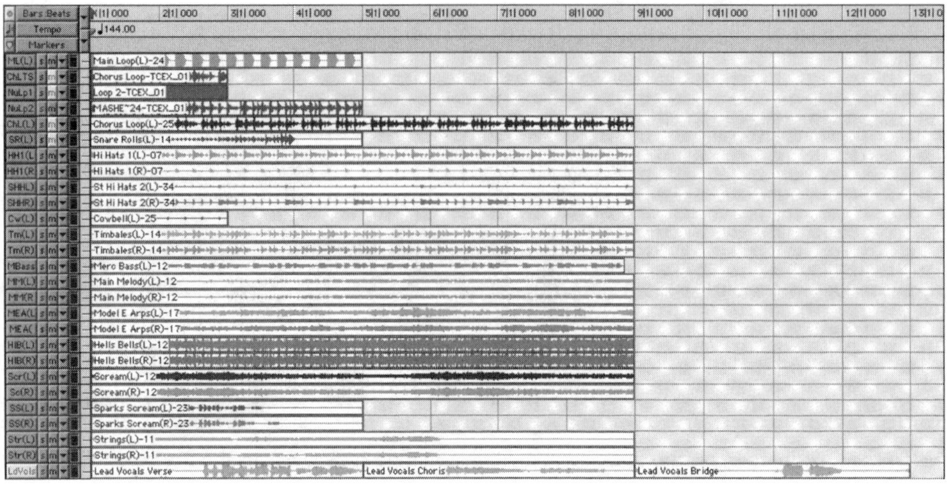

FIGURE 8.11 Tempo-Corrected Loops Ready for Arranging. All of the breakout loops of a song have been tempo-corrected and lined up on individual tracks in preparation for arranging.

CHAPTER 9

Working with Lead Vocals

Not every remix you do will include a complete lead vocal track, but when this is the case, part of preparing the tracks for that remix is time correcting these vocals. However, sometimes changing a song's lead vocal to a new tempo can be frustrating. No matter what you do, time stretching just doesn't hit the mark. Regardless of the processing settings, the vocal track ends up sounding like the soundtrack to a bad horror movie. Occasionally, you may be able to convince the lead vocalist to re-sing their parts at the new tempo. This is an option if you are a friend of the artist, or the remix is for an independent artist that you have developed a good working relationship with. However, if the artist you are remixing is a big star, or deceased, then having them re-sing their parts is out of the question. Fortunately, there are a handful of special production tricks that can work wonders in this situation.

Before you produce a final lead vocal track, you should create a rough lead vocal track. Just use time compression/expansion to make the entire vocal track the right tempo. Don't worry about any strange sounding artifacts, right now. The rough vocal track will serve as a template around which to arrange the basic elements of your remix. When your remix's structure is finalized and the music production is nearing completion, then you can put together the final lead vocal track. Don't throw away the original, unprocessed lead vocal track. Keep it handy in your remix's project folder because it will be instrumental in creating the final vocals.

The method behind creating a vocal track that sounds like it was sung to your remix is to cut and paste together, at the micro-editing level, several lead vocal tracks with different types of processing to assemble one contiguous, flawless track. The completed track is a composite of the original, unprocessed track and up to three copies of the original that have been processed with time compression/expansion, pitch correction, and time compression/expansion followed by pitch correction. You may need all of these versions, or just the original and the time compression/expansion version; it all depends on the original track's performance and how it responds to time compression/expansion in the first place.

WHERE'S THE BEAT?

Remember that if you're working with an *a cappella* single and you're having problems lining it up to a beat, find the full version of the song and use this as a template. Start by figuring out the song's original tempo, and match it up to the session's click track at this tempo, making sure to line up the odd and even beats with the session's grid. Then match the *a cappella* version up to the full version (when the lead vocals sound like they are tightly doubled, the two tracks are aligned). Take note of the vocal track's total number of bars at the original tempo (for example, ninety-two bars). Reset the project's tempo to the new remix tempo, then time-compress or expand the vocal track to match that same original number of bars, at the new tempo; that's your reference vocal track. You can mute the song's full version, and time-compress/expand it for use as another reference track (such as for figuring out the chords behind a particular vocal section).

> *Very seldom do we actually get a vocal, throw it in time compression/expansion, and then that's the one we use. Sometimes there will be days of editing. Sometimes it's not just the processing but also a timing issue, like they sang it in a certain meter or with a particular feel and we need it to be different. So, we'll cut it up syllable by syllable to get it in our groove. It's the longest, most painstaking process of the whole thing, and it's so important.*
>
> —Chris Cox, Thunderpuss

CD 3

Vexing Vibrato

The biggest problem with time compression is that it turns a singer's vibrato into something that sounds like a braying goat. This artifact affects sustained notes with vibrato the worst. Short, staccato notes that have only a little vibrato are usually passable. Time expansion makes vibrato sound bad as well, but more like a sick cow. However, by combining the original, unprocessed vocal track with the time-compressed or expanded track, it is possible to edit out nearly all such farm animal artifacts.

STEP 1. Listen to your entire reference lead vocal track (the time-compressed or expanded version), and use your digital audio sequencer's bookmark feature to mark each problem spot. Depending on the material, you may have just a few marks, or a whole bunch.

STEP 2. Import the original lead vocal track into your project, place it on its own audio track, and very roughly, line it up with the reference vocal track. It won't line up perfectly because the tempos of the two tracks are different.

STEP 3. Cut the original lead vocal track up into sections that roughly mirror the reference track's problem spots. Then slide these regions into place so that they closely parallel the reference track's waveforms (see figure 9.1).

STEP 4. Next, replace a note that sounds bad in the reference track with its parallel, unprocessed note from the original vocal track (see figure 9.2). Do this by trimming the unprocessed note so that it perfectly matches the processed note, then copy and paste it over the processed note. Try to make the in and out edit points at zero crossing points, so that the waveform's appearance from one take to the next looks as natural as possible (without jagged edges or big amplitude jumps). Make very short crossfades at the edit points to smooth the transitions. You usually don't need to replace the beginning of a note, just its sustained portion where the artifacts appear.

STEP 5: Repeat this operation for every bad note. The process may take a while, if there are a lot of problem spots, but the final result is well worth the effort.

> *What happens to legato and vibrato phrases when they are time stretched is what makes the performance sound fake. Pair up the original vocal with the time-stretched version, and whenever there is a held note—not a succession of notes but a flourish, like a legato phrase that has vibrato on it—take it from the original and crossfade into it. That's how you make a really natural sounding vocal comp.*
>
> —(BT) Brian Transeau

> *I can't stand billy goat vocals, that sound that happens to notes sung with vibrato when they are time compressed. We work hard to make the processed vocals sound like they are the original performance.*
>
> —Barry Harris, Thunderpuss

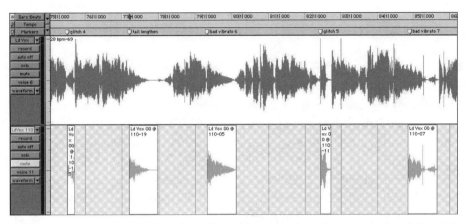

FIGURE 9.1 Prepared to Edit. The reference lead vocal track's problem spots have been marked, and the original, unprocessed lead vocal track has been cut up and its parts roughly aligned in preparation for creating a composite vocal track.

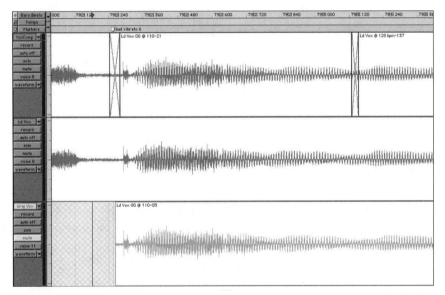

FIGURE 9.2 The Edit. The good note from the unprocessed vocal track is perfectly lined up to the bad note in the processed vocal track (bottom). Then that note is cut and pasted over the bad note (top).

Timing Issues

When you change a vocal track's tempo and put it over a new beat, the *performance's swing*—where it sits in relation to the song's original groove—is going to be affected. Phrases may drag or sound rushed, and in the case of speeding up a tempo, lyrics can become too dense and start sounding nonsensical. The most common approach to fixing timing problems is to simply nudge the vocals forward or backward in time by small amounts until they "feel" right. The best digital audio sequencers let you nudge whole sections using your computer keyboard, by a set amount of time, either in samples, seconds, frames, or beats. The magic number for nudging a performance in order to adjust its feel is in 10 millisecond increments.

There are also more radical ways of dealing with groove and timing issues, such as lyric editing and Synchro Art's *VocAlign* software (see figure 9.3). However, these methods seriously change an artist's performance. At this level, you are reinterpreting their performance, and depending on the project, this may not be kosher. If you're just cooking up a remix for your own personal pleasure, it's not going to be a problem, but if it's a remix for hire, you should check with the artist and their label before doing anything too extreme.

CD 4

LYRIC EDITING

Often, an idea can be expressed with fewer words than originally used. There may be single words, or entire lines of a verse or a chorus, that can be omitted without destroying the lyrics' meaning. Creating space between words and phrases can even give a line greater weight, making it stand out more. However, when editing lyrics, be careful not to leave gaps that sound unnatural, since this can have the opposite effect—causing the lyrics to sound choppy and confusing. It's a good policy not to go crazy deleting individual words, since this can cause a disturbing lilt. Instead, concentrate on removing entire phrases that seem redundant or unnecessary.

After a phrase has been removed, it's often nice to scoot the following lyrics forward, closing the gap left by the deleted line. However, if this doesn't work, and the gap sounds as if the last note of the previous line should have carried over longer, you can sometimes grab just that note from the unprocessed, original track. This trick will only work if your remix tempo is faster than the original song because the unprocessed note is longer than the processed note. Using the same micro-editing, cut-and-paste technique described for repairing time-compression/expansion artifacts, replace the last note before the deleted line with its unprocessed counterpart, creating a held note where before there was none. When needed, you can also fade out the held note so that its ending is in time with the music, giving it a totally natural feel.

At times, actually rearranging lyrics to cause the vocalist to say something different is appropriate. For example, the line "Right about now, the funk soul brother. Check it out now, the funk soul brother." from the song, "The Rockafeller Skank" by Fatboy Slim (who is renowned for his cut-and-paste, and low-fi approach to vocals), is a vocal line that was rearranged in an Akai sampler. Creating an entirely new hook out of a series of words is always a lot of fun. And there's no rule (unless the artist or label says otherwise) against using a line other than the song's chorus for your remix's hook.

CD 5

WAVEFORM ALIGNMENT WITH VOCALIGN

Synchro Art's *VocAlign* allows you to line up the waveforms of one track with the waveforms of another track. It's available as both a stand-alone application, or as an extra, off-line, processing application within *Digital Performer* and *Pro Tools*. Common applications include lining up background vocal harmonies to make them all sound perfectly in sync (no flammed consonants or tails that end at different times), causing a voice-overdub-to-picture to perfectly match the actor's original source recording (a standard post production practice that the film industry calls ADR, Automatic Dialog Replacement), and even making a sloppy bass guitar performance line up better with the drummer's kick drum rhythm.

VocAlign can also be employed to re-groove a vocalist's recorded performance. This operation should only be attempted after you have repaired all the time-compression/expansion artifacts, and you've done you're best to nudge the vocal performance into time with your remix. Having the original vocalist re-sing the part is preferable, but if the vocalist is unavailable, you can give this method try. Hire a session singer whose vocal tone and range are similar to the recorded vocalist, and use them to create a timing template to which you can align the remix vocals. Keep in mind that this method can't turn a country singer into a house music diva, but it can correct for the type of subtle timing differences causing a performance that's not sitting in the pocket to really lock in and groove with your rhythm tracks.

STEP 1. Find an experienced session vocalist who can sing the part the way you hear it in your head, who can groove with your track while at the same time following the melody of the not-so-perfectly timed original (processed and edited) vocal track.

STEP 2. Record their performance on a separate audio track. Make sure to have a lyric sheet for them to follow, and be sure that it reflects any lyric editing you may have done.

STEP 3. Open *VocAlign* and select a short phrase from the re-sung vocals to use as the Guide track.

STEP 4. Select this same phrase from the original vocals as the Dub track, the performance to be corrected.

STEP 5. Click the Align button to let VocAlign calculate the matching operation. A waveform trace of the Guide appears superimposed on the Dub to illustrate the final result. You can adjust the time correction to be more or less rigid to the Guide, though the software's default setting usually provides goods results right off the top.

STEP 6. Click the Process button to process the audio. Some programs will let you assign *VocAlign's* time corrected audio to a track in your session, otherwise, save the file to the project's Audio File's folder and import it into your digital audio sequencer, manually.

STEP 7. Repeat this process for each phrase that needs re-grooving. Though it would be faster to process the entire vocal track all at once, processing smaller chunks one at a time usually produces cleaner results.

IF THE VOCALS FIT

If it's not paramount that you feature the original song's vocalist, and if the session vocalist you hire nails the song, consider using their performance for the remix. At the very least, since you have them in the studio and you're paying for their time, have them sing a few different takes over the remix just for kicks. You never know, something might stick. And if you do decide to release it, paying for a song's performance rights alone is cheaper than also paying for the performance rights of a name artist's featured performance. If it ends up that your remix doesn't contain any of the song's original recordings, that another vocalist sings the leads, then you've produced what is commonly called a "cover" tune.

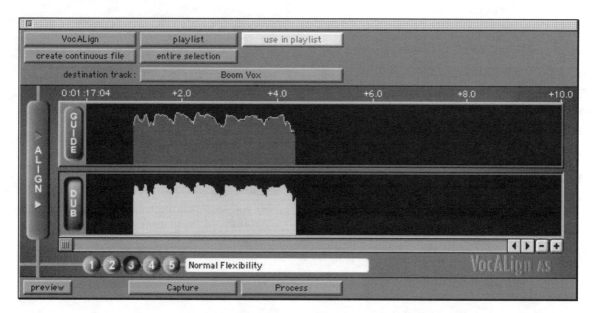

FIGURE 9.3 VocAlign. Synchro Art's *VocAlign* waveform alignment software can be a powerful tool for re-grooving a recorded vocal performance.

CD 6

Intonations

Sometimes, a vocal's wavering pitch will sound fine against its original arrangement, but against the electronic sounds of a remix, it will sound out of key. For example, the vocalist might have sung in perfect tune with a slightly out-of-tune acoustic guitar. Listening to these vocals over a perfectly in-tune synthesizer is going to sound bad. Fortunately, pitch correction plug-ins (such as Wave's UltraPitch or Antares Auto Tune, see figure 9.4) can be employed to fix an out-of-tune vocal track.

The method for repairing a vocal track's intonation is identical to repairing time-compression/expansion artifacts, and is a step that should be performed after tempo-changing a complete vocal performance. By combining the processed and repaired vocal track with a pitch-corrected version of itself, a single, composite performance with great intonation can be assembled. Replacing only those notes that really need pitch correction lets you create a very natural-sounding performance, by not destroying all of the vocalist's pitch inflections.

STEP 1. Run the processed and repaired vocal track through a pitch correction plug-in. Set the plug-in's scale to chromatic and its *sensitivity setting* (the threshold for pitch correction) to maximum (so that it catches everything). If after processing, the vocal track sounds late, don't worry; most pitch correction programs introduce a processing delay. This will be fixed in the course of creating the composite track, as will any funny sounding pitch-change artifacts.

STEP 2. In order to print the effect to an audio file that you can edit, bounce the effected track to disk. You may want to remove the pitch correction plug-in when this is complete in order to reclaim some DSP power, but be sure to save any custom settings, in case you need to repeat the bounce.

STEP 3. Import the audio file of the bounced track to its own separate audio track and line it up with the repaired and processed, original vocal track. The two tracks should line up nearly perfectly. When you can hear them phasing on top of each other (doubling so closely that their individual volumes are at times decreased), they are well aligned.

STEP 4. Listen through to the track that has not been pitch-corrected, and mark the notes that need replacing.

STEP 5. Carefully cut the pitch-corrected notes out of the processed track, and paste them over the out-of-tune notes in the unprocessed track. Be sure to make your cuts at the zero crossing points, and crossfade the edits when necessary to smooth out any bumpy transitions. Replacing notes at this stage is less tedious than fixing time-compression/expansion artifacts because you can usually cut and paste whole notes (since the tempos of the two takes are identical), instead of working to blend portions of notes.

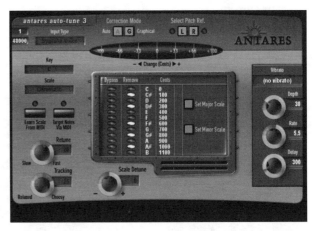

FIGURE 9.4 Auto Tune. Auto Tune by Antares is a powerful pitch correction plug-in that's available in all the most popular plug-in formats.

The Whole Process

Successfully tempo-changing a song's entire vocal performance is a time-consuming and detail-oriented process. It isn't something that's done all at once, in one fell swoop. It requires several distinct steps that must happen over the course of the remix. An overview of these steps is outlined below.

STEP 1. Time-compress or expand the song's original vocal track. Don't worry about odd-sounding artifacts at this stage, because it's just a reference track.

STEP 2. Write the remix's basic music (chapters 10 and 11) and create a song structure (chapter 12). Nudge the vocals into time with the basic beat, then cut the reference vocals up into sections that follow the remix song structure.

STEP 3. Repair the reference vocal track's time-compression/expansion artifacts by replacing them with duplicate, unprocessed notes from the original vocal track.

STEP 4. Fix any timing problems that have become apparent after hearing the tempo-changed vocals against the remix's final beat. This might involve nothing more than a 10 millisecond nudge here and there, or more radical editing to alter the performance's phrasing and swing.

STEP 5. Deal with intonation problems by running the vocals through a pitch-correction plug-in and printing the effect to disk. Then, applying the same micro-editing techniques used to repair the time compression-expansion artifacts, replace any out-of-tune notes.

STEP 6. With the vocal track complete, return to the final stages of music production (see chapter 13).

We work with a lot of major artists because they know we aren't just going to destroy their vocals in the process of making a phat beat. If we're hired to do somebody's record, it's about them, so we make sure that the vocals sound the best they possibly can. We've actually rejected projects based on the vocals, if the stretch to a new tempo isn't going to work, then we would rather just pass on the project. If it's going to come out sounding awful, it's not worth it.

—Chris Cox, Thunderpuss

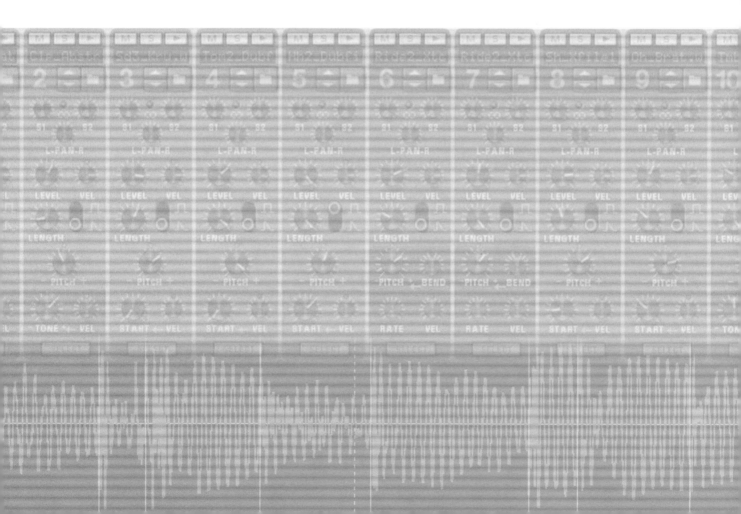

Composition Basics

CHAPTER 10

Writing the Basic Beat

At this point, you should have a good idea of the tracks you're going to use from the original song, and have targeted a dance music style for the remix. If vocals are part of the mix, you should have a reference lead vocal track that includes verses, if any, and the hook, whether it's the same as the original or reinterpreted for the remix. The next phase is to build up a basic groove and instrumentation that will serve as the musical foundation of your remix.

Don't worry about giving your remix any song structure, yet. Instead, focus on creating a 4- to 8-bar loops with lots of rhythmic and musical elements that work well together. Write a loop that grooves and evolves over time, using whatever means are at your disposal (samples, loops, MIDI instruments, recorded performances, etc.). Make sure to include drums, percussion, bass, and chords that fit with the vocal performance's key. Compose all the elements you can think of now so that there will be plenty of parts to layer up, break down, and move about when we begin forming the remix song structure, mapping out where its energy will wane, hold, and peak. Build up the loop under the chorus section of the vocals (or other lead instrument line) because this will likely be a peak energy area of the remix—where instrumentation reaches its climax.

There are no rules about how to begin the composing process, but most people start by finding a drum loop or writing a beat. Then, usually a bass line and chord progression is written over the beat (which is discussed in the next chapter). These are the fundamental parts of every song. Other instruments follow, like guitars, synthesizers, and percussion. Neither are there any rules regarding what's better, playing your parts live, programming, or just finding loops that work well together. If you are a proficient musician, playing your parts in live is probably the fastest, but programming and loops are equally valid ways of composing. The fact is that each has its own merits

and imparts a different flavor to a track. Using all three techniques is really the best. But if you're more of a programmer than a player, that's not a problem, because what really matters is the music you produce, not how it was created.

When I start working on a remix, I usually begin at the chorus, because that's the important part of the song, the high point of the song. I'll get a kick drum in there, decide on a tempo, map the vocals out so they're in some kind of arrangement. Then I'll just start looping things and throwing stuff in, just to get an idea of where I'm going. Once I get there, to the place I'm going to end up musically, then I go back and hit the verses, work on getting the verses to go into the chorus nice.

—Dave Audé

Building a Better Drum Loop

The three most popular ways to create a drum beat are by finding a sampled drum loop, recording a live performance using MIDI drums, or programming the beat. Often, all three techniques are combined to make a "groove." The key is to find or write several different drum parts that all mesh in terms of swing and complimentary tones. Most people start by recording a basic kick (bass drum) and snare MIDI pattern or finding a sampled drum loop. On top of these elements, layer more drum and percussion parts using a combination of instruments and samples. As you add parts, make sure that each loop's swing works with the beat's main elements (usually the kick, snare, and hi-hat pattern), as well as each other, or you'll end up with a drum beat that sounds like a train wreck.

Using similar swing quantize settings (see "Quantization Explained," p. 78) for each drum pattern can help keep different parts' grooves locked

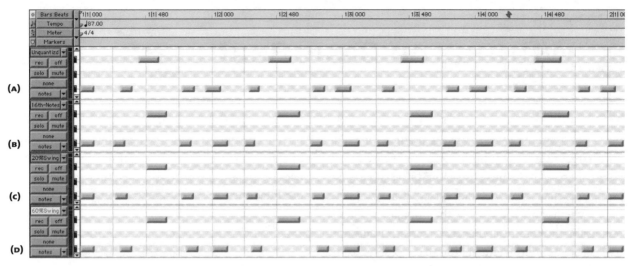

FIGURE 10.1 The Effects of Quantization. A basic hi-hat pattern **(A)** unquantized, **(B)** quantized to straight sixteenth notes, **(C)** with 20 percent swing, and **(D)** with 60 percent swing.

together. Most basic dance music parts can be written using either eighth- or sixteenth-note quantization with a swing value of between 20 to 60 percent (play with the swing percent on different drums for a different "feel"—for example, a tight versus a loose sounding groove). Getting sampled loops that don't naturally fit with your MIDI tracks to really groove with your beats is possible, but it's more complicated than straight quantizing, involving groove templates and breakpoint editing (see "Making Tracks Groove Together," p. 84).

QUANTIZATION EXPLAINED

When a note is quantized, it gets snapped to the nearest beat, or division of a beat. The quantize setting you choose determines the resolution of the quantize grid (such as quarter notes, sixteenths, thirty-second-note triplets, etc.). Swing is a function of quantization that gives you the ability to offset notes on the upbeats by a set percentage (see figure 10.1). Judiciously applied, swing helps quantized performances and programmed parts feel less mechanical and more human. Quantization is traditionally used on MIDI notes, but good digital audio sequencers can also quantize audio regions.

CD 7

FOUND DRUM LOOP

STEP 1. Find a sampled drum loop that's close in tempo and the proper style for your remix. It's a good idea to choose a fairly simple drum loop, without too many extra percussion and sound effect elements, in order to leave yourself room to add custom parts on top. A loop that features kick, snare, and hi-hat is a good place to start.

STEP 2. If the loop isn't at the right tempo, you should either time-compress/expand it (for small tempo changes, like +/−5 BPM), or recycle it (for tempo changes that are greater than +/−5 BPM). Breakpoint editing a drum beat has the added advantage of providing the opportunity to extract a groove template from the loop that can be used to groove quantize other audio regions and MIDI performances (see "Making Tracks Groove Together, p. 84).

STEP 3. If the loop's hi-hat pattern is weak, adding a few choice hi-hats of your own can spice up the rhythm. For example, playing an open hi-hat on the upbeats can give a straight hi-hat pattern a solid house feel.

STEP 4. Over a simple loop, add extra percussion instruments to taste, such as electronic drum samples, world percussion instruments, and hand drums. These performances might be MIDI drums, sampled loops, or some combination of the two.

PLAYING IT LIVE

STEP 1. Turn on your sequencer's click track, and assign it to either an internal sound or a MIDI sound module—something you'll be able to hear while recording your beat.

STEP 2. If you're timing isn't perfect, turn on Input Quantize, and set it to sixteenth notes with a swing of 35 percent. Input Quantize will help you create a tight performance right off the bat, and avoid needing to quantize tracks post performance.

STEP 3. Load a drum-kit preset on your virtual drum machine, sampler, or external MIDI instrument, and assign this instrument to a MIDI track. Make sure that the instrument's audio outputs are connected to an aux input, in your digital audio sequencer's mixer, for sound.

STEP 4. Record-arm the MIDI track, and you should be able to play the drum kit. Each note of the preset should have a different drum sound. Locate the kick and snare on your MIDI controller.

STEP 5. Set your sequencer to loop two bars and the record mode to overdub, so that when the sequence loops around, your last recorded performance isn't erased.

STEP 6. Some people like to record the kick and the snare at the same time on the same MIDI track. Others prefer to record each drum separately, on its own MIDI track. Recording on the same track lets you view and edit all of your drum performances in a single window, while recording on separate tracks gives you faster editing control over individual drum performances. Whatever method you prefer, record a kick and snare pattern, then label the track(s) accordingly.

STEP 7. Locate the hi-hats (open and closed) on your MIDI controller, record a hi-hat pattern, and then name the track.

STEP 8. Add extra percussion instruments to taste, such as electronic drum samples, world percussion instruments, and hand drums. These performances might be MIDI drums, sampled loops, or some combination of the two.

TOO FAST TO PLAY?

With most dance music running at such fast tempos, it can be difficult to play a complex rhythm pattern. To get around this problem, slow the project's tempo down until you can perform the part comfortably. Record the part, and then speed the project's tempo back up. Remember to mute those tracks that can't follow the tempo change (like audio loops that aren't breakpoint edited) while you're recording; otherwise, everything will sound very confused.

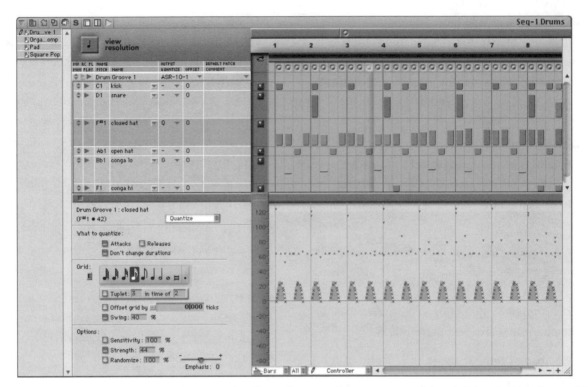

FIGURE 10.2 *Digital Performer's* Drum Editor. *Digital Performer* has one of the most powerful and slickest looking drum editing windows of all the digital audio sequencers.

PROGRAMMING A BEAT

Beats can be programmed using your sequencer's built-in drum editor (see figure 10.2) or a software drum machine that has built-in pattern sequencer, like *Reason's* ReDrum Drum Computer module (see figure 10.3). If you are at a loss for a pattern to write, figure 10.4 illustrates a standard drum pattern for each of the main dance music styles.

FIGURE 10.3 *Reason's* ReDrum Drum Computer. *Reason's* ReDrum Drum Computer module has a great built-in pattern sequencer that mimic's the classic Roland drum machines.

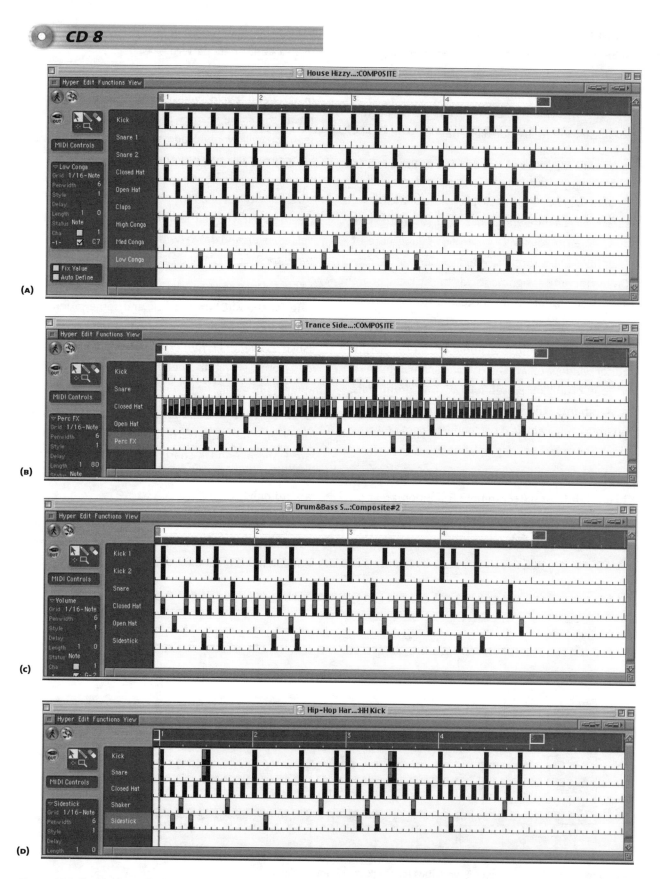

FIGURE 10.4 Typical Drum Patterns. A typical drum pattern for each of the main styles of dance music: **(A)** house, **(B)** trance, **(c)** drum-and-bass, and **(D)** hip-hop.

DRUM EDITOR

STEP 1. Load a drum kit preset on your virtual drum machine, sampler, or external MIDI instrument, and assign this instrument to a MIDI track. Make sure that the instrument's audio outputs are connected to an aux input, in your digital audio sequencer's mixer, for sound.

STEP 2. Record-arm the MIDI track, and you should be able to play the drum kit. Each note of the preset should have a different drum sound. Locate the kick and snare on your MIDI controller, taking note of their MIDI note numbers (standard General MIDI, or GM drum note assignments for the kick and snare are C1 and D1, note numbers 36 and 38 respectively; see Appendix A for the complete list).

STEP 3. Open your digital audio sequencer's Drum Editor window. Locate the kick and snare note rows. If your drum kit preset follows GM drum note assignments, the note rows should already be appropriately named. If not, name the note rows so that they reflect your drum samples.

STEP 4. Make sure that the drum editor's grid is set to an eighth- or sixteenth-note resolution, and that the window's magnification is set to view at least four bars comfortably.

STEP 5. Select the program's pencil tool, and draw in a kick and snare pattern.

STEP 6. With a pencil tool, notes are usually drawn in at a default velocity (like 100). Having every beat hit at the same velocity makes for a very robotic feel. You will want to add some variations to the velocities, making sure that the downbeats are stronger than the upbeats. Open up the drum editor's velocity curve editor, and make these changes (see figure 10.5) by either clicking and dragging the velocities up and down (with either the selection or hand tool), or by using the pencil tool.

STEP 7. Most programs let you assign a swing setting for the MIDI drum track, and some programs can assign a swing value to individual note rows (such as *Digital Performer*). If not, you will want to add some swing to the programmed drums by quantizing using the program's swing function.

STEP 8. Locate the hi-hats (open and closed) and draw in a hi-hat pattern (the standard GM note are F-sharp 1 and A-sharp 1, numbers 42 and 46 respectively). Program the velocities and swing accordingly.

STEP 9. Program in extra percussion instruments to taste, such as electronic drum samples, world percussion instruments, and hand drums.

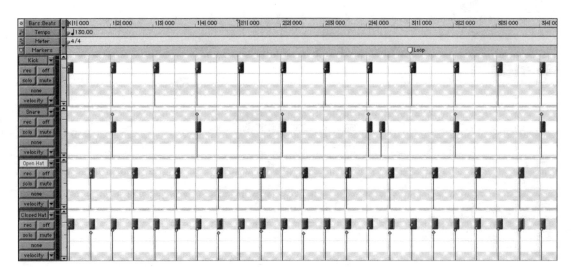

FIGURE 10.5 Velocities. Examples of velocities for a kick, snare, and hi-hats.

REDRUM

STEP 1. If you have a digital audio sequencer that supports ReWire, boot it up first, then *Reason*. This will automatically slave Reason to your digital audio sequencer. To verify that a connection has been made, the ReWire Slave Mode indicator will turn on. (If your digital audio sequencer does not support ReWire, see "Missing ReWire.")

STEP 2. Starting with an empty rack in *Reason*, create a Mixer 14:2, then create a ReDrum Drum Computer module. With nothing else in the rack, ReDrum will automatically connect to channel 1 of the mixer.

STEP 3. Make sure that the ReWire Mix L/R coming from *Reason* into your digital audio sequencer is enabled.

STEP 4. Load a preset drum kit into ReDrum. *Reason's* stock ReDrum patches are great kits for building beats. (Check out the House Kits as a place to start.)

STEP 5. If there's a sample in the kit that you don't like, replace it with a sample that's more to your taste. Then save the modified preset under a different name.

STEP 6. Set your digital audio sequencer to loop-play four or eight bars of the remix's chorus section. When you click Play, *Reason* should follow along.

STEP 7. With the Steps set to 16, and the resolution set to sixteenth notes, program a beat. With ReDrum's Shuffle setting turned on, the Pattern Shuffle dial on *Reason's* main transport bar can be used to adjust the drum pattern's amount of swing. You should "earball" this setting to best match ReDrum's swing with the swing of any sampled loops or MIDI performances already on your digital audio sequencer.

MISSING REWIRE?

If your digital audio sequencer doesn't support ReWire, there are alternatives for integrating *Reason's* wonderful programming and virtual instrument features into your system.

• *Reason* exports Standard MIDI Files (SMF) that can then be imported into your digital audio sequencer and assigned to play any instrument. ReDrum and Matrix patterns can both be transferred to one of *Reason's* MIDI tracks using the Copy Pattern to Track command, then exported as an SMF. Though with this method you lose the sounds of *Reason's* instruments, you do still get the advantage of being able to program MIDI patterns using ReDrum and Matrix.

• Creating sampled loops with *Reason* is a snap, using its Export Loop as Audio File command. Simply set your Left and Right loop markers, make sure *Reason's* tempo is set to your remix tempo, mute the tracks you don't want to hear, and export the audio. Then, import the loop to a stereo audio track of your digital audio sequencer. Though you get the sounds of *Reason's* instruments with this method, because the exported loop is a stereo mixdown, you have no mixing control over the loop's individual elements (unless, of course, the loop contains only one element, like a single drum).

• *Reason* will synchronize with MIDI Clock, and almost all digital audio sequencers can output MIDI Clock. On a Mac, you can use an Interapplication Communications bus (IAC) to send MIDI Clock from your digital audio sequencer to Reason on the same computer. For audio, simply plug the output (analog or digital) of *Reason's* sound card (such as the computer's stock sound card) into the input of your digital audio sequencer's audio interface.

Drum Pattern Creation Tricks

Beyond the traditional methods of recording and programming beats, there are several other commonly employed tricks to creating unique drum rhythms and sounds.

CD 9

RHYTHMS FROM DELAYS

A simple way to add really interesting rhythmic elements to a straight beat is to use delay. For example, add a rhythmic ambient backdrop to a straight four-on-the-floor kick, or create an actual poly-rhythmic bongo line from a single quarter-note bongo pattern. Any standard delay plug-in can work, but a multi-tap delay with the ability to set delays in note values (like *Waves'* SuperTap delay) produces the best results fast. Rather than implementing the delay as an aux effect, insert it directly on the source channel for maximum control of the delayed rhythms and the wet/dry mix ratio.

IMPORTING MIDI SAMPLES

Don't forget that besides programming, playing, and finding sampled loops, you also have MIDI samples at your disposal. Click and drag from your desktop, or use the Import SMF command to get a MIDI sample onto a MIDI track of your sequencer. Assign the MIDI track a drum kit for playback; most MIDI samples use GM drum note assignments.

Since most MIDI samples are recorded live by top session players, each has a distinctive groove with a wonderful human feel that can't be duplicated by programming and normal quantize settings. However, it is possible to extract a MIDI sample's groove and apply it to other performances (see the sidebar "Making Tracks Groove Together"). In fact, stealing a MIDI sample's groove is an excellent way of creating your own custom quantize template, commonly referred to as a "groove template." You can use it just for the current remix, or save it in your groove library for other projects.

CD 10

MAKING TRACKS GROOVE TOGETHER

The Groove Quantize feature (see figure 10.6) allows you to create a custom quantize setting template based on a MIDI performance or beat-mapped (breakpoint edited) audio loop. All the top digital audio sequencers have a Groove Template feature. It's a truly invaluable tool because it allows you to quantize your programmed patterns to match any other performance, from an expertly played MIDI sample to a rare groove lifted off an old record. Groove templates aren't just for drum parts either; they're useful for keeping all of an arrangement's music parts in line with the main groove too.

The procedure for creating a groove template is fairly standard across all the most popular digital audio sequencers. Pretty much every digital audio sequencer can create a groove template from a MIDI performance. Those that can import REX files and have built-in breakpoint editors can also extract a groove template from an audio loop. All digital audio sequencers can groove-quantize MIDI notes, and most can groove-quantize audio regions.

STEP 1. Select a region of MIDI notes or breakpoint-edited beats on which to base the groove template (selections with mostly sixteenth notes work best). Most programs allow a groove template to be as long as your selection, and sometimes to start on any beat. However, keeping the looped, repetitive production values of electronic dance music in mind, you should make your selection two, and no more than eight even bars.

STEP 2. Execute your program's "Make Groove from Selection" command, and the selection's groove will be added to the program's Groove Template folder, and then show up in the Groove Template menu.

STEP 3. Select the MIDI performance or breakpoint-edited beats that you want to groove-quantize.

STEP 4. From the program's Groove Template menu, apply the custom groove template to your selection. If the effect is too heavy handed, there are usually additional parameters for tailoring the amount of groove quantization applied (such as the Timing, Velocity, and Duration controls in *Digital Performer*). Another trick is to carefully select only the events that you want to groove-quantize (such as all the eighth notes after the third beat of each bar). This way you're only groove-quantizing a few notes instead of the entire bar.

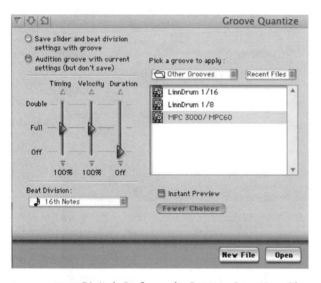

FIGURE 10.6 *Digital Performer's* Groove Quantize. The Groove Quantize window in *Digital Performer* is nicely implemented, offering all the groove control features you need in a single window.

Rearrange and Double Time

Once you have breakpoint-edited a sampled drum loop, there's no rule that says the samples must be played back in their original order. In fact, rearranging the beats of recycled drum loops is a classic drum-and-bass production trick.

Beats can be rearranged as short audio regions in an audio track, or loaded into a sampler and triggered by their assigned MIDI notes. Working with the beats as audio regions creates a tighter, more choppy feel because you can abruptly cut beats off using overlapping regions and super-fast crossfades (see figure 10.7). However, scooting lots of tiny audio regions around to create a custom beat can be tedious. In contrast, triggering the beats as samples in a sampler makes rearranging them a snap. But because the beats are from a MIDI sound source, which introduces very slight delays in playback and how the samples' amplitude envelopes are handled, that super-tight feel you get with audio regions is missing.

However, there is another trick you can do with MIDI that is more difficult to accomplish with audio regions. You can create wonderfully complex-sounding drum patterns that are perfect for drum-and-bass and breakbeats by playing back a MIDI performance in double time. Most digital audio sequencers can time-compress a MIDI performance (such as *Logic Audio's* Double Speed Transform function) to make, for example, a 4-bar pattern into a 2-bar pattern (see figure 10.8). Time-compressing an actual audio file by this amount would sound awful, but because the MIDI notes are simply being played faster, the audio quality of the samples is not affected.

EXS24 MEETS REX

Logic Audio's proprietary sampler, the EXS24 mk II, can import a REX file's samples and MIDI performance directly. This makes loading a recycled beat into a sampler, and coordinating the playback of all its samples via MIDI, extremely fast and convenient.

STEP 1. Open the EXS24 Instrument Editor and from the ReCycle Convert menu choose "Slice loop and make new instrument." A new instrument is automatically created and the loop's slices are mapped chromatically beginning at C1. (You can also add a REX file's slices to an already existing instrument by selecting the "Slice loop and add samples to current instrument.")

STEP 2. The REX loop's associated MIDI performance file is automatically extracted at the same time you import its samples, and dropped to your selected track in the Arrange window at the play-bar's current position. If this location is incorrect, scoot the MIDI performance to the proper position.

STEP 3. Assign the MIDI performance's MIDI track to an active EXS24 mk II in the audio mixer. Load the appropriate REX instrument preset, and click Play. With everything properly configured, the MIDI performance will play the samples back and recreate the original loop.

STEP 4. Get creative and rearrange the MIDI performance to play back the samples in a different order. You can even experiment triggering the samples with another REX file's MIDI performance for some really interesting drum beats.

CD 11

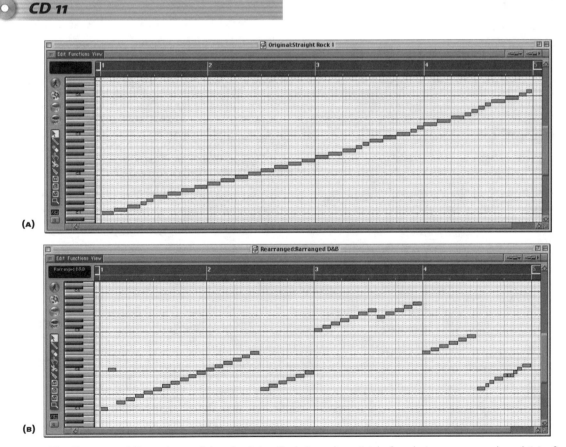

(A)

(B)

FIGURE 10.7 The Rearranged Drum Loop. A breakpoint edited drum loop **(A)** before being rearranged, and **(B)** after being rearranged.

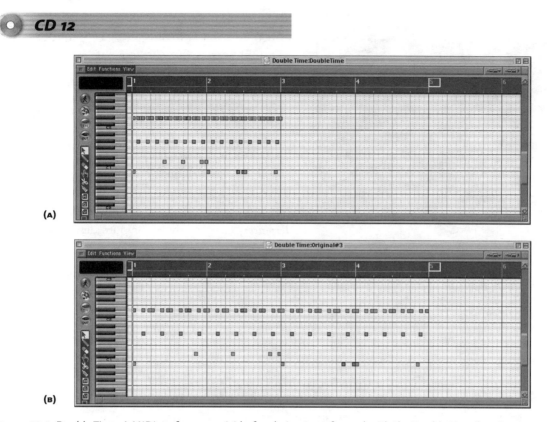

FIGURE 10.8 Double Time. A MIDI performance **(A)** before being transformed with the Double Time function in *Logic Audio,* and **(B)** afterwards.

Triggering New Sounds

A neat way of adding new drum sounds and rhythmic parts to a sampled drum loop is to trigger samples from the loop's waveform peaks. This has traditionally been done using an audio-to-MIDI trigger device (such as the Alesis DM5 drum module), but now, software is available that allows the entire operation to happen right in your computer, without the need for any external hardware. Many of these programs are plug-ins, but there are two distinct schools of the software: those that are modeled after traditional audio to MIDI trigger devices, and those that skip the audio-to-MIDI trigger step altogether and jump right into creating audio files based on the loop's waveform peaks.

AUDIO TRIGGERING MIDI

An excellent example of an audio-to-MIDI trigger application is *Digital Performer's* built-in Trigger plug-in (see figure 10.9). It can be used to trigger any MIDI sound source, from sampled drums, to a percussive synth patch, or a recycled funk guitar loop that has been loaded into a MIDI sampler. A Threshold control lets you determine how sensitive the trigger is to the waveform's peaks, and peak amplitudes can even be translated into MIDI note velocities. Once a sound is being triggered, the MIDI performance can be recorded to its own MIDI track for further manipulation.

SOUND REPLACEMENT

A perfect example of the second software type is Digidesign's Sound Replacer (see figure 10.10), an AudioSuite (offline processing) plug-in for all versions of *Pro Tools.* Instead of using the audio peaks to trigger MIDI sound sources, the samples you want triggered get loaded directly into the software, then the performance that's created can be exported as an audio file, straight to a track. This method is very convenient, circumventing the need for MIDI altogether. As with audio-to-MIDI triggers, a sample's playback velocity can be derived from the waveform's peak

FIGURE 10.9 *Digital Performer's* Trigger. *Digital Performer* features a built-in audio-to-MIDI trigger plug-in appropriately named, Trigger.

amplitudes. Up to three different samples can be loaded into Sound Replacer at once, and each can be triggered by its own peak amplitude zone.

TRIGGERING A HI-HAT PART

The following directions outline the steps to creating a dynamic hi-hat pattern from a basic drum loop and three hi-hat samples. Though the focus is on *Sound Replacer*, many of the techniques described can also be applied to an audio-to-MIDI trigger setup as well.

STEP 1. Select the loop for which you want to generate a hi-hat pattern.

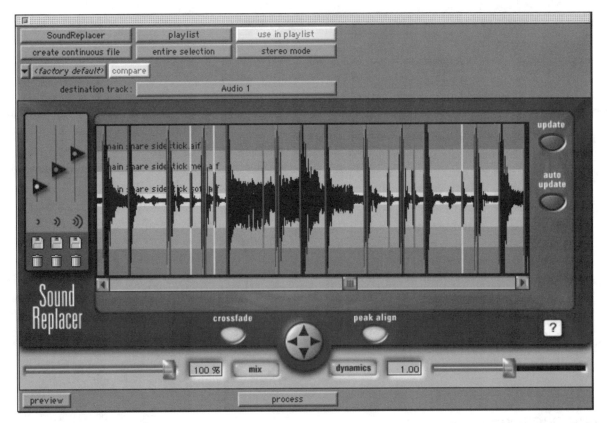

FIGURE 10.10 Digidesign's Sound Replacer. Digidesign's Sound Replacer for *Pro Tools* is a perfect example of a trigger application that doesn't use MIDI to play back samples, and instead allows you to load samples directly into the program itself for triggering.

STEP 2. Open *Sound Replacer* and load the selection into its Waveform Overview window by clicking on the Update button.

STEP 3. Load three hi-hat samples (click on the floppy disk icons to the right of the Waveform Overview) into *Sound Replacer*, two different closed hi-hat samples for the lower velocity zones, and an open hi-hat for the top velocity zone.

STEP 4. Set each threshold marker to its appropriate zone (see figure 10.10). You can audition the results by clicking the Preview button. Make any changes that are necessary to smooth out the triggering.

STEP 5. To print the results to a track, click the Process button. The Mix setting should be at 100 percent wet so that only the triggered sound is audible. Though you can select to overwrite the original drum loop, instead, deposit the processed audio to a separate track so that you can mix the two sources together.

CREATING TWO TRIGGERS FROM ONE

Let's say that you are only able to generate an eighth-note pattern from the original loop, but what you really want is a sixteenth-note pattern. Here's the trick: make a copy of the eighth-note pattern on a separate track, then shift it later in time by a sixteenth note. Turn its volume down relative to the original eighth-note pattern to mimic lower velocities on the sixteenth notes, then playback both tracks at the same time, and you should hear a sixteenth-note hi-hat pattern. The tracks can be left separate for further processing or mixed down to a single file to conserve audio voices.

That's the Beat

After applying the techniques discussed in this chapter, you should have a good, solid 4- to 8-bar drum groove. Now its time to start writing the music parts that go with the groove. This process is explained next, in chapter 11.

Building the Music Bed

With the basic beat constructed, you have a good rhythmic foundation on which to write the bass line and chord progression. These are the root musical parts of the remix and will determine much of its final mood and harmonic content. Writing pitched instrument parts is very different than writing drum and percussion parts because you must now pay attention to the song's key. The parts that you write must be in the same key, have the same tonal center, or be in a harmonically related key to the original song's breakout tracks. This doesn't mean that you need to follow the original song's chord progression. But if the parts you play are in a key that clashes with the original song, your remix won't sound right.

Learning music theory and harmony can take years, and is a subject best left to a different book. However, if you aren't tone deaf, you should be able to distinguish between different notes, and like the ability to see colors, that's the only real skill necessary to form an opinion about which notes sound good together and which notes clash. To find the notes that work with a song's breakout tracks, simply play the notes of a sampled piano one at a time and carefully listen for the notes that sound best with the music. You will discover that some notes sound "sweet" and others sound "sour." Locate at least four sweet-sounding notes, and you're well on your way to writing a part that's in the proper key.

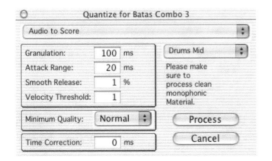

FIGURE 11.1 *Logic Audio's* Pitch to MIDI Converter. *Logic Audio* features a built-in pitch to MIDI converter as part of its Transform functions.

CD 14

A LITTLE HELP FINDING THE NOTES

If you feel unsure about your ability to find notes in the proper key, let your computer give you a hand by employing a pitch-to-MIDI converter program. It lets you convert the pitches in an audio file into a MIDI note performance. The translation isn't often perfect, so don't expect miracles, but it can narrow your choices by giving you a performance from which to start picking and choosing notes.

Many digital audio sequencers have a built-in pitch-to-MIDI converter feature, like *Logic Audio's* Audio to Score (see figure 11.1). If your program does not, and your system is PC, there are a lot of inexpensive programs available (such as *Music Composer* by AKoff, www.akoff.com) that can generate a SMF document from any WAV file.

Write a Bass Line

Traditionally, popular music has been written starting with a melody and a chord progression. Then the bass line underpins the chords, usually playing the root on the downbeats and following along with the progression. However, because the bass line plays such an important role in electronic dance music, many remix producers start by writing the bass line, followed by the chords. Choices for a bass line's key are usually constrained by the original song's breakout tracks, as are the choices for chords.

A bass line's rhythm should reflect, or work in partnership with, the kick-drum pattern (see figure 11.2). It may closely follow the kick pattern, accentuating the beats for that driving, throbbing, bass-heavy dance sound. Or, it may play off the kick rhythm, hitting on the upbeats, letting the sound of the kick

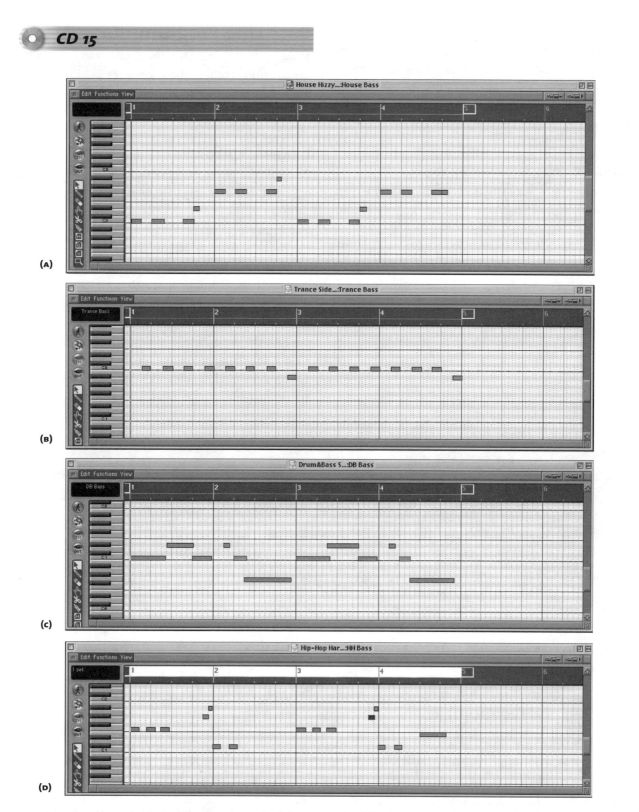

Figure 11.2 Bass Lines. A standard bass line for each of the main styles of dance music: **(A)** house, **(B)** trance, **(C)** drum-and-bass, **(D)** and hip-hop.

come through for that bouncy, happy, exciting feel. The bass sound should also be complementary to the kick drum, adding to each other so that the sum of their parts is greater than each individual tone. Avoid tones that interfere with each other's frequencies, such as a bass sound that phase-cancels low frequencies on the kick drum.

As with writing a beat, a bass line may be recorded live or programmed. If you are a proficient musician, playing it live will likely be the fastest way to create the bass line. However, programming a bass line also has advantages, such as the ability to very precisely control a synth bass patches' performance and affect parameters such as portamento and velocity filtering. Whether played live or programmed, it's usually a good idea to quantize the bass line to the same settings as the kick drum for a really tight groove.

Bass Line Programming

Since recording a MIDI bass line live needs little explanation (other than connect a MIDI bass instrument, assign it to a sequencer track, and record a performance), let's jump right into programming.

GRAPHIC EDITOR

Also called a Piano Roll Editor for its resemblance to an antique player piano's music roll, the Graphic Editor window lets you view and edit notes on a grid (see figure 11.3). The Y-axis is for note pitches and the X-axis is for note length. The grid can usually be set to display a variety of different beat divisions (such as whole bars, eighth or sixteenth notes, or dotted and triplet values), and notes can be made to snap to the grid. Velocity values for the notes are either displayed beneath the notes or as a translucent, colored overlay. Control Change events (such as Continuous Controllers, modulation and pitch bend, see appendix B) are also displayed in this same fashion.

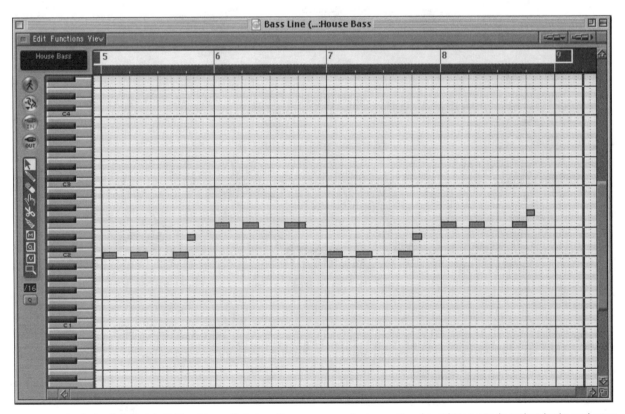

FIGURE 11.3 *Logic Audio's* Matrix Editor. Many digital audio sequencers feature a Graphic Editing window that looks and operates similarly to *Logic Audio's* Matrix Editor.

A Pencil tool is available for drawing in notes and a Grabber tool is employed for adjusting note lengths. The Pencil and Grabber can also be used for scaling velocities and Control Change data. When you draw in a note, its velocity is set to a default value. So after programming a series of notes, you should edit their velocities to give the bass line dynamics that pulse with the beat (such as making the velocities for the downbeats harder than the upbeats). A grid setting of either eighth or sixteenth notes is fine for composing most bass lines. The Graphic Editor is also excellent for editing a MIDI bass line that was recorded live.

MATRIX PATTERN SEQUENCER

Reason features a module that is perfect for sequencing bass lines: the Matrix Pattern Sequencer (see figure 11.4). Though it can only control one note at a time, this is fine because most bass lines are monophonic.

STEP 1: In *Reason*, create a 14:2 Mixer, then create a Subtractor Analog Synthesizer. It should automatically connect to channel 1 of the Mixer.

STEP 2: Subtractor has some great bass presets. Find the Subtractor Bass folder and select a patch.

STEP 3: With the Subtractor selected, create a Matrix Pattern Sequencer. It should automatically connect to the Subtractor. If not, connect the Matrix Note CV and Gate CV to the Subtractor Note and Gate, respectively. These connections give the Matrix sequencing control over the Subtractor.

STEP 4: Set the Matrix editing mode to Keys, its octave to 2, the resolution to sixteenth notes, and the Steps to 32 for a 2-bar pattern.

STEP 5: Program notes in the grid and their velocity values below, in the Gate display area. To create eighth and held notes, enable the note Tie feature. Be sure to program harder velocities for the downbeats than the upbeats to give the bass line dynamics that groove with the beat. If you are uncertain about how to perform these operations, you should consult the *Reason* Operation Manual.

STEP 6: To create more movement in your bass line, connect the Matrix Curve CV to the Subtractor Filter 1 Freq or Filter 1 Res and turn the associated Modulation Input knob up to at least 75 percent. Switch the Matrix edit mode to Curve and draw in a modulation curve (see figure 11.5). At playback, you should hear the modulation curve affecting the Subtractor's Modulation Input parameter.

CD 16

ACID HOUSE BASS SLIDE

To create that classic synth bass slide sound popularized by Acid House, turn the synthesizer's Portamento control up to at least 50 percent. Then make sure that the first note of the slide runs over into the note that you want to slide up to (that its Note Off message falls after the second note's Note On message). For the best sounding slides, be sure that the interval between the notes is at least a third.

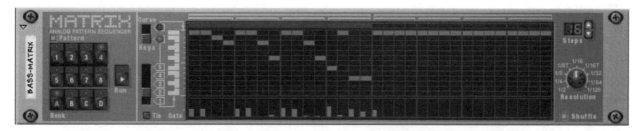

FIGURE 11.4 Matrix Pattern Sequencer. *Reason's* Matrix Pattern Sequencer module is perfect for programming bass lines.

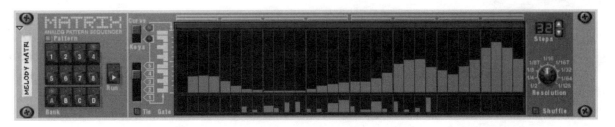

Figure 11.5 Modulation Curve in the Matrix Pattern Sequencer. By switching the Matrix's edit mode to Curve, a modulation curve can be created and used to control a synthesizer's parameter (such as filter frequency or resonance).

Chord Progressions and Arpeggios

At the most basic level, a chord is three or more notes that sound good together—notes that are harmonically related. Play the notes together that you know are in the key of your remix, and that's a chord. A *chord progression* is a series of two or more chords, usually evolving from a chord that has tension (such as a minor) to a more resolved chord (like a major), or vice versa. Getting into the theory behind chord structures is a deep subject, but don't let a lack of formal training deter you from having fun, making up your own chords. Let your ears and fingers guide you to find chords that move through a cycle of tension and release, and that sound good with your remix. (If you're looking for a place to start, figure 11.6 illustrates a standard chord progression in each of the most popular dance music styles.)

CD 17

Chords are generally played in one of two ways: either with a rhythmic cadence or very straight, on the downbeats. Of course, there are permutations, but generalizing like this helps you to choose an appropriate chord sound. The synthesizer patch assigned to play your chords is closely related to the rhythm with which a chord progression is played. For example, a busy rhythmic style should be played by a sound that has a fast, aggressive attack (see figure 11.7), such as a piano or electric guitar patch. A chord progression playing a simple rhythm pattern can be assigned to a sound with a slow, soft attack, such as bowed strings or a synth pad.

CD 18

Arpeggiating your chords, playing one note at a time, can produce interesting melodic movement, especially if you arpeggiate more than one chord back to back. To arpeggiate a chord, play its individual notes sequentially, with a steady rhythm (eighth or sixteenth notes work well), in a continuous loop. The note sequence may be played up, down, up and down (or vice versa), or be some random, repeating pattern. Some synthesizers (both hardware and software) have a built-in arpeggiator. Make sure that if you use this feature, the synthesizer is receiving MIDI Clock from your sequencer so that the arpeggiator plays in tempo with your remix. Many digital audio sequencers also come with an arpeggiator feature (such as *Cubase SX's* Arpache 5 MIDI plug-in, see figure 11.8). Whether you use an arpeggiator in your sequencer or your synth, the effect is pretty much the same. When you hold down a chord, it will be arpeggiated.

CD 19

A classic way to add movement and dynamics to your chord progression, especially simple progressions, is to automate a *filter sweep*. The filter effect can be a plug-in (like *Logic Audio's* ever-popular AutoFilter), or a parameter in the synth's own filter section. Move either the Cutoff, Resonance, or Frequency controls of the filter while the chords are playing. The move might be a slow, steady, upward sweep or one that dips and peaks continuously over the course of the loop. Automate the parameters by recording their movements to a MIDI track, assigned to the synth, in your sequencer.

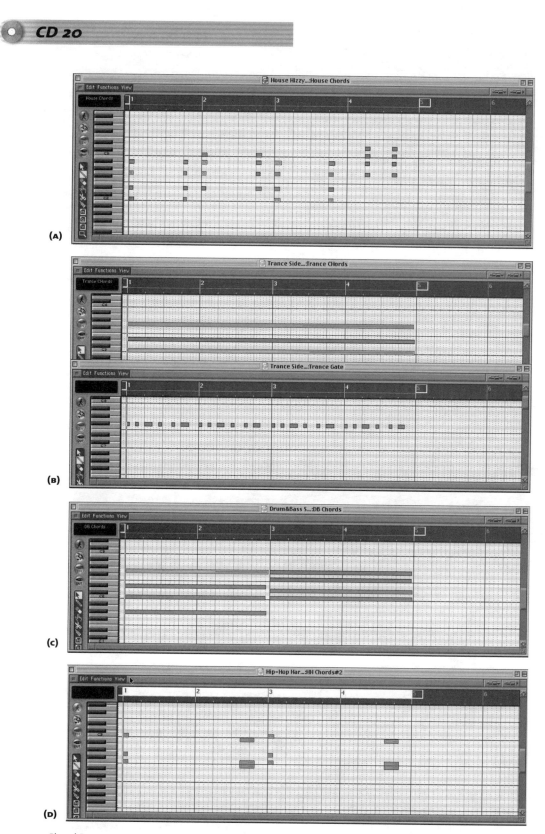

FIGURE 11.6 Chord Progressions. A standard chord progression for each of the main styles of dance music: **(A)** house, **(B)** trance, **(C)** drum-and-bass, and **(D)** hip-hop.

Our favorite filter is the band pass [discussed in chapter 14], especially the one on the Emu EOS series samplers. Band pass sounds great on big beefy pads, and it can help turn a sound that would normally hog the mix into a manageable yet lush musical element. Filter sweeps are great for adding motion to a sound that would otherwise come across as flat and uninteresting. Low-pass filter sweeps are also a great way to introduce new sounds into a mix. It may seem like a played-out method, but low-pass sweeps allow the producer to introduce elements into the mix in a subtle fashion and gradually bring them to the listener's attention.

—J. Scott G., Deepsky

UNDERSTANDING ADSR

Every sound has an amplitude envelope whose shape is composed of four basic stages: attack, decay, sustain, and release (ADSR, see figure 11.9). *Attack* is how fast, or slow the sound starts. *Decay* determines how long the sound takes to reach the "sustain" stage. *Sustain* is how long the sound lasts. The *release* determines how long the sound takes to fade out after the note has been released.

It's important to understand the ADSR envelope so that you can modify synth and sampler patches to fit your production. For example, a sound that needs to hit harder can have its attack time shortened to come in faster. Or, a sound that needs to cut off quicker, for a more "staccato" sound, can have its release time shortened. Synthesizers and samplers also employ ADSR envelopes to shape other sonic building blocks, like filters.

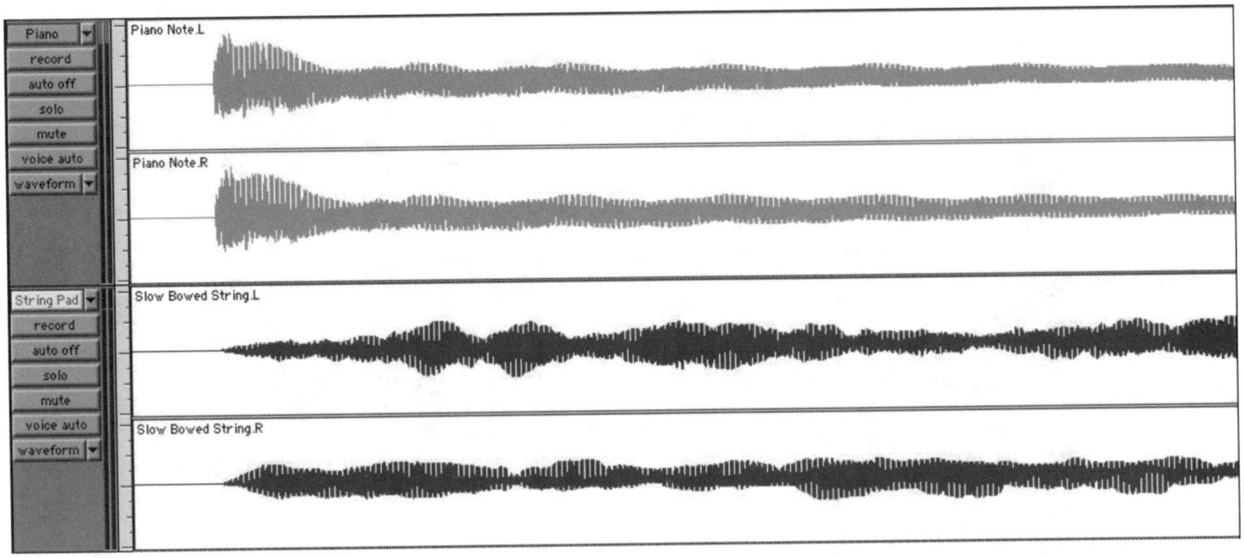

FIGURE 11.7 Fast and Slow Attacks. A piano note has a fast attack. In contrast, a slowly bowed string has a slow attack.

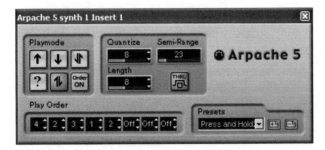

FIGURE 11.8 Arpeggiator MIDI Plug-in. *Cubase SX* comes standard with a MIDI plug-in for creating arpeggios.

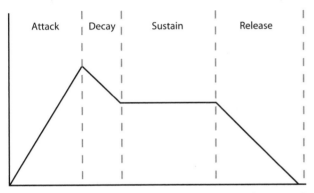

FIGURE 11.9 ADSR Envelope. The four stages of a typical amplitude envelope.

QUICK CHORD CONCOCTION

If you have found three notes in the key of your remix, you have what it takes to make a simple chord progression.

STEP 1. Find a voicing (the order of the notes) for the three notes that will work for your first chord (for example, C, E, G).

STEP 2. Create a second chord with more tension (or possibly less tension, depending on your initial three notes) by *flatting* (lowering by one note, called a half-step) the middle note of your first chord (so the first chord becomes, C, E-flat, G).

STEP 3. You can stop at just these two chords, or continue and develop a couple more. Create an *inversion* of your first chord by moving the bottom note of the chord to the top of the chord (so the first chord becomes, E, G, C). You might also try the reverse (G, C, E). The notes of the chord are still the same as your first chord; you're just changing the chord's *voicing*.

STEP 4. Create more variations by again, flatting the middle notes (so the two last chords would become E, G-flat, C, and G, B, E).

STEP 5. You should now have four chords. Play around with their order of playback to create a chord progression that works for the remix. Rearranging a chord's initial voicing to create more chords, and flatting notes within the chords to create more, or less, tension are tricks for generating chords that are most always useful.

Program a Chord Progression

As with most music and drum parts, a chord progression can be recorded live or programmed. If you are a good enough musician to play it live, you probably know how to record a MIDI track into your sequencer. If not, you should refer to your program's user manual. Programming a chord progression is more technically involved and time consuming than playing it live, but creating chords this way can also produce wonderfully musical results. If you're not a proficient keyboard player, the only choice may be to program your chords. Fortunately, there are features in most sequencers to make the task easier. (For ideas on chord construction, see the sidebar, "Quick Chord Concoction," p. 97.)

GRAPHIC EDITOR

The Graphic Editor is the window of choice to program chords in most sequencers. All the same tricks for programming a bass line apply to programming chords. Draw your notes in using the Pencil tool, lengthen or shorten notes with the Grabber tool, and be sure to go through and edit note velocities after the chords are programmed to create dynamics. The only difference now is that you are programming *polyphonic* (several notes played at the same time) chords rather than a *monophonic* (just one note at a time) bass line. Generally, each note of a chord is about the same length, though this is not a hard-and-fast rule. Unless you are decidedly going for a programmed sound, varying note lengths, velocities, and even start times will give your programmed chords a more human feel (see figure 11.10).

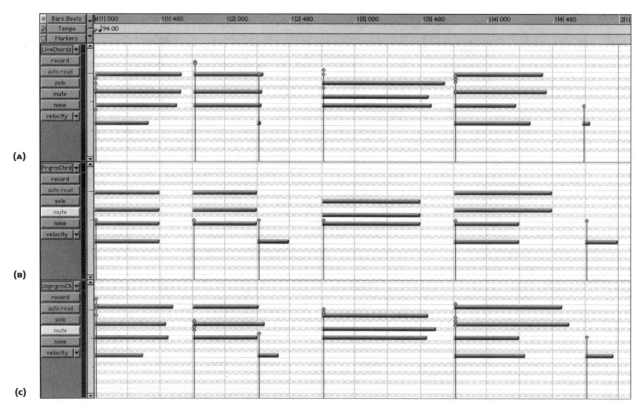

FIGURE 11.10 Comparing Live and Programmed Chords. The same chord progression **(A)** played live, compared to **(B)** programmed, and then **(C)** after editing to give them a more human feel without removing all of the programmed feel.

FIGURE 11.11 *Logic Audio's* Keyboard Window. An onscreen keyboard in *Logic Audio* can be used to enter notes and chords one note value at a time directly into the Matrix Editor.

STEP SEQUENCING AND CHORD PRESETS

Most sequencers have a *step-sequencing* feature that allows you to program in notes and chords one note value at a time. There are generally three ways to enter notes: from a MIDI keyboard (or other MIDI controller), using the computer's keyboard, or from an onscreen keyboard (see figure 11.11). Though every program's step sequencer works differently, the general operating principle is to select a note value (like an eighth or sixteenth note) and then enter a note, or the notes of a chord. Once the notes have been entered, the sequencer's playbar will jump to the next beat over, where you again enter a note value and a note or a chord (or a rest, if you don't want anything to play on that beat).

If you are entering the notes from a velocity-sensitive MIDI controller, the velocity for each note you play usually gets recorded. However, if you're entering the notes from your computer keyboard or onscreen keyboard, these are not velocity-sensitive controllers, and you will need to choose a velocity value for each step. An alternate, usually faster method is to step sequence the part and then draw a velocity curve for the notes in your program's Graphic Editor. It can take getting used to, but with patience and practice, remixers that prefer to program rather than play their parts can learn to compose very efficiently with a step sequencer.

A few sequencers and synthesizers offer a selection of chord presets (such as Bitheadz *Unity* DS-1 or *Cubase SX's* Chorder, see figure 11.12). Features such as these allow you to select a chord type (such as minor or major 7), and play a note, and a chord is generated

with that note as its root. Chord presets can be a quick way of entering chords into a step sequencer using just one finger.

Lead Lines

Even if there is already a vocal hook, adding a memorable synth lead line can propel your remix to a whole other level. Catchy melodies are an important element of any song, and a strong synth line that either stands on its own or helps to underscore the lead vocals can really make your remix stand out. A good lead line brings another musical element to your production that can be used to build energy in and out of transitions and differentiate sections.

Like most drum and pitched-instrument parts, a lead line can be recorded live or programmed. All the same techniques employed for writing chords and, especially, bass lines can be applied to writing lead lines. You can program the line using a Graphic Editor or Step Sequencer, and *Reason's* Matrix is particularly suited for writing lead lines. Add velocity changes and automate filter sweeps for dynamic and interesting lines. Incorporate a synthesizer's portamento parameter, pitch bend, and the Mod wheel to articulate pitch

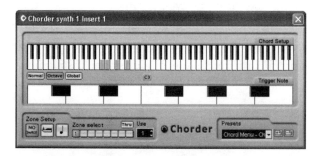

FIGURE 11.12 Chorder. The Chorder MIDI plug-in comes standard with *Cubase SX*. It allows you to select a chord to be generated when you play a single, root note.

and vibrato. There are no rules as to what constitutes a lead sound, as long as it can rise above the mix, and it doesn't interfere with the bass, get buried by the chords, or conflict with the lead vocals. And you can always adjust a patch's ADSR, tailoring its sound to match the part.

The very same notes that worked for your chords and the bass line will also work for the lead line, only at a more appropriate octave (usually, two or three octaves above the bass, and at least one octave above the chords). A few sequencers (such as *Digital Performer*) will let you draw or paint (using a Brush tool), key-constrained lines directly into the Graphic Editor (for example, you could only paint in notes that were in the key of E-flat minor). This is a powerful feature that frees you up from worrying whether you're playing in the right key, and instead lets you concentrate on programming the performance. Keep in mind that a lead line doesn't need to be complex. In fact, a simple line is often the best line (see figure 11.13).

CD 22

COUNTERPOINT MELODIES FROM LOOPS WITH ODD BEAT COUNTS

Any program that has the ability to create loops with an odd number of beats, not just an even number of beats, can create wonderfully sophisticated counterpoint melodies. For example, a lead or arpeggio line that is three beats long, playing against a line that is a whole bar (four beats long) will create a 3-bar melodic cycle (see figure 11.14). Add a loop to this same example that is five beats long, and the entire cycle becomes fifteen bars; the downbeat of all three loops doesn't come around again until the downbeat of the sixteenth bar. This production technique produces great sounding trance melodies.

Recording Live Tracks

Just because you're producing a dance remix doesn't mean that you can't add you own live-recorded tracks. Maybe you hear an extra vocal line, a rhythm guitar part, or a lead trumpet line; samples and MIDI tracks aren't everything as long as your new parts are tasteful and don't overshadow the original song's breakout elements, turning the production into an original track instead of a remix. Also, keep in mind that the "feel" behind dance music is largely loop driven, and you should stick with this production value even though you are recording live tracks. Think of the process more like sampling custom loops than traditional multitrack recording. Fortunately, most digital audio sequencers have a loop recording feature that make this task a breeze (such *Pro Tools* Loop Record mode or *Digital Performer's* unique RAM-based loop recording tool, Polar).

With a bass line, chords, and possibly a lead synth loop, you've crafted the essential musical elements for your remix. Now, along with the groove, it's time to begin forming all of these elements into a cohesive song structure, instead of just a repetitious loop.

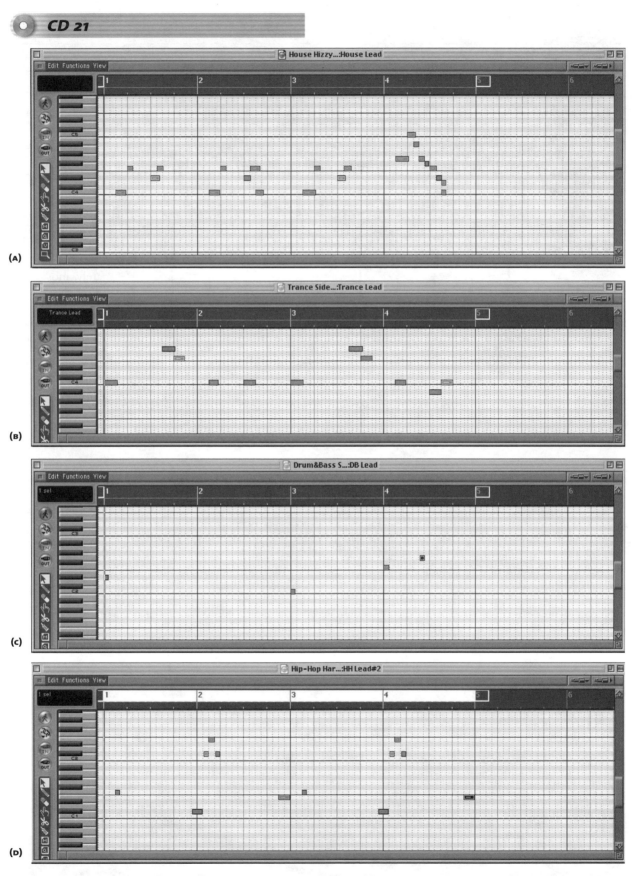

FIGURE 11.13 Lead Lines. A standard lead line for each of the main styles of dance music: **(A)** house, **(B)** trance, **(C)** drum-and-bass, and **(D)** hip-hop.

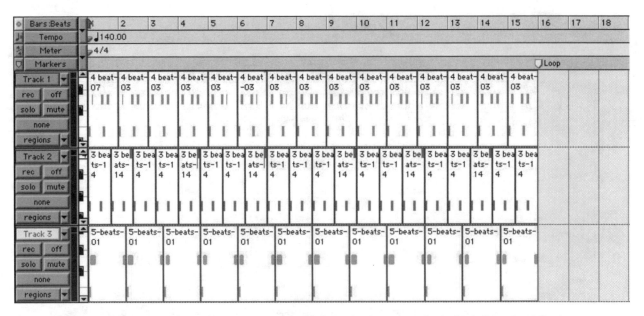

FIGURE 11.14 Counterpoint Melodies and Loops with Odd Beats. Track 1 has a standard 1-bar, 4-beat loop. Track 2 contains a 3-beat loop. Track 3 has a 5-beat loop. Playing against each other, the downbeat of all three loops doesn't come around for fifteen bars, until the first downbeat of the sixteenth bar.

Arrangement and Production

CHAPTER 12

Structure and Arrange

The last two chapters covered the fundamentals of composing—how to build up the remix's basic musical elements over a 4- or 8-bar loop. With these essential ingredients complete, it's now time to begin the arranging process, using your loops as the building blocks in the creation of the remix's song structure. But first, it's important to understand the concept of "song structure," and how to plan your remix's direction and form. Then you will have a framework around which to start arranging.

You may be familiar with the conventional, popular song structure, of verse, chorus, verse, chorus, change (or bridge), a return to the chorus, and out to the end. Though much less formulated, remixes also adhere to a standardized structure. However, this structure is far less apparent than that of popular songs because you rarely hear a complete song on the dance floor. A good DJ keeps the energy and flow of their set seamless by continuously mixing between records. It's mainly for this reason that a set of simple guidelines has evolved for remixes, so DJs know what to expect from one record to the next.

> Dance music follows a structure that I like to call "house music song structure."
>
> —(BT) Brian Transeau

Remix Song Structure

A remix's energy must ebb and flow over the course of the track in order to stay interesting and keep people motivated to dance. Creating this ebb and flow is achieved first by arranging and then by production, creating dramatic and seamless transitions between sections. Think of it like building a sonic roller coaster. The remix's emotional highs and lows are the ride.

The first rule of remix song structure is that there should be a clean, uncluttered beat, with few to no pitch elements (nothing that might infer a key), for about thirty-two bars, at the remix's beginning and end. These beats are often referred to as the "mix-in" and "mix-out," respectively. They provide the time and space necessary for DJs to beat match between records, without worrying about matching keys. What goes on between these beat-driven bookends is more loosely structured and open to interpretation. (See figure 12.1 for a structural analysis of one hit remix.)

A section commonly inserted midway through a remix is the "breakdown." This is a return to the track's basic beat, interspersed with light musical elements, or the beat may drop out altogether, with layers of chords and arpeggios taking over, carrying the track's rhythmic pulse through careful arrangement and production techniques (such as the gated rhythm effects, covered in chapter 13).

> What we're doing is creating tools for the DJ so that they can mix in and out of tunes. We'll save musical elements for later in a track because most DJs don't do "harmonic mixing" [playing records on top of each other that have lots of pitched parts]. It can lead to two things: either you'll get a weird clash melodically, or you get a DJ who is riding their turntable's pitch slider to adjust the record's tempo. If you have a string line, for example, its pitch is going to start sliding around, and this may not sound pretty. By having mainly percussion, with just a little vocal hook or effect, on a tune's beginning and end, you're giving the DJ what they need to mix records—to beat mix.
>
> —Chris Cox, Thunderpuss

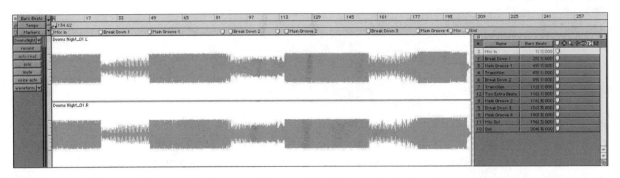

Figure 12.1 Structural Analysis. Timo Maas's remix of "Dooms Night," by Azzido Da Bass, is an example of a typical remix song structure.

> *Timo Maas and his producer Martin Buttrich took a decent dance tune ["Doom's Night" by Azzido Da Bass] and turned it into something completely different, that barely resembles the original tune. The remix was a bigger hit than the original version, and it made Timo into a household name on the dance music scene. Timo's version of "Doom's Night" has great sounds, an irresistible beat, and an imaginative buildup. Even though I've heard it probably a thousand times, it still sounds fresh and gets me out on the dance floor whenever the DJ drops it.*

> —Chris Gill (Gilla Monsta),
> editor of *Remix* Magazine (1999–2002)

Creating a Basic Structure

Once all of your basic loops are written, chiseling out a basic structure is pretty straightforward. It's mainly a process of copying loops throughout the duration of your remix, and then deciding which ones should be muted or unmuted for each section.

STEP 1. Begin by making sure that all of your loops are lined up at bar 1, and that the 4- to 8-bar multi-track groove you have built up starts at the beginning of the project. For example, if you were creating the groove under the vocal chorus section, copy all of the tracks less the lead vocals and paste them at bar 1.

STEP 2. Working with these same loops, mute everything but the most fundamental parts, so that all you're left hearing are the basic drums, bass, chords, and lead vocals, if any. Mute the individual loops, not the tracks. Most good sequencers have this feature; it's usually also available as a keyboard command (such as, M or Option-M). To mute more than one sequence at once, select a group of sequences and mute them all at the same time.

STEP 3. Copy and paste this multitrack section, muted sequences and all, back-to-back until you reach an appropriate length for the remix, say between five and seven minutes. This operation can usually be completed in one fell swoop with a Repeat command. (The keyboard command is often R or Option-R.) For example, an 8-bar loop at 130 BPM would need to be repeated twenty-five times in order to surpass the six minute mark (see figure 12.2).

STEP 4. If there is a lead vocal track, and you have not cut it up into discrete sections yet (as into verse, prechorus, chorus, bridge, and so on), do so now. Be sure to make the cuts on downbeats where there are no vocals recorded so that moving the vocals around, later, is a piece of cake. To accomplish this, a section may need to be cut a bar ahead of its downbeat. For example, a vocal that starts between the downbeat and the 4-count of the previous bar, say on bar 32, should be cut on the downbeat of bar 31.

(You can make a note in the audio region's name or comments area to remind yourself that the section has this extra bar.)

STEP 5. Returning to the task of creating the remix's song structure, place song markers (also called bookmarks) in the Arrange window, at each bar where you want a different section to begin. (If you aren't sure how to do this, refer to your program's user guide.) These markers show just a rough outline of the remix at this point, and will likely be moved as you flesh out all of the production elements (such as the track's high and low energy points). You can use the section names and bar counts shown in figure 12.1 as a place to start. (The section names given in figure 12.1 are the standard nomenclature, but feel free to make up your own labels where appropriate.)

STEP 6. Drag any lead vocal parts to their appropriate section markers, making sure that the performances stay properly lined up with the beats. For example, a verse that originally began on an odd bar (such as bar 31) should only be moved to an odd bar (such as bar 17). This will help keep the vocals in beat, both rhythmically and melodically.

STEP 7. Go through and begin unmuting loops in each section. Don't worry about unumuting everything right now. This is just a rough arrangement so that you can distinguish differences between sections. For example, bring loops in at the choruses, drop them out on the verses, introduce a new loop for the bridge, and so on (see figure 12.3). Refining the arrangement, transitions between sections, and the overall ebb and flow of energy come next.

WHY NOT JUST LOOP THE PARTS?

Most sequencers have a function that will let you loop a selection of bars a specific number of times—or even infinitely. Though this function can come in handy when you're sequencing the remix's basic music loops, it is not ideal for arranging. The reason for making real copies of a loop all the way through the remix is so that each loop can be treated individually. For example, you can mute or unmute one loop, or dramatically edit a sequence's performance without affecting the copies.

I usually have an extended intro, verse, chorus, break—the break comes after the chorus, like an 8- bar second intro, just some space before the second verse. And if it sounds good, I'll double the second chorus, going into the next break.

—Dave Audé

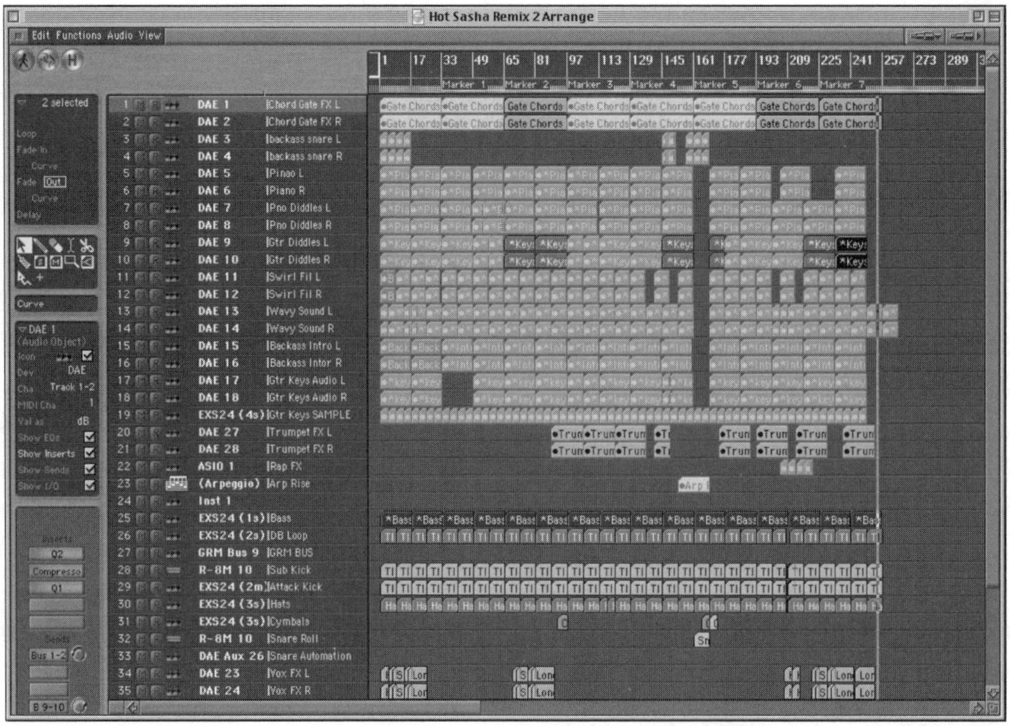

FIGURE 12.2 Copied Through and Ready for Arranging. The multitrack loops have been copied through to reach the remix's six-minute mark. At this stage, most of the parts are still muted and awaiting arrangement, when they will be selectively unmuted.

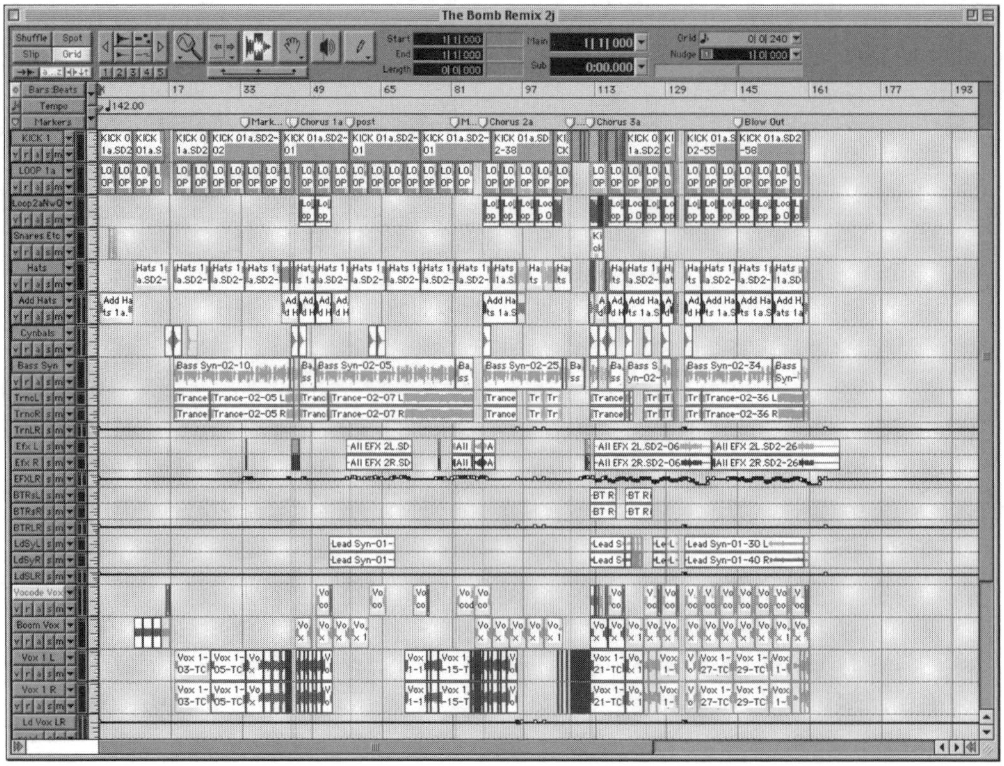

FIGURE 12.3 A Basic Structure. Looking at the big picture, you can see that more loops are playing during the choruses than any other section, and that over the course of the entire remix, additional loops are slowly introduced.

It's like classical music where you have a theme, variation on the theme, and a recapitulation of the theme. House music follows a similar structure. Start with a beat, then introduce the vocal, go off somewhere new, then usually in the middle of somewhere new, you'll have a breakdown, then you come back with the hook. Generally, you'll have a rise, fall, rise farther, and level out sort of structure. That's typically the pattern my compositions follow.

—(BT) Brian Transeau

Energy Ebb and Flow

With the remix's basic structure taking shape, it's time to start setting up the track's energy—where it will peak or dip. Arranging the multitrack loops in combination with different production tricks (such as drum fills, synth swells, and dramatic breaks) are the means for realizing this ebb and flow of energy, but before beginning the process, you should create a roadmap to follow. This will let you see the big picture, so you know not only where your arrangement is headed, but also where it's been, in order to make the most effective arrangement and production choices possible.

A great technique for making such a roadmap is to draw a diagram that shows target energy levels in relation to bars elapsed (see figure 12.4). The Y-axis is the energy level and the X-axis shows the remix's sections and bars. The end result is a chart that looks something like a landscape elevation map. Leave plenty of space for yourself beneath the X-axis to scribble production notes and other related reminders (such as the loops you want to bring in or out, and ideas for fills or other transitional parts).

Paul Van Dyke got me started on something he'd been doing for years. He draws a map of how he wants the track to feel in terms of a build. It's drawn as if you were looking at the side of a mountain that's been cut away. You can see it rise in some in parts and fall away in other parts. For example, you can see right on your map that bar 16 to 32 is building, the line is going up, and then at 33 we drop, but we only drop this far. At bar 33, you only want to take the intensity down a little bit, meaning leave the kick drum in but drop a bunch of the elements out. It's such a handy thing, a visual way of thinking.

—(BT) Brian Transeau

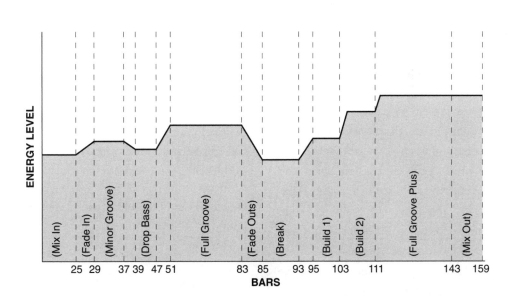

FIGURE 12.4 Energy Level Roadmap. The Y-axis shows the energy level and the X-axis lists the remix's sections and bars.

Differentiating Sections

Instead of just having a loop start playing because it's been unmuted, you want to find creative ways to introduce it. By the same token, you don't necessarily want a loop to just stop playing simply because it's been muted. You want to figure out how to take it out subtly. In so doing, you are creating *transitions*—introductions into different sections that may be obviously dramatic or so smooth that they slip by without notice. How you craft these transitions greatly influences listeners' emotional ride. Great transitions will take listeners on a wonderful and seamless journey, while poor transitions are like taking the same journey in an old broken down car with flat tires.

There are a variety of basic techniques for producing great transitions, including standard drum fills, the careful arrangement of loops, and creative special effects. It's a good idea to start with loop arrangement and drum fills, then experiment with the more innovative special effects transitions, and even try combining effects and drum fills. Once you have two or three basic fills and a couple of unique transition arrangements, you should have your section introductions covered. It's fine to use the same fill or transition arrangement more than once, and adding or subtracting background parts can make them sound very different.

KEEP IT SIMPLE

A busy arrangement and tons of brilliant production elements that work for a pop radio song may not sound so hot on the dance floor. A club's sound system is very different from a car or home stereo system. Most big clubs feature huge speakers, lots of amplification, and a listening environment that's saturated by room tone (such as reverb, frequency cuts and boosts, and even slap-back delay). For example, too many extra percussion parts and poorly mixed pads can sound awful in a club, echoing off the walls and drowning the beat in an annoying drone. Keep your productions simple and uncluttered for the dance floor, because the music always sounds bigger and more impressive over the club's system than at your home studio.

DRUM FILLS

A fill that sounds like it was played by a real drummer qualifies as a standard drum fill. Most fills incorporate kick, snare, toms, cymbals, and the occasional hi-hat, and a crash or splash cymbal usually lands on the first downbeat following the fill. It may be an audio loop, a MIDI sample, or a live recording, and can be manipulated by breakpoint editing (recycling) if it's audio, or via your program's graphic editing window if it's MIDI. Though there are no real rules regarding types of drum fills and dance music styles, standard drum fills are most predominant in drum-and-bass, hip-hop, and down tempo (see figure 12.5).

Another type of drum fill that has been a staple of electronic dance music (especially for trance and house) is the drum-machine snare roll (see figure 12.6). The rolls developed their characteristic sound because they were originally created using the step sequencers of classic drum machines like Roland's TR-808 and TR-909. Today, this same step-sequenced feel can be programmed with a software drum machine (like ReDrum) or by drawing or painting, notes into your sequencer's graphic editor. The drum of choice for the rolls is usually an electronic snare sample, but really, almost any drum sample can be employed (from an acoustic snare sample to a kick drum).

The typical roll is created by stringing a series of eighth- or sixteenth-note snare hits together over one or more bars. It's usually slowly faded in (with a velocity curve, and sometimes a fader) to create a *crescendo* effect—a sense of rising anticipation with the volume peaking just before the downbeat of the next section. A filter effect is occasionally added for more dynamics. Timing of the roll is often doubled near its climax for extra punch, for example an eighth-note roll will become sixteenth notes on the last few beats of the roll's final bar. Trills (short double-time embellishments) and pauses may also be inserted over the course of the fill to add extra energy and more anticipation.

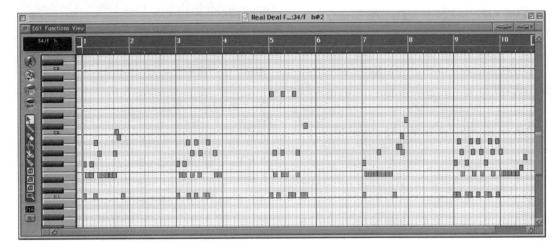

Figure 12.5 Realistic Drum Fills. Several standard drum fills as seen in *Logic Audio's* Matrix Edit window. Real sounding drum fills are most predominant in drum-and-bass, hip-hop, and down tempo dance music styles.

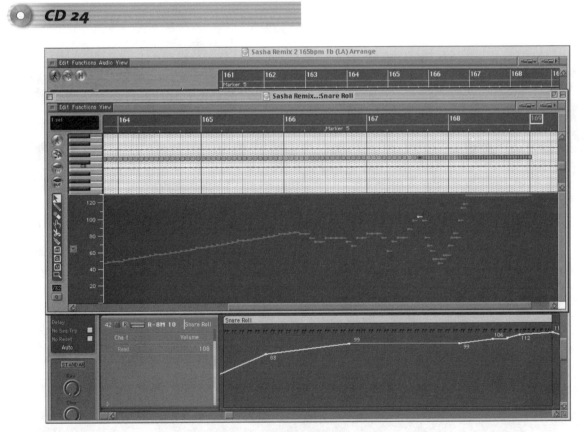

Figure 12.6 Drum Machine Snare Rolls. Drum machine style snare rolls, typical of trance and house styles, as seen in *Logic Audio's* Matrix Edit window. The velocity curve for each roll is shown below the notes.

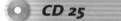

CRESCENDO AND DECRESCENDO

Slowly adding in loops to build up to a peak energy section works wonderfully. Keep in mind that while the kick pattern and bass line act as the remix's heart beat, the mix's busier, syncopated, mid- and high-frequency parts (like an open hi-hat on the upbeats, or a funky, wah-wah guitar) create all the excitement. To make a loop buildup even more effective, fade the loops in. Fading them in quickly can create a dramatic crescendo effect, while fading them in over several bars will manifest a more subtle transition—a shift in energy that listeners will feel but not necessarily be conscious of (see figure 12.7).

Removing loops one at a time to introduce a new section is also effective. However, simply muting a loop with no warning can sound abrupt. The solution is to wean listeners off of the loop by slowly fading it out over several bars, a decrescendo (see figure 12.8). This technique also creates a subtle shift in energy that is more felt than heard.

DRAMATIC PAUSE

There are times when you want to create a very dramatic shift or break in the remix's energy. After you have built a section all the way up to its peak, drop everything out but the most basic elements (like drums and bass). Make the mutes on a downbeat, and let a little reverb or delay trail over from the muted loops to create the impression of a quick, DJ-style crossfade (see figure 12.9). This technique proves that it's often the parts you take out that create the drama and excitement, not just the loops that are being continually added.

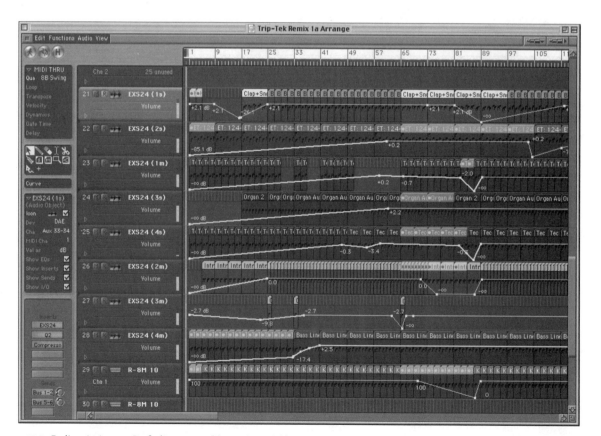

FIGURE 12.7 Fading In Loops. By fading several loops in quickly, you can create a dramatic crescendo effect. Conversely, fading several loops in slowly, over several bars, will create a more subtle transition.

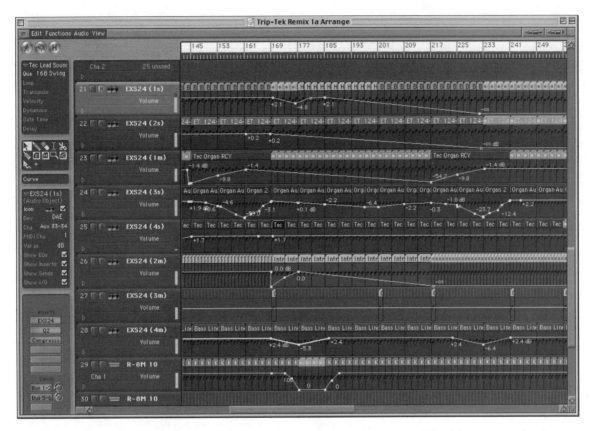

Figure 12.8 Fading Out Loops. Slowly fading loops out over several bars can create a subtle shift in energy that listeners will feel but not necessarily be conscious of.

Along these same lines, muting beats or actually inserting a bar of silence immediately after a peak can create lots of drama. Experiment with dropping drums and parts of loops out in a bar's fourth beat—a sort of anti-drum fill, creating a momentary break in the remix's energy before beginning the next section (see figure 12.10). Or, after a big fill or climactic build, instead of giving listeners a downbeat, which is exactly what they expect, create tension by delaying the downbeat (see figure 12.11). Insert a bar of silence immediately before the downbeat, pushing the entire arrangement that follows back by one bar. (Most good sequencers have this feature; refer to your program's user manual if you aren't sure about how to proceed.) The downbeat of the new section will then come as a wonderful sense of release.

PAUSE FOR A WORD

If your remix includes lead vocals, dropping beats out, or even muting everything for a beat or two while the vocals are still playing can be very effective. This trick was pioneered by hip-hop artists, and always sounds great with rap, but when tastefully done, works equally well with sung notes.

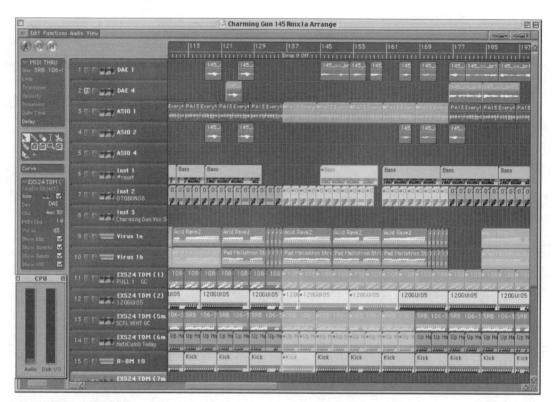

Figure 12.9 The Drop Off. Once a section has been built up to its peak, dropping everything out but a few basic parts can be very dramatic.

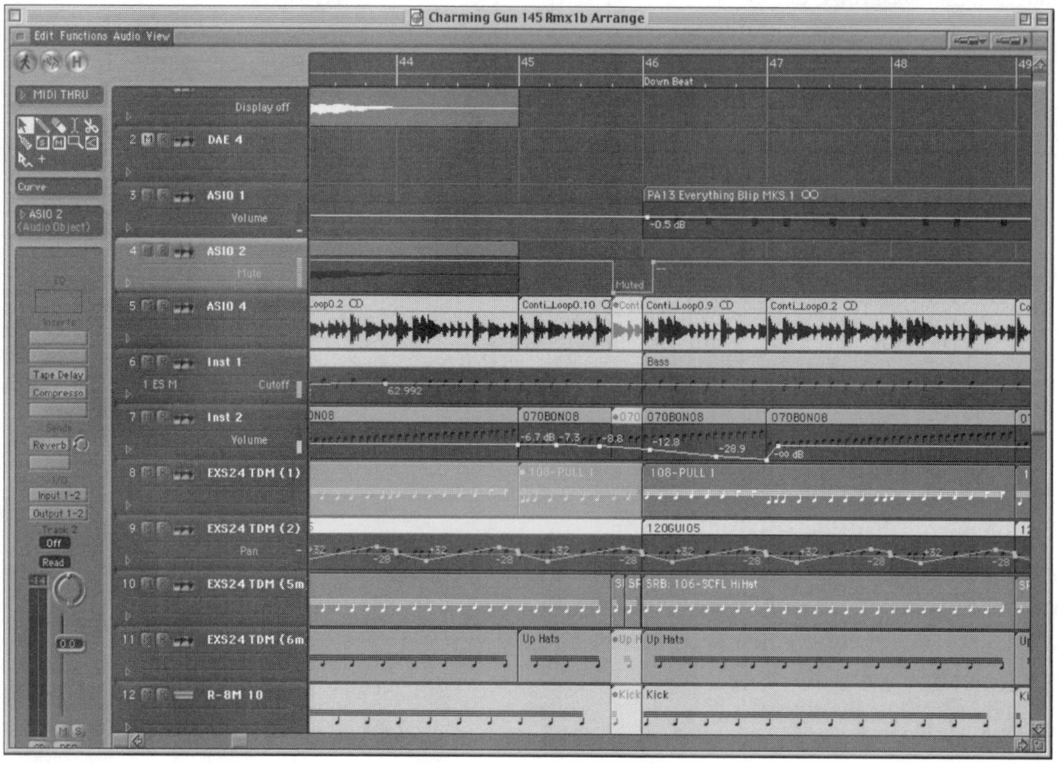

Figure 12.10 Changing a Bar's Fourth Beat. By dropping out drums and parts of loops in a bar's fourth beat, you can create a momentary pause in energy before the next downbeat.

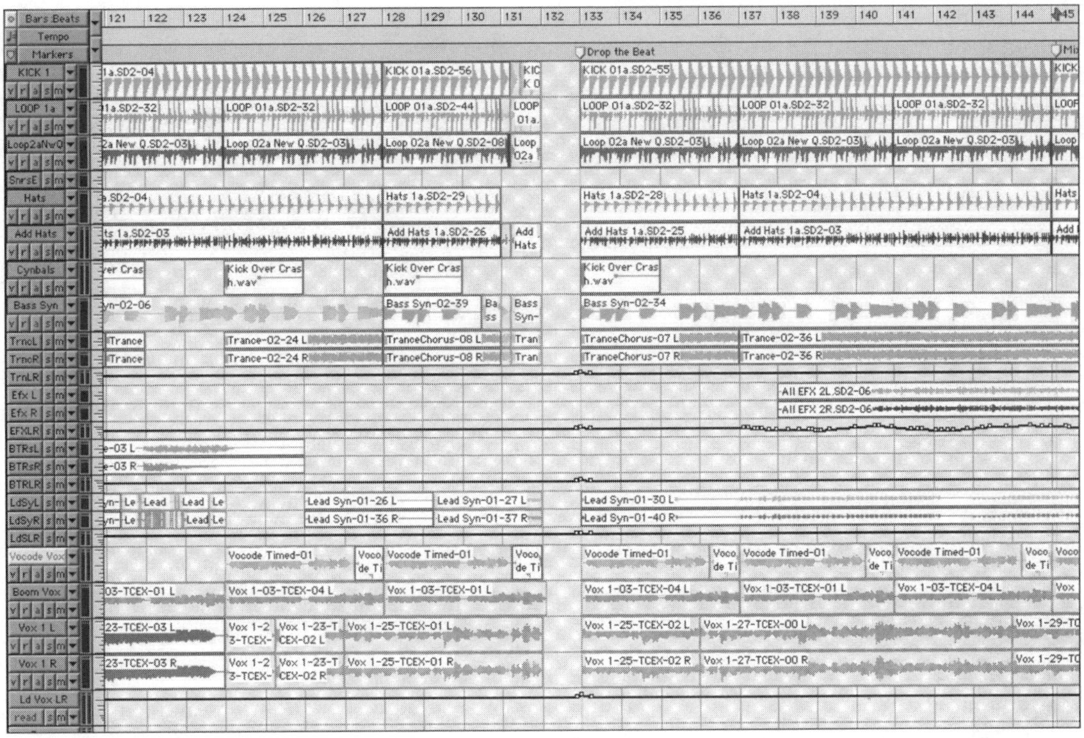

FIGURE 12.11 Dramatic Pause. After a big fill or climactic build, and before the downbeat of the next section, insert a bar of silence to create tension.

CD 27

SYNTH SWELLS

Any synthesizer sound that slowly crescendos over time can be used to create a build. With thick or complex patches, holding down a single note often sounds better than a chord. It's usually the patch's Attack parameter that determines how long the crescendo will take. You may also want to turn down its Release parameter so that the note cuts off right when it's released, on the downbeat. Try layering a synth swell under a loop arrangement that's being faded in to create extra drama.

CD 28

BACKWARDS REVERB

An old production trick that's still in use today is the *backwards reverb* effect. It's perfect for creating an ambient sweep that slowly builds to a downbeat. In the days before computers, a reverb return signal was recorded to tape, then the tape was played in reverse and synchronized with the main multitrack tape machine. Today, it's a much simpler operation. You must still record the reverb return (like a snare hit running through a reverb plug-in, with the wet/dry ratio set to 100 percent wet) to an audio track, but then you just reverse the waveform. (Most digital audio sequencers have this function; see figure 12.12.) Then scoot the waveform to a spot just in front of a downbeat, so that its peak meets the downbeat. For more punch, you can trim the effect's end so that it cuts off right on the downbeat. Sometimes, sliding the effect earlier in time by an eighth or sixteenth note, creating a brief pause right before the downbeat, can add extra tension.

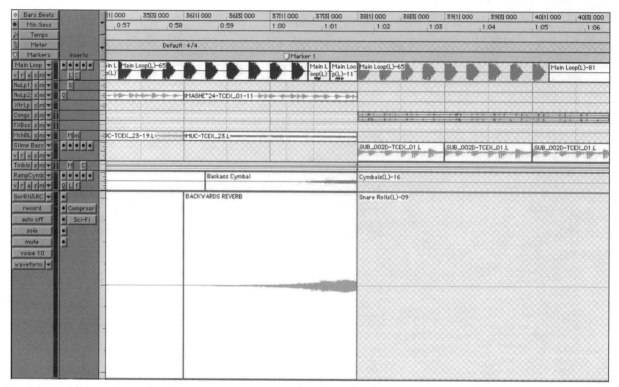

FIGURE 12.12 Backwards Reverb. After recording a 100 percent wet reverb, return to an audio track, reverse the waveform, and scoot it up to a downbeat.

I do a lot of reverse reverbs, on everything, from vocals to drums, it's a cool effect. Back in the day, they used to do it using tape machines. You'd record a nice long reverb to tape, on a second machine, then flip the reel over and play it back in time with the first machine. Now all you have to do is record the reverb to hard disk, then just reverse its waveform.

—(BT) Brian Transeau

Putting It All Together

Here's a quick overview of all the steps in creating the remix structure and basic arrangement.

STEP 1. Following a standard house-music song structure, create a rough outline of the remix, first with song markers, then by muting and unmuting loops in the different sections.

STEP 2. Map out how you would like the remix's energy to flow.

STEP 3. With the map as your guide, begin forming your rough arrangement into a final arrangement, adding the necessary transitions and production elements to create a direction and flow of energy.

STEP 4. With all the transitions in place, and the remix's ebb and flow of energy taking form, it's time to add the final production touches that will make your remix really stand out from the crowd. The next chapter explains several guarded production secrets used by the world's top remixers.

CHAPTER 13

Advanced Production

When the remix has a set structure, and all of its sections and transitions are clearly demarcated, it's time to begin adding the final production touches. These are the elements that will give your remix that polished, professional-sounding edge. Sophisticated production elements that are tastefully interwoven into your track, and are equally compelling heard on the dance floor or the home stereo, make the difference between a remix that's dull and one that truly dazzles.

The production techniques explained in this chapter are not meant to be used all in the same remix. That would probably just sound ridiculous and self-indulgent. Read about the different approaches, and then decide which ones will work best with your remix. Keep in mind that some techniques are more adept at steering the remix in a particular direction than others. For example, if you want to take the energy of your bridge down several notches, consider slowing the beat down using the "tempo change" technique. Or for a very dramatic textural change without affecting the energy level, you might consider a global effects-processing trick.

Rhythm, Tempo, and Key Changes

When poorly executed, changes in key, tempo, and rhythm can seriously throw off a beat. However, when done properly and with finesse, such changes can add a whole lot of excitement to the remix without messing up the beat.

KEY CHANGE

Introducing a key change can make a very effective bridge or break. The trick to making the change without detracting from the beat is to keep all of the rhythms the same, regardless of the key. For example, if the chords are playing a samba–like rhythm in the key of C, and you make a minor third key change to E-flat, the samba rhythm should not be affected. Minor-third key changes (up three half-steps) always sound dramatic, as do simple half-step key changes.

If the bass line is simple, steady, and repetitive, it's possible to change keys simply by shifting its notes (keeping the same rhythm), without touching the chords. This is because a bass note can act as a chord's root. For example, a C-major chord (C, E, G) played with a C bass note is C-major, but it becomes an A-minor7 when played with an E bass note. The rule with key changes in dance music is not to go overboard. Too many chord changes, even if all the rhythms remain steady, will end up distracting listeners from the beat.

TEMPO CHANGES

Always make tempo changes gradual so that they don't disturb the remix's groove. Keep the tempo change to one section—preferably in the middle of the remix, such as the bridge or a break. It's a bad idea to put a tempo change at the remix's beginning or ending; otherwise, it will be impossible for a DJ to beat-match the remix between other songs. Introducing a slower tempo right after a dramatic pause is usually more effective than gradually slowing down to that tempo (which can diminish a dance crowd's energy). However, gradually bring the tempo up, from slow to fast, can be very effective—a fabulous technique for building energy. All the best digital audio sequencers have a feature for creating gradual tempo changes over a selected area (see figure 13.1).

Dropping a remix's tempo to half-time is an innovative way of dramatically bringing a remix's energy level down while still maintaining a semblance of the original beat. You can drop the tempo to half-time without actually changing the project's tempo: just halve all of your note values. For example, quarter notes would become half notes and sixteenth notes would become eighth notes. You can quantize your performances accordingly, and some programs (like *Logic Audio's* Half Speed Transform function) will let you time-expand a MIDI performance, causing it to play back in half-time. Try introducing the half-time tempo immediately after a big buildup, then gradually speed the tempo back up to the original BPM (beats per minute).

NOT ALL LOOPS FOLLOW TEMPO CHANGES AUTOMATICALLY

MIDI performances and REX files (that have not been converted to contiguous audio files) will follow all tempo changes—even gradual changes. However, audio tracks and loops will not automatically follow tempo changes. Audio files must either be recycled or time stretched accordingly.

We did tempo changes in the remixes of Mary J. Blige's "No More Drama" and "Rainy Days." Like Ja Rule's rap on "Rainy Days," we tried putting it at 130 and it sounded ridiculous, so instead, we put it around 115 and it still had a groove. Then we bookended that with the 130 tribal house anthem stuff. And, I really love where "No More Drama" went. We gave that song a lot more drama. There were actually three tempo changes. It starts off as a tribal thing, breaks down to a total hip-hop record, then goes to this big dramatic instrumental, Pink Floyd–esque middle section, then back into the big tribal house anthem. Not everything has to be this really redundant 130 BPM 4x4 kick. There isn't just one particular production technique or effect; it's thinking like musicians and making an arrangement that takes you on a journey.

—Chris Cox, Thunderpuss

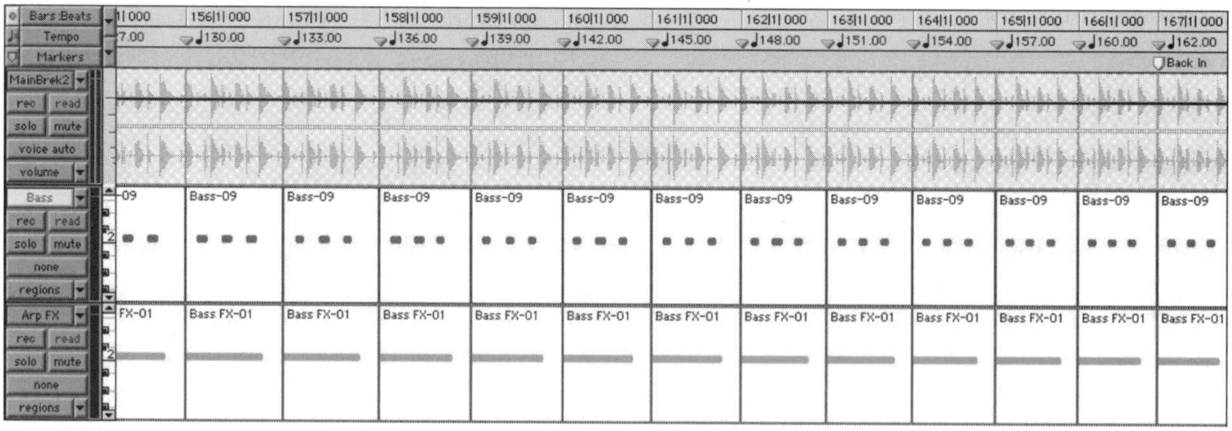

FIGURE 13.1 The Gradual Tempo Change. The Tempo ruler in *Pro Tools* shows that the tempo is gradually changing starting at bar 9 and ending at bar 33.

CD 31

RHYTHMIC CHANGES

Generally speaking, it's a bad idea to throw rhythm changes into the midst of a dance track. Though there are no rules that say you can't switch from a straight four-on-the-floor beat to a samba rhythm mid-stream, doing so will interrupt the groove and cause dancers to lose their stride. A good trick to bringing in any sort of rhythm change is to do it subtly, adding new rhythmic elements slowly, smoothly morphing from one rhythm to the next.

Changing from a quantize setting with little to no swing into a setting that's funkier is an excellent way to pick up the mood of a groove. Since swing only affects the off-beats, it's easy to leave a groove's downbeats untouched and bring in a little funkiness by adding swung sixteenth notes. For example, add sixteenth-note grace notes to the snare drum pattern (see figure 13.2). Try this with other drum and percussion performances (such as the kick or a tambourine), or even musical instruments (such as a bass). By carefully incorporating off-beat sixteenth notes, rhythm variations can be created that don't interfere with the main, steady beat. Introducing a new rhythm following an ambient break, then carrying that theme out to the remix's end, is a smooth way of transitioning from straight to funky.

Effect Tricks

There are many creative processing techniques that have become staple production tricks in electronic dance music. Several of these tricks are inspired by the sounds turntablists make with records, turntables, and a DJ mixer (effects such as scratching and transforming). Others are derivative of mixing strategies developed by club DJs (such as using a DJ mixer's EQ like a filter sweep), and some are the pure inventions of remix producers and dance music artists working in their personal studios (such as MIDI controller effects and stutter editing).

CD 32

GLOBAL AUDIO EFFECTS

DJs often run the main stereo output of their DJ mixer through an effects unit in order to process the entire mix. This technique is wonderful for creating dramatic breakdowns, funky segues, or very subtle, overall timbral changes. DJ-inspired hardware that's perfect for this type of processing includes the Alesis AirFX (pictured on page 54) and Korg's Kaoss Pad 2 (see figure 13.3). Both units have innovative interfaces that allow multiple parameters to be controlled in real-time. Plug-ins may also be employed, though few have the same type of real-time control. The exceptions are plug-ins made by Ina-GRM (the GRM-Tools series) and Ableton's *Live*, which has some excellent proprietary plug-ins featuring similar controls (like Erosion and Grain Delay).

Common types of effects applied to the stereo mix include: filters, phasers, flangers, distortion, pitch shifting, and delays. To use a plug-in, insert it directly on your digital audio sequencer's master fader (see figure 13.4). If you want to employ an external effects unit, you will need to set up an external effects send and return loop. (See "Bringing in External Effects" on page 53.) For whole-mix processing, you should assign the outputs of all the channels to the external send going to the effect unit, then assign the aux return (that's receiving the effect unit's input signal) to the master stereo output (see figure 13.5). This way, you can process every channel through the effects loop before it reaches the master output.

Employ a group effects bus (pictured on page 144) if you want to process select groups of channels (such as the drums or vocals), instead of the entire mix. An effect loop for a plug-in is identical to that of an external hardware unit, only you assign the input of the aux return channel to the effect bus directly, and insert the plug-in right on the aux channel. Plug-ins and hardware equipped with MIDI (such as the Kaoss Pad 2) can be automated, letting you record an effect

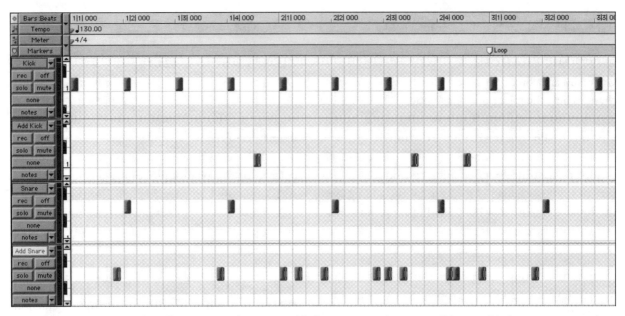

FIGURE 13.2 The Funk is in the Off-Beats. Straight snare and kick patterns with swung off-beats added on separate tracks to spice up the rhythm.

sweep in real time, and then tweak the performance to perfection. If your effects unit doesn't have MIDI (such as the Alesis AirFX), you will need to perform the effect in real-time while recording the mix to a new track. (See "Tape Style Splicing," on page 136.)

FIGURE 13.3 Kaoss Pad 2. Korg's Kaoss Pad 2 features a touch sensitive pad that can be tapped and stroked to change several effect parameters simultaneously. Producer/Songwriter Joe Solo demonstrates how it's done.

CD 33

AUTOMATING EFFECTS

There are the obvious stable of plug-ins for processing a track, filters, phasers, flangers, and so on. Inserting such an effect directly on a mixer channel needs little explanation. The key to taking these effects to another level is to automate their parameters in time to the remix's tempo. The easiest way of doing this is to draw a periodic wave shape that snaps to your sequencer's tempo grid (see figure 13.6).

Another powerful effect-automation trick is to automate a channel's send going to a delay or reverb plug-in. This can be done using the input level on the plug-in itself (a good choice when the plug-in is inserted directly on the channel), or via an effect send (best used when the plug-in is inserted on an aux channel). Slowly turning up the input to a delay plug-in with a high feedback setting (see figure 13.7) can create an amazing cascade of sound that is perfect for dramatic crescendos. Automating the effect send to a reverb can make a track sound like it's moving off into the distance (more reverb return and less dry signal), or coming forward into the foreground (more dry signal and less reverb return). This can be a powerful vocal effect.

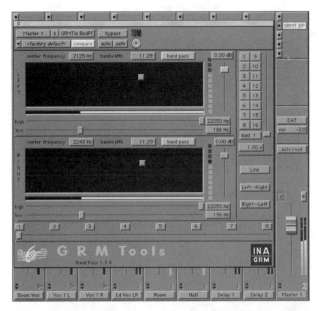

FIGURE 13.4 Effect Insert on Master Fader. The GRM Tools' BandPass filter plug-in inserted on a master fader in *Pro Tools* for whole-mix processing.

KEYED GATE EFFECTS

An old trick, but always amazingly fresh sounding, is the "keyed gate." This effect is produced by a gate plug-in that has the ability to be triggered (or "keyed" also called a "sidechain"), by a signal other than the track it is inserted on (see figure 13.8). For example, you could key gate a straight pad sound using the remix's hi-hat track, for a much more rhythmically interesting pad. There's no obligation to use a preexisting track either. You could use a MIDI cowbell and write a custom key pattern just for that track. Quantize, or "groove quantize," the cowbell's performance to lock the gated rhythm into the remix's groove.

Play with the gate's parameters to change the way the gate opens and closes. This is the envelope of the

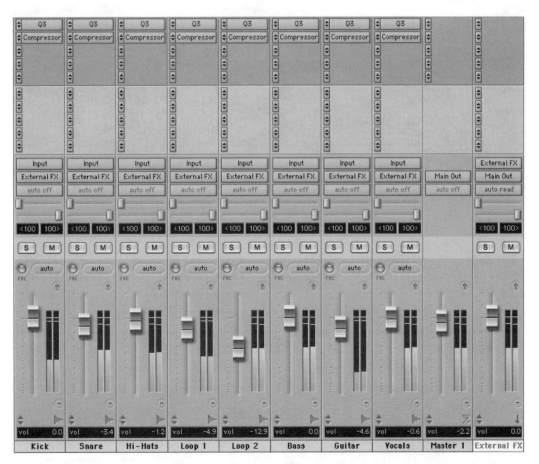

FIGURE 13.5 Effect Loop Pre Master Fader. To send a channel through an effects loop pre the master fader, the channel's output should be assigned to the effect send, and the related aux return channel then assigned to the master stereo output.

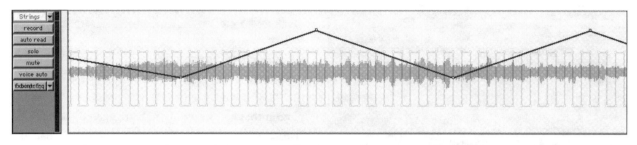

FIGURE 13.6 Automation Waveshapes Locked to Tempo. A filter's center frequency is automated by a triangle wave that cycles every bar, while its input gain is automated by a square wave that cycles every eighth note.

FIGURE 13.7 Delay with High Feedback. Slowly turning the input level up to *Logic Audio's* TapeDelay, with a high feedback setting, is great for creating a huge crescendo of sound.

triggered sound. (For example, increase the attack parameter for a less staccato performance.) You can pull out unique trigger patterns and remedy false triggers from audio using EQ, before sending it to the gate's sidechain (for example, roll off all the highs and lows of a drum loop to leave just its mid-range tablas). What is especially wonderful about key gating, verse simply replaying a sound, is that held sounds can evolve over time underneath the gating effect. (This is because when a note is held, the synthesizer's envelopes for that preset are allowed to run through their natural cycles.) The result can be a continually changing sound: the gate opening and closing in time with the beat, providing glimpses of the progressing waveforms beneath.

> *Putting a keyed gate on a pad sound can really make things interesting. Try keying the gate by your hi-hat pattern.*
>
> —Dave Audé

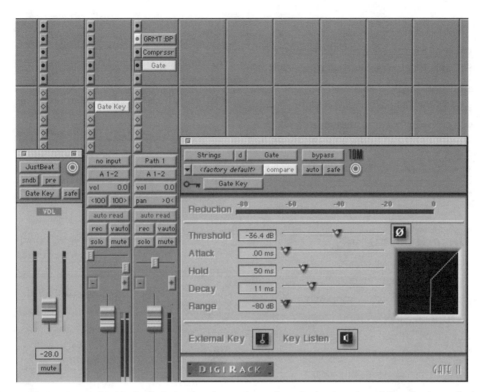

FIGURE 13.8 Gate with Key Input. Digidesign's Gate plug-in can be assigned a key input, and there's even a feature to monitor the input right on the plug-in itself.

CD 35

GRAINTABLE SYNTHESIS

An extremely unusual effect that's wonderful for adding different textures and dimensions to leads and vocals is *graintable synthesis*. This effect is characterized by a "breaking up" of the processed sound, with the ability to scatter or coalesce the pieces of sound at will.

There aren't many plug-ins that do graintable synthesis well, though there are a few standalone programs that sound great, such as *Kyma* by Symbolic Sound, and *Live* has a proprietary plug-in called Grain Delay. Since these programs operate outside of your digital audio sequencer, you will need to export the audio you want processed as standard WAV files, import them into the standalone program, process them, and export them again as WAV files. The final step is to import the processed WAV files back into your digital audio sequencer and line them up with the original performances. (This practice is handy for capturing any effects that are not available from within your host program.)

> *I use Kyma a lot. It's such a powerful tool for sound design. It has these grain synthesis algorithms that are amazing. With normal grain synthesis, it's like you have a sound drawn on a piece of paper that you can cut up into a thousand pieces and scatter them around the room, then make them re-congeal at will. The new Kyma algorithms allow you to take 10,000 different phasers and apply one to every single piece. Or, you could shift the formants of every single piece in different directions. It sounds like the sound is shredding apart. You can hear different styles of grain synthesis processing on the vocals of "Dreaming" and my remix of *NSync's "Pop."*
>
> —(BT) Brian Transeau

MIDI Control Effects

There are several unique effects that can be employed to manipulate MIDI performances using MIDI Control Change messages. Some of these effects mimic an audio effects plug-in (though they require far less processing power because they are just MIDI data), while others are totally original and can only be achieved using MIDI.

PERIODIC CONTROLLER CURVES

Just as audio plug-ins can be made to respond to tempo-synchronized automation curves, so too will MIDI instruments respond to tempo-synchronized Continuous Controller (such as modulation or pitch bend—any controller that can respond to a continuous stream of control change data) curves. Instead of drawing a periodic automation curve for a mixer channel, you draw a periodic Continuous Controller curve, that snaps to your sequencer's grid, for a MIDI instrument (see figure 13.9). There are a total of 128 Control Change Events (see Appendix B). Some have standard assignments (like #7 for controlling volume, which is great for simulating a keyed gate effect), while others are left unassigned so that they may be used to control different parameters (like filter cutoff) on different products.

Try sending several curves at the same time to the same MIDI instrument to create very complex, rhythmic tonal changes. The results can be similar to the sounds produced by Korg's well-known Karma synthesizer (pictured on page 161).

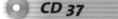

RANDOM PATCH CHANGES

If you have been searching for some radically different special effects to spice up your production, try the random patch-change trick. Using the remix's MIDI chord track as the performance source, throw a series of rapid patch changes at the assigned MIDI sound module or soft synth (like somebody was frenetically twirling the unit's patch change dial). If the module responds to MIDI patch change messages, automate the patch changes. (Otherwise, you will need to make the patch changes manually.) Send the sound module's output through a multi-effects unit (such as TC Electronic's FireworX or Ensoniq's old DP-4), and send it a series of random patch changes as well.

Record the results to a stereo audio track in your digital audio sequencer. Not all of the sound effects will be useful, but there are sure to be a few gems. Cut out and save the sound effects that work, and discard everything else. Be sure to make the cuts on beat so that scooting copies of the sound effects around to different parts of the remix is a piece of cake.

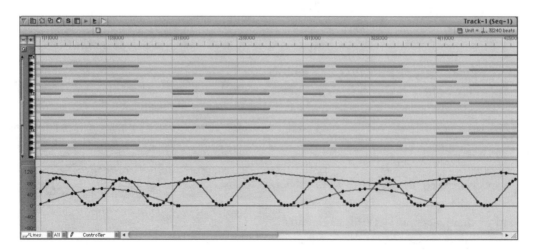

FIGURE 13.9 Periodic MIDI Continuous Controller Curves. Multiple periodic controller curves, whose cycles have been locked to tempo, can breathe complex, rhythmic tonal changes into a boring preset.

CD 38

ECHOING LEADS

An effective way of underscoring a vocal hook or instrumental lead line is to "echo" (double) it using a different sound. Use your digital audio sequencer's pitch-to-MIDI converter (see "A Little Help Finding the Notes," page 98) to create a MIDI note performance from an audio track. Edit out any bad notes that are generated in the conversion process using your program's graphic editor. Then find a synth sound that blends well with the lead track.

To double the lead line, simply mix the MIDI performance in under the audio track. Some reverb and delay can help to set it off, in the background. To echo the lead line, offset the MIDI performance later in time. Anywhere between an eighth and a quarter note usually sounds okay. Another alternative is to have it play after the lead line entirely, as sort of a mirror of the main hook.

> Sometimes I'll use a piano, strings, or synth lead sound to double, or echo the lead vocal melody. Drop the part in after the chorus as sort of a B-section to the vocal hook.
>
> —Dave Audé

Advanced Audio Editing Tricks

The ability to easily cut and paste audio waveforms has given rise to a couple of innovative editing tricks that are employed regularly by many top remix producers. One technique is best known as "stutter editing," a method for precisely cutting up and rearranging audio tracks to create mind-blowing fills and breaks. The other technique was inspired by analog, tape-style, 2-track editing. It's a process of splicing fully mixed, stereo files together to create arrangements and effects that would be very difficult to duplicate in a multitrack environment.

CD 39

STUTTER EDITING

The idea behind stutter editing is to chop up an audio file into a variety of beat segments, which are then snapped to the tempo grid and played back at very high note resolutions. The results sound something like your computer is stuttering, but only on particular tracks, and in perfect time with the project's tempo.

The note value of a stutter is usually between a thirty-second and a ninety-sixth, but may be higher or lower. The stutter may be a single, isolated event, or a series of stutters strung out over several bars to create a break. Stutters are often interspersed with triplets (such as twelfths, twenty-fourths, forty-eighths, and so on) to give the feeling of the tempo slowing down and speeding up. Distortion and stereo panning effects may also be employed to enhance a stutter's dynamics and excitement level. Follow these steps to create a basic stutter edit.

STEP 1. Choose an audio track for stutter editing. Drum and percussion loops always work well, but so too can chords, lead, and bass lines.

STEP 2. Find an area that will lend itself to a stutter. Usually, the third and fourth beats of a bar work well, but there are no set rules. The only thing to keep in mind is that you will want the orchestration to open up at the moment of the stutter, to avoid conflicting tones and rhythms. Look for spots like this to make your stutter edit.

STEP 3. Begin making your cuts. Start with eighth notes because when you slide the pieces together, the audio regions beneath each subsequent layer will be automatically muted (see figure 13.10). This is one instance where you don't need to worry about always cutting at zero crossing points. In fact, sometimes using audio regions that don't begin at zero crossing points can make for punchier stutters. (The pops and clicks caused by non-zero crossings can be cleared up with quick, very short crossfades.)

STEP 4. Set your digital audio sequencer's grid resolution to thirty-second notes. Make a copy of an audio region, and paste it a thirty-second note later. (You will probably need to zoom in to see what you're doing.) Most programs have a feature for dragging and copying a region at the same time. For example, with the Hand tool selected, hold down Option (Mac) or Control (PC), and drag-copy from the original audio region to the new location, a thirty-second note later. This is a fast way of working.

STEP 5. Listen to the edit to hear if there is a click or a pop at the splice. If there is, make the smallest crossfade possible to clear it up. It's important that the crossfade be very short or you will diminish the stutter's percussive punch (because a long crossfade creates a slow attack).

Some programs let you apply a series of crossfades, between multiple audio regions, simultaneously (such as when you perform a Digital Mixdown in *Logic Audio*). If your program can do this, then you can skip this step, and wait to smooth out a stutter's pops and clicks when you bounce the completed stutter edit to disk, in step 8.

STEP 6. Repeat step 4 (using the region with the crossfade created in step 5, if applicable) until you have a series of thirty-second note regions, one after another for the duration of a beat. To save time, you can create eight stutters and then copy that section three times for one full beat of thirty-second notes.

STEP 7. Play with different grid resolutions to create a variety of stutters with different note timings. Cut up other tracks in the same bar to create simultaneous and sequential stutters across several different sounds (see figure 13.11). Apply automated effects to the stuttered audio regions to create additional stereo movement and excitement (such as distortion with a filter sweep, and auto or doppler panning).

STEP 8. To make a track's complex stutter edit or break easy to move (in case you want to slide it to a different spot in the remix), consolidate its audio regions into a single, contiguous audio file. If your program allows you to apply crossfades during the consolidation process, you should do that now. Repeat this procedure for each track that contains stutter edits so that multitrack stutter sections can be easily moved about.

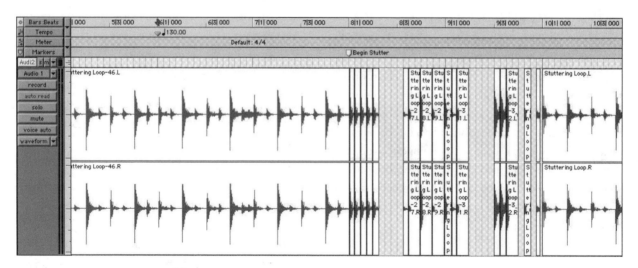

Figure 13.10 Drum Loop Prepared for Stuttering. The loop has had several eighth-note divisions made at the beginning of the fourth beat. A few of the audio regions have already been slid forward to show how they cut off the preceding region.

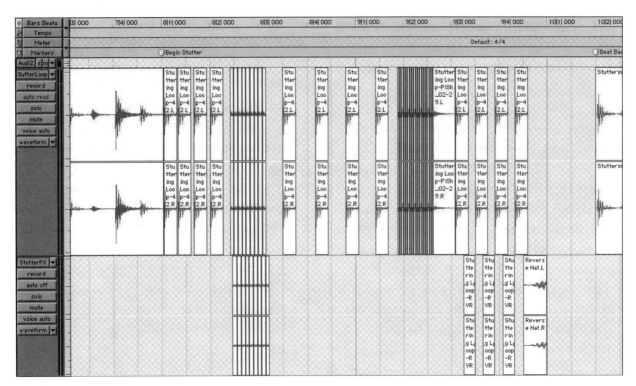

FIGURE 13.11 Completed Stutter Edit. A break composed of multiple stutter edits and triplets.

Stutter edits are just sounds cut into small increments (twenty-fourths, thirty-seconds, sixty-fourths, etc.) that are assembled into a riff. There are different ways to accomplish this, but we mostly cut them up manually on the Arrange page of our sequencer. The tightest results are typically achieved by slicing up audio clips into sixty-fourth and one-hundred and twenty-eighth note bits, copying each slice a few times, and shuffling them around until something desirable comes out. Good stutter edits and fills are as much art as science— experimentation is key. An easy way to spruce up flat stutter edits is by applying different audio effects to each slice or group of slices.

—J. Scott G., Deepsky

EXTRAORDINARY STUTTER PRODUCER

While there is argument over who exactly invented stutter editing, there is little doubt that BT developed the technique to its fullest. His mind-blowing breaks are composed of multiple, multitrack stutters combined with innovative effects for stunning results. In fact, listening to his breaks (such as those found in the track, "Hip Hop Phenomenon," or his production of "Pop" for *NSync remix) is an excellent way to learn about the technique.

I've spent as much as forty hours working on just a 2-bar break; that's how complex I get. I'll actually time stretch individual waveforms to make their shapes fit to tempo.

—(BT) Brian Transeau

MIDI STUTTERS

The concept of stutter editing can also be applied to MIDI notes. However, the result has a distinctly different feel. The sound of precision, razor sharp edits that you get with audio can not be exactly duplicated with MIDI. For example, a MIDI kick drum's release will naturally ring over, despite close, fast note repeats. Though this can be remedied with a few parameter adjustments (such as setting the preset to mono, turning its attack to zero, decay to zero, sustain to 100-percent, and release to zero), the timing with external MIDI modules is just too slow to create truly tight sounding stutters above thirty-second notes. The exception to this rule are virtual instruments, which don't suffer anywhere near the timing delays of external MIDI gear.

 CD 40

TAPE-STYLE SPLICING

Splicing together completely mixed, stereo audio files lets you make razor sharp, and very radical changes in sound. A section of the remix that is ambient, with lots of reverb and delays, can become a dry, pounding section with a simple butt splice. This type of edit leaves no overhanging reverbs or delays to soften the transition, only the remix's tempo and musical themes (like the rhythms, chords, and lead lines) carry over. Furthermore, a loop of a section, or even of a single beat, can be repeated like a record, skipping in time to the music.

Creating changes that sound like a 2-track butt splice in a multitrack session is a logistical nightmare. Every audio and MIDI track and every effect send must be muted perfectly on the downbeat of each new section. For extra bar repeats or beat skips, bars and beats must be carefully inserted and repeated across multiple

tracks. The fact is, there is no ideal way of simulating the sound of a 2-track butt splice in a multitrack session. To make those tight, surgically precise changes, you need to work with a stereo mix file.

STEP 1. Editing 2-track tape-style needs to happen after the remix is mixed (mixing is discussed in the next chapter), but before it is mastered. You should bounce several different versions of the remix to disk so that you have plenty of material to work with. For example, in addition to the final mix, record versions with just beats, without any beats, with bass only, with extra delays, etc. To save time and hard drive space, some of the mixes you intend to use for 2-track editing can be loops (eight bars or longer), rather than bouncing down the entire remix every time, for every version.

STEP 2. Create a new project file that will be used exclusively for the 2-track editing. Set the new project to the tempo of your remix, and import all of the remix's stereo mix versions.

STEP 3. Bring the stereo files into the Arrange window, and line them up on a few different tracks for easy visibility (see figure 13.12).

STEP 4. If your remix was done entirely at one tempo, you can enable the program's snap-to-grid feature for easy cutting and pasting. If not, you may need to cut and splice by visually cueing up downbeats by their waveforms, and using your ears to hear if a spliced beat comes in early or late.

STEP 5. Edit the sections together, and create a new version of the remix. Keep in mind that there's no reason to go overboard here. If the remix is already structurally sound and well arranged, you may just want to make a couple of 2-track edits. That will be plenty to add the 2-track sound to your remix. (A final 2-track editing session can be seen in figure 13.13.)

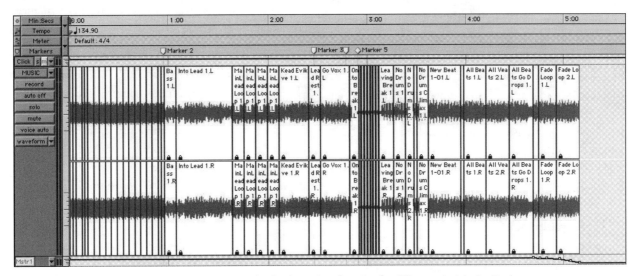

FIGURE 13.12 Setting Up a Session for 2-Track Editing. The remix's stereo mixdowns are lined up in *Pro Tools'* Edit screen for easy visibility.

FIGURE 13.13 Completed 2-Track Editing Session. The final results of a 2-track editing project in *Pro Tools*.

QUARTER-INCH TAPE

There was a time when pioneering engineers and producers (like Tom Moulton and Walter Gibbons) cut up, and pasted together quarter-inch analog tape to create different versions of a song (such as editing an extended mix down to a shorter, radio mix). They had no waveforms for reference as they cut and spliced sections together, on beat. All they had was a tape head for cueing the beats, a grease pencil for marking in and out points, a razor blade, an aluminum splicing block, splicing tape, and their ears. Though 2-track editing on a computer is a stroll in the park by comparison, you must still use your ears to hear if a splice is on time (even when you're depending on a grid to make your cuts).

Turntablist Inspired Tricks

As mentioned, a wealth of creative production tricks have grown out of the sounds turntablists make with records, a turntable, and a DJ mixer. The most common practice is to incorporate scratching into the groove, where the scratches act like another percussion instrument. There are lots of options available now for scratching your own sounds, from software plug-ins and stand-alone applications, to CD DJ decks that can scratch audio CDs. There are also several ways to mimic the sounds of a turntablist (such as back-spinning, transforming, and the sound a record makes when the turntable's power is turned on or off) right in your digital audio sequencer, with no additional hardware or software.

CD 41

SCRATCH YOUR OWN TRACKS

For years, turntablists have been pressing their own tracks to acetate one-offs (referred to as "dub plates") for the ability to scratch their own beats, and spin their own tunes. However, this process can get expensive because dub plates can wear out when used heavily for scratch performances, and lots of back-cueing. Fortunately, the most recent crop of scratch-capable CD DJs can mimic turntables better than ever (units like the CDJ1000 by Pioneer). If you own one of these amazing CD players (and a DJ mixer), simply burn an audio CDR of the track you want to scratch (like the lead vocals or a drum loop), pop it in the player, and cut it up. Record the performance to an audio track, and edit where necessary.

Another alternative is Serato's *Scratch-Studio Edition* application (see figure 13.14). This amazing piece of software operates similarly to Stanton's *Final Scratch*, only in the form of a plug-in instead of a stand-alone application. Using a proprietary, time-coded piece of vinyl and a turntable, you can scratch audio that has been loaded into the plug-in. If you don't own a turntable, you can also scratch the audio using the computer's mouse, though of course it's impossible for a mouse to produce the same feel and control as a piece of vinyl on a turntable. Serato's Scratch system does require real turntable skills, so if you aren't a turntablist and you want a convincing performance, consider hiring a professional.

Mixman's *Mixman StudioXPro* application (see figure 2.2), for PC, is not only handy for converting Track files into WAV files; it can also be used for scratching. Any WAV file or Track file loaded into a sound slot in *StudioXPro* can be scratched using the computer's mouse or Mixman's custom controller, the DM2. Simply exporting a WAV file from the remix, converting it to a Track file with *ReCycle*, then loading it into *StudioXPro* gives you an amazing amount of control for creating a convincing scratch performance. Record the scratches in Mixman's own sequencer, edit the performance if necessary, export it as a WAV file, and then import it back into your digital audio sequencer. If your system is PC based, *StudioXPro* along with the DM2 is a very cost-effective setup for scratching your own tracks.

FIGURE 13.14 Scratch-Studio Edition. An audio file that has been loaded into Serato's Scratch-Studio Edition plug-in can be controlled via a time-coded piece of vinyl, allowing you to scratch the audio as if it was a real record.

CD 42

TRANSFORMING WITH RECYCLE

Transforming is an effect that's created when a turntablist rapidly switches the DJ mixer's channel on and off in time with the music. Transforming sounds particularly neat over long, sustained sounds. The effect can be created by automating a virtual mixer channel's volume or mute. However, this may not create the tightest transforming performance possible because of volume automation ramp times. ReCycle provides a unique way of creating a very tight sounding transforming effect, and its Show Grid feature makes programming the transforming rhythm a snap.

> **STEP 1.** Load a perfectly trimmed loop, and enter its number of bars in the Bars field. Entering the loop's actual number of bars will give you a quarter-note grid; doubling this number will give you an eighth-note grid, and so on.

> **STEP 2.** Under the View menu, enable Show Grid.

> **STEP 3.** Under the Process menu, select Add Slices to Grid.

> **STEP 4.** Under the Process menu, enable Silence Selected.

> **STEP 5.** Enable the Preview Toggle button so that you can hear the effect. If you have doubled or tripled the loop's actual bar count in the Bars field, you will need to enter the BPM that appears in the Orig. Tempo field into the Tempo field, or the loop will not play at the proper speed.

> **STEP 6.** Play the loop, and while the audio is looping, select a series of slices to mute, keeping in mind that you want to create a rhythmic pattern (see figure 13.15). You will need to hold down Shift on your computer keyboard to select and retain more than one slice at a time.

> **STEP 7.** When you have a sequence of muted slices that sound good, save the loop to your hard drive, and import it into your digital audio sequencer for playback. You can save the loop as a REX file for tempo control of the performance, or as a straight-ahead, set-in-stone WAV file.

CD 43

DIRTY SOUND

That unmistakable, "low-fi" sound that's caused by an old scratchy record or a vintage sampler can add a lot of personality to a track. But if all the loops in your remix are high-quality, perfect-sounding recordings, then you will need to purposefully create this classic dirty sound. A standard trick that has been used for years is to add a loop of record noise throughout the entire remix. You can either sample your own scratchy record and create a loop, or find a sample library that includes a record noise loop. Hip-hop and down-tempo productions often employ this trick to create the illusion that loops were lifted from vinyl, even though that was not the case.

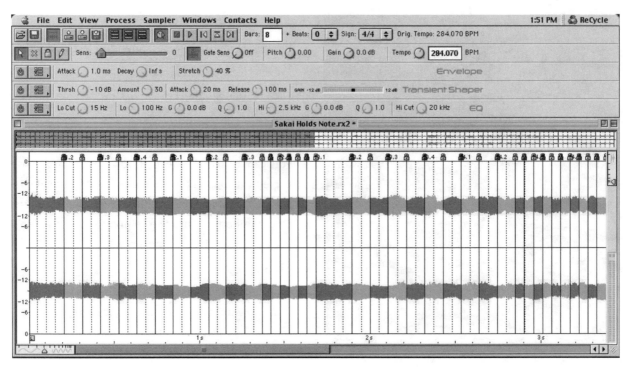

FIGURE 13.15 Transforming in ReCycle. A DJ style transforming effect has been created over a sustained note in ReCycle, by muting select slices in a rhythmic pattern.

Down sampling a high-quality loop can create the illusion of a worn out record needle or an old 8-bit sampler. The "low-fi" sample sound has become such a staple in contemporary music production that there are a ton of great plug-ins designed specifically to degrade sound quality (such as Digidesign's Lo-Fi or Steinberg's Grungelizer). Causing a 48 kHz, 24-bit sample to sound like it was recorded at 11 kHz, 8-bit may sound ridiculous at first, but it creates a very distinct type of distortion that seems to work particularly well with breaks-style drums and stutter editing. But you can down-sample just about any type of loop with pleasing results (like guitar and synth loops), and down sampling vocal hooks is particularly popular. (Listen to "The Rockafeller Skank" or "Sunset [Bird of Prey]" by Fatboy Slim.)

CD 44

TURNTABLIST MIMICRY

Here are a few other ways to mimic a turntablist. The sound you hear when the turntable's needle is on the record and power to the turntable is turned off, or switched on can be imitated using an AudioSuite plug-in in *Pro Tools* called Vari-Fi. If you don't have *Pro Tools*, try loading the audio into a sampler, and automating the sample's playback pitch for a similar effect. The sound of a record being back-cued can be simulated by simply reversing a waveform. All good digital audio sequencers have an off-line processing function for reversing audio files.

By employing just a few of the techniques discussed in this chapter you will have added another dimension to your production. Indeed, the remix should be sounding pretty good by now, having all of its structure and production fleshed out. The only steps remaining are to smooth out the mix's rough edges, and after that, create a final stereo master.

Mix and Master

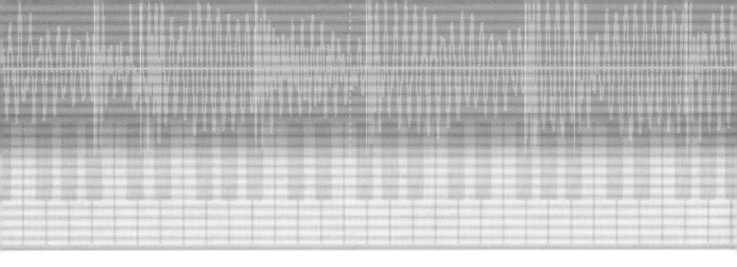

CHAPTER 14:

Mixing

With the arrangement and production of the remix complete, it's now time to begin the final mixing process. This is the stage for sculpting the remix's overall sound by massaging its individual tracks with EQ, reverb, stereo effects, and dynamics processing. The idea is to chisel out a space for each track in the remix's aural landscape, ensuring that frequencies and parts aren't clashing and that all the tracks are working together to paint a balanced sonic picture.

In the past, mixing was traditionally done after all of a song's tracks had been recorded. The phrase, "We can fix it in the mix," was significant because it was expected that performances would be enhanced and repaired during mixing. Thanks to computers and home-studio technology, mixing is now something that also happens during a track's composition stages. Since digital audio sequencers allow you to save your remix, along with all of its EQ and effects settings, at each step of the production process, you have been refining your mix already, for some time.

Remixing is so heavily sound-design driven, the sounds you are using during the writing and production stages need to work well together sonically from the very beginning. Subsequently, mixing a remix is not nearly so complex as mixing a traditional, multi-track song; it is just a last step in refining your existing mix. Furthermore, since you're using some tracks from a song that has already been mixed, chances are that these tracks already sound pretty good. Keep in mind, too, that it's more acceptable for a remix to have a slightly raw edge. Electronic dance music owes a big part of its personality to the creative use of low-tech, home studio gear. That dirty sound is part of its heritage.

Labels are expecting everything to sound pro, they're expecting a remixer to turn out stuff that's as good sonically as tracks being mixed on a big budget by name mix engineers. So you have to start thinking about the mix from this angle early on. The way to work is to make everything sound good as you are writing the music. Sort out the effects that you're going to use, make sure that every sound gels, mix your track as you're working out the arrangement. Certain sounds might sound great on their own, but when you put them together, everything gets muddy; if a sound isn't working, find another one that does. You need to start hearing and listening to stuff like this from the very beginning.

—Pablo La Rosa, Tune Inn Records

Ready, Set, Mix

The process of mixing closely parallels the composing process. Start with the drums and bass, and work up from there. The kick drum and the bass must work together to create a tight, punchy bottom end. The drums should sound crisp and cohesive, as if they were all recorded at the same time, in the same location. Once these elements are forged, you have the foundation over which to layer all the other tracks. The rhythm instruments (like strummed guitar or staccato synth chords) are usually mixed in next, making sure that they mesh well with the high- and mid-range percussion tracks (such as hi-hats and congas). Pads, strings, and background vocals follow, finding their own mid-range space where they won't make the mix muddy or interfere with other instruments. Finally, the leads are set to sit atop the mix, but not so loud as to be a distraction from the beat.

CD 45

Remember to employ group effects buses in order to save on DSP (see figure 14.1). Use your virtual mixer's "solo" feature to audition individual tracks, and to hear how groups of tracks are gelling. Good digital audio sequencers will let you set group-effect aux returns to solo-safe mode so that channels can be soloed with their respective group effects "in place." (To learn more about this function, read up on your program's "solo" feature.)

Define each instrument's basic frequency, level, and pan position before diving into the automation of the mixer's channels. Though each track should sound solid on its own, never forget that it is the sum of all the parts that make a great mix. As often as you listen to and make changes on tracks one at a time, also listen to all of the tracks together, as a whole, while you fine-tune individual tracks.

EQ

Equalization (EQ) is employed to boost or cut specific frequencies (and consequently, is often referred to as a "filter"). This allows you to mold each sound to fit neatly into a particular frequency range. For example, if a pad has too many low frequencies that are interfering with the bass line, then EQ can be used to "roll off" the offending frequencies. In contrast, a bass line with a weak low end can be enhanced by using EQ to bring out these low frequencies. Keep in mind that it's generally better to subtract frequencies, rather than boost them, because too many boosted frequencies will result in a brash, unpleasant sounding mix. EQ may be placed pre- or post-compression, but with different outcomes. Compressing the EQ generally produces rounder, warmer tones, while EQing the compression will give you brighter, crisper tones.

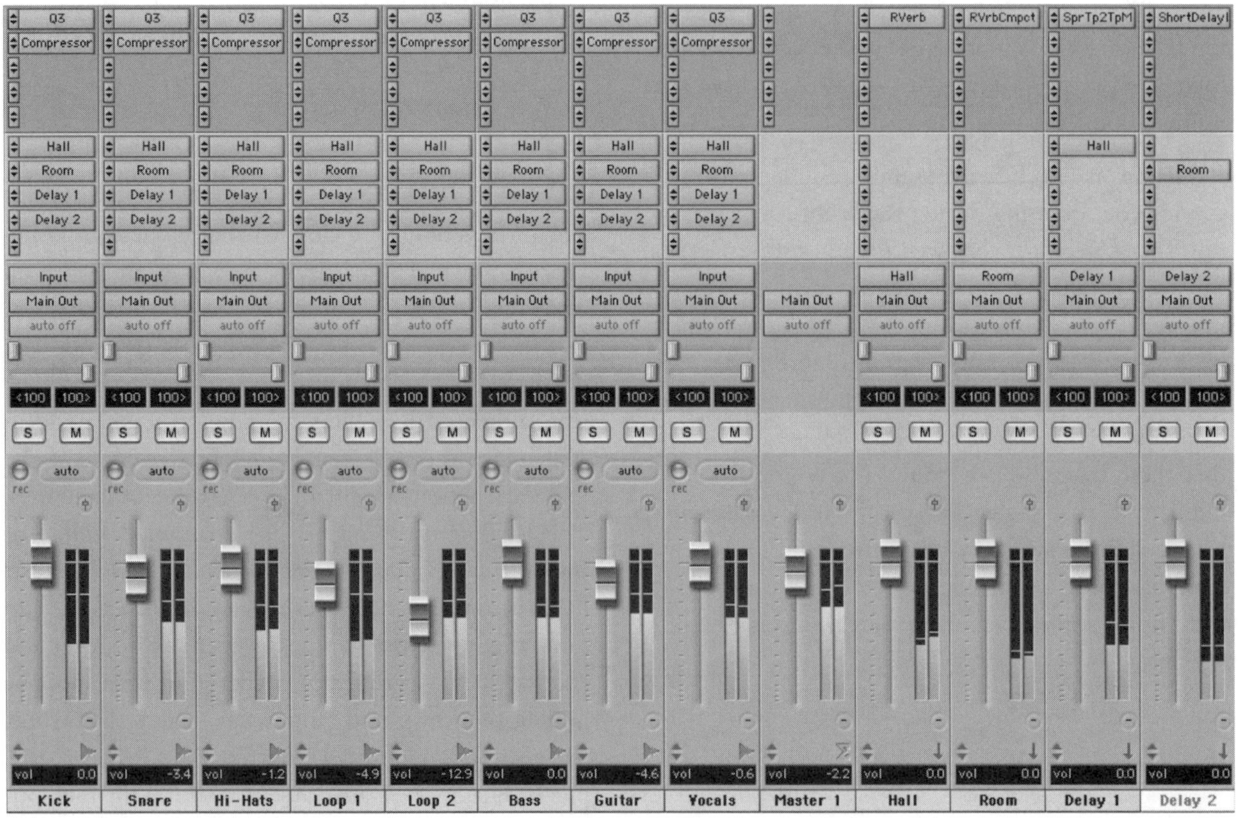

FIGURE 14.1 Group Effects Buses. Several channels in *Pro Tools* with their effects sends assigned to reverb and delay group effects.

Every analog EQ unit, despite having nearly identical parameters, has its own unique sound because of its electronics. Many EQ plug-ins are designed to emulate vintage gear (like Waves' *Renaissance EQ*, see figure 14.2). These plug-ins impart a warm, round, analog-like tone to signals. In contrast, there are also EQ plug-ins that are relatively colorless (such as Digidesign's stock *EQ II* plug-in). Some digital audio sequencers feature EQ built into their mixer channels (such as *Cubase SX* and *Logic Audio*). When selecting an EQ, take into account whether you need to warm a signal up or simply, and very precisely, shape a specific frequency without coloring the entire signal.

Pretty much every EQ plug-in includes a *Frequency* parameter, for selecting the center of the frequency that will be cut or boosted, and a *Gain* control, for boosting or cutting the selected frequency. Several bands of EQ are provided per plug-in, for maximum sound shaping control. In addition, there are five basic types of EQ curves to choose from (see below). Most plug-ins feature all five, and they are sometimes available to every band.

HIGH PASS Attenuates all of the frequencies below a selected cutoff frequency and allows all of the frequencies above that cutoff frequency to pass through unaffected. The Gain control does not apply to this type of EQ curve. Use this curve to remove low frequencies, as in cutting the low end out of a pad.

LOW PASS Attenuates all of the frequencies above a selected cutoff frequency, and allows all of the frequencies below that cutoff frequency to pass through unaffected. The Gain control does not apply to this type of EQ curve. Employ this curve to remove high frequencies, as in cutting the brightness out of a bass line.

HIGH SHELF Provides a uniform boost or cut above a selected frequency. This curve is good for enhancing or removing high frequencies, as in the brightness of a hi-hat.

LOW SHELF Provides a uniform boost or cut below a selected frequency. Use this curve for enhancing or removing low frequencies, as in the resonating lows of a bass tom-tom.

PEAK Also called "notch." Boosts or cuts only those frequencies centered around a selected frequency, and at a selected width as determined by the Q parameter. (When a Q parameter is present, the type of equalization is called "parametric.") This is the most useful curve for pinpointing specific frequencies, as in notching out an offensive mid-range ring for a snare drum.

> *If there's one thing I can't stress enough, when you're doing a remix for club play, it is to make sure that everything in the entire mix, with the exception of the kick drum and the bass line, are shelved at 150 Hz. It makes for a clean sounding mix. If you're not doing this, your mix is going to sound muddy.*
>
> —(BT) Brian Transeau

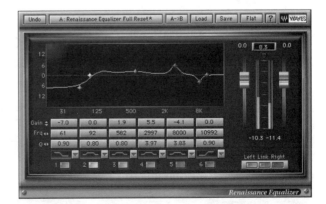

FIGURE 14.2 Waves' Renaissance EQ. Waves' Renaissance EQ emulates a vintage EQ unit, imparting a warm, round tone to signals.

EQ COPYCAT

With a lot of practice, it's possible to copy the EQ of a hit song. This is an important skill that will help you craft excellent sounding mixes. For example, if you love how a particular song's kick sounds in a club, pick up the record and EQ your kick to sound similar. If this task sounds daunting, Steinberg distributes a plug-in called *FreeFilter*, which can copy the EQ of one sound and apply it to another sound. Though the software can't perform miracles, if the original sound is clean and well isolated (such as a solo beat or break-out track), then the resulting EQ can sound very good. Even if *FreeFilter* doesn't nail the EQ perfectly, at the very least, it provides a place from which to start making your own adjustments.

 **CD 46**

Compression

The key to controlling a performance's dynamics—its loudest peaks and softest passages—is compression. Compressors operate by automatically pushing a signal's level down whenever a selected threshold level is exceeded. This effectively reduces the overall loudness of a track, and is visible as shorter distances between a waveform's peaks and dips (see figure 14.3). Tracks that are compressed generally sit better in the mix because all of a performance's nuances get brought to the surface, instead of being buried in the mix. (Several standard compression settings are shown in figure 14.4.)

The downside to compression is that in the process of squashing a performance's peak levels, you are also raising the track's noise floor. With a high compression ratio and gain "make up" setting, a track's noise floor can get pretty loud. In some instances, a gate can be employed to reduce the noise floor in silent passages (the times when an instrument isn't playing).

Most compressors (both software and hardware units) have several universal controls. If you understand these parameters, you should be able to operate most compressors.

THRESHOLD   Sets the level above which signals will be compressed. Signals below the threshold setting will be unaffected.

RATIO   This control sets the compression ratio—the increase in input signal needed to cause a 1 dB increase in output signal. For example, with a ratio of 4:1, an 8 dB increase of input will produce a 2 dB increase in the output.

ATTACK   Sets the compressor's attack time. The faster the attack, the more rapidly compression is applied. Employ a short attack to squash transients, and create round, fat tones (like a thudding, thumping kick drum). Use a long attack to create tight, punchy sounds (like a firm, taut kick drum).

RELEASE   Controls how long it takes for compression to stop after the input signal drops below the threshold level. A long release setting should accompany high compression ratios, to smooth the transition between super compressed and uncompressed signals, and avoid the "pumping" sound.

KNEE   Sets the speed at which full compression is achieved once the input threshold level has been exceeded. A high value produces a "hard knee" setting that is good for squashing signals fast (for example, "in your face" vocals). A low value produces a "soft knee" setting that is better for slow attack sounds (like slowly bowed strings).

GAIN   This control is used to bring up the level of highly compressed signals. It is often referred to as a "make up" gain stage.

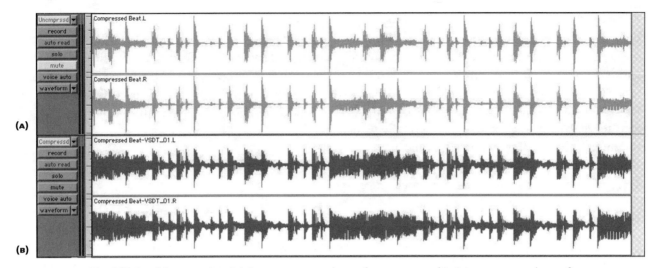

FIGURE 14.3 The Affects of Compression. **(A)** An uncompressed waveform, compared to **(B)** a compressed waveform.

	RATIO	ATTACK (MS)	RELEASE (MS)	KNEE (FROM 100)
Kick	5:1	30	64	32
Snare	3.5:1	16	44	80
Vocals	2.5:1	14	40	80
Bass	3:1	14	100	80
Electric Guitar	4:1	20	20	90

FIGURE 14.4 Typical Compression Settings.

The kick, in particular, you really want to compress the heck out of that. I go so far as an 8:1 compression ratio, and I'll crank the attack up to make it really crack so that it cuts through the mix. I used to think that using such an extreme compression ratio was wrong, but forget engineering rules and just do what sounds good.

—Pablo La Rosa, Tune Inn Records

Noise Reduction

A gate, or "noise gate," can be employed to remove unwanted background noise. It operates by only allowing signals above a selected threshold level to pass through unaffected. Signals below this threshold are fully, or partially, attenuated. Gating works particularly well on noisy drum and vocal tracks—anything with clean, distinct attacks that can accurately trigger the gate. A downside to gating is that the effect can cut off the very beginning of a signal that fades in, and may also chop off a sound's tail as it fades out. Most gates generally have pretty similar controls.

THRESHOLD Determines the level at which the gate opens, or begins opening, according to the processor's other parameter settings.

REDUCTION Sets the amount of attenuation. For example, a setting of –80 dB is a full gate; no sound is heard when the gate closes. By contrast, the audio below the threshold level may still be audible with a setting of –20 dB. Less gain reduction is useful when you just want to reduce a performance's background ambience, not cut it out altogether (as for a snare drum that was recorded with a big room tone).

ATTACK Use this control to set the gate's attack time. The shorter the attack time, the faster the gate opens. Longer attack times will open the gate slower, creating a smooth "fade in" effect.

DECAY Controls how much time it takes for the gate to close after the input signal falls below the threshold level. The shorter the decay time, the faster the gate will close. Longer decay times will close the gate slower, creating a less abrupt, "fade out" effect.

HOLD Sets the length of time the gate will remain open after its attack cycle is complete. Use this control to keep the gate open for longer durations at a shot. For example, it can help to decrease gate chatter caused when an input signal rapidly and repeatedly crosses the threshold level.

An alternative to gating is a denoiser application (such as Waves' X-Noise, part of the Restoration plug-in bundle; see figure 14.5). Denoisers are good at

greatly reducing steady, broadband noise. They operate by sampling a section of the offending noise, then applying noise reduction to just that frequency spectrum. The downside to these types of applications is that they can remove too many of a signal's frequencies, resulting in a dull, muffled-sounding track.

[CD 48]

Panning and Stereo Effects

How sounds are placed in the stereo field is an important part of creating a space for each instrument. For example, two busy, mono (not stereo), funk guitar parts with similar frequency ranges, both panned center and sitting on top of each other, are apt to sound pretty confusing. But pan one part hard left, and the other hard right, and they suddenly become distinct performances, each clearly heard in the stereo field.

Positioning a sound in the stereo field, called *panning*, is usually done using a channel's *Pan* control, most often found just above the Fader. Though there are no hard rules about where instruments are

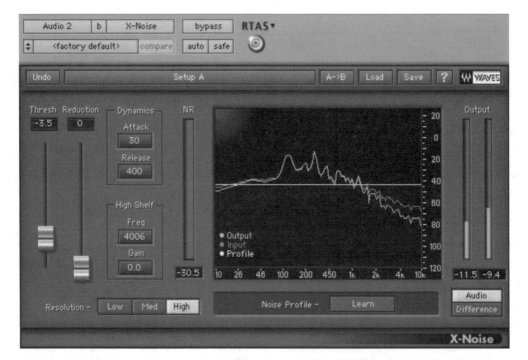

FIGURE 14.5 X-Noise. The X-Noise plug-in operates by sampling a section of a track's offending, broadband noise, then applying noise reduction to just that frequency spectrum.

FIGURE 14.6 Typical Pan Positions. The generally accepted pan positions for traditional instruments and some standard remix elements in a stereo field.

supposed to be panned, there is a set of generally accepted pan positions (see figure 14.6).

There are plug-ins available for turning a mono sound into stereo (like *Logic Audio's* Spread'er plug-in). These plug-ins are useful for broadening a mono signal, making it sound larger by diffusing it in the stereo field. For example, giving a mono pad a wide, stereo spread can make for a much grander sound. Plug-ins that automate panning (such as *Digital Performer's* stock AutoPan plug-in) can also be fun. Employ these plug-ins to automatically move a sound back and forth across the stereo field at varying speeds. This is a useful trick for giving a sound that was recorded in mono (like an old field recording of some East Indian hand percussion) lots of extra movement.

CD 49

Reverb

Creating the illusion of depth in your mix is done with reverb. Every physical location has its own sound—a series of reflections and delays that define the space. The bigger a space, and the more reflective its surfaces, the more reverberant it will be. Reverb

plug-ins (like Waves' TrueVerb or TC Electronic's MegaVerb, see figure 14.7) emulate the sound of different rooms and halls in varying sizes, shapes, and surface composition.

The mix between a "dry" sound and its "wet" return (the reverb effect) determines how near or distant a signal sounds. The drier a signal, the closer it sounds, while the wetter a signal is, the further away it sounds. Every mix usually requires at least one hall reverb, and more complex mixes often employ a hall and a room reverb. The goal is to impart a cohesive sound to your mix by creating a virtual space in which all of the instruments seem to be playing. If the breakout tracks you're working with already have their own reverb, then you should apply a similar sounding reverb to your remix tracks. Always apply reverb conservatively, primarily to push sounds to the rear of the mix. Too much reverb will cause a muddy sounding mix, especially when heard in a large reverberant club.

The better a reverb plug-in sounds, the more DSP it requires, so be sure to always set up the remix's main reverb on an effect send, as a group effect. Though reverb plug-ins can vary greatly in sound and controls, there are several nearly universal parameters (see following pages).

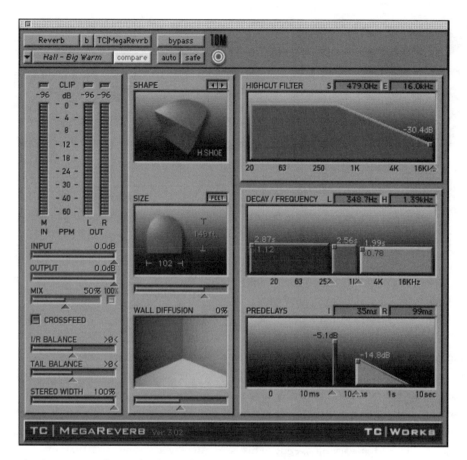

Figure 14.7 MegaVerb. The MegaVerb reverb plug-in by TC Electronic is excellent sounding, and a perfect example of a well-designed and complete set of reverb shaping parameters.

PREDELAY The time it takes, after the dry signal hits, for the reverb effect to be heard. The longer the predelay time, the more distinct the reverb will be from the dry sound.

DECAY This controls the duration of the reverb. The larger the decay value, the longer the reverb's tail, and the larger the space sounds.

DIFFUSION The complexity of a reverb is determined by its diffusion. A space with lots of surfaces and reflective objects has a high diffusion value, producing a reverb with many distinct echoes. In contrast, a room with four barren walls and no furniture has a low diffusion value, and produces a much smoother sounding reverb with fewer distinct echoes.

BRIGHTNESS (OR HI FREQ CUT) Use this control to roll off the high frequencies of the reverb. The more high frequencies you remove, the darker and more ominous the reverb will sound.

MIX This controls the wet to dry mix. When you have the reverb set up on an effects send, and returning via an aux return, you should have the mix set to 100-percent wet.

REVERB EVENS OUT ROUGH EDGES

If you have a breakpoint-edited loop that has been slowed down to the point where you now hear gaps between the samples, adding a touch of reverb can help smooth out the edges, making the holes less noticeable.

To us, reverb is a key element in mixing music, and we still haven't come across a plug-in that comes anywhere near the quality and clarity of outboard units like Lexicon's PCM91. As technology continues to progress this will no doubt change, but right now, we rely on the PCM91 for nearly all of our reverb. We run 24-bit signal out digitally to the PCM91 and print a 100 percent wet signal to a separate track. This gives us plenty of flexibility controlling the reverb mix and opens up a whole gamut of new possibilities, like chaining new plug-ins or doing stutter edits on the reverb while leaving the dry signal unaffected.

—J. Scott G., Deepsky

DELAY INSTEAD OF REVERB

It's possible to employ a delay in place of a reverb as a means for creating ambience. Set up a tempo-synchronized, multi-tap delay (such as Waves' SuperTap) on an effect send, just as you would a reverb plug-in. Enable two of the taps, and give them eighth- and quarter-note delay values, and a stereo spread. Adjust the feedback so that it decays slowly over about a second (like the duration of a small hall reverb tail). Apply the delay similarly to a hall reverb. The difference is that a multi-tap delay doesn't push signals back into the mix quite so distinctly. Instead, the wetter a signal, the more ethereal and spread out it sounds.

I rarely use reverb on vocals, I use a delay. Delay just seems to make the vocals smooth out, but adding presence, and carry more without making things muddy. The delays should be matched to the tempo of your remix, which is easy to do with today's plug-ins. I'm a big fan of Logic Audio's TapeDelay. I use that all the time on vocals, instruments, and drums too.

—Pablo La Rosa, Tune Inn Records

Automation

For many years, comprehensive automation was only available in major recording studios via their large-format, expensive mixing consoles. Now, all of the industry's top digital audio sequencers have automation features that equal, and in some cases rival, these antiquated consoles—at a fraction of the price. Good automation allows you to record fader and knob movements for every facet of a mixer channel, including plug-ins. This provides an extremely high degree of control over all types of levels and related parameters. For example, you can program a fader to dip at the exact moment of a vocal pop, or automate an effect send so that a performance sounds as if it's moving slowly off into the distance.

The automation features of most virtual mixers are usually pretty easy to understand. Despite what may be unfamiliar names for the automation modes, operations are similar to a MIDI sequencer with modes for record, play, add, and overdub (see below). Recording automation is done by choosing a "Write" mode (i.e., Write, Touch, or Trim), then selecting a parameter for the channel or plug-in that you want to automate, clicking the sequencer's Play key, and moving the associated control.

READ   For the playback of existing automation data. Automation is played back in this mode, and cannot be written.

WRITE   Allows the recording of automation data. This is a destructive record mode; any previously existing automation data will be overwritten. In this mode, recording begins when the digital audio sequencer enters play, and ends when playback stops.

TOUCH   An overdub mode that punches in when you move the control for the parameter that has been selected for automation. When movement stops, automation write ends, and any previously existing automation data is read from that point forward, or until the control is moved again.

OFF Disables all automation data for the selected track.

TRIM This mode allows you to add or subtract values from a track's existing automation data. For example, you could add +6 dB to an automation curve without affecting the shape of the curve. It is most often used in conjunction with Write and Trim modes, though it is not so common a feature as the other four modes.

FADER GROUPS

When you need to move several faders at the same time, gang the faders together to create a fader group. Not all programs have this feature, but fader groups are really handy for creating refined, professional mixes. (To find out about your digital audio sequencer's fader grouping capabilities, consult its user manual.) For example, to slowly fade out all of the drum tracks in a break, assign all of the drum channels to one fader group. Then you can write the fade for all the channels simultaneously. Or, to adjust the level of all the background vocals at the same time, relative to the entire mix, assign all of the backing vocal channels to a fader group.

If your digital audio sequencer does not have fader groups, an alternative is to remove all of the channels for a group from the main stereo mix, and instead bus them all to a stereo aux input. Then assign the aux input's output to the main stereo mix. Use the aux input's fader to control the stereo sub mix of the bused channels. The downside to this alternative is that it isn't nearly as convenient as fader groups, and you may introduce some delay to the tracks being routed through the aux input (because you're adding another stage of processing).

Best Reference

In order to produce great sounding mixes, it's crucial that you know how your speakers and your room sound. For example, what frequencies do your speakers emphasize? Or, what frequencies does your room absorb? The best way to discover and understand these attributes is to listen to lots of commercially released material—songs you know sound good in the dance clubs—in your studio. This will help to give you a clear picture of where each instrument should sit in the mix, in terms of level and tone, ensuring that your mix will translate well from your studio to the dance floor.

Along with your main, pro audio, powered speakers and a quality set of headphones, it's also wise to have a small (like a 3- or 4-inch woofer) pair of consumer-level speakers hooked up (such as Edirol's MA-10 or –20 series). These speakers will provide a real-world point of reference, to give you an idea of what your remix will sound like through a television's speakers, a stock car stereo system, or a cheap boombox. While you're mixing, be sure to switch back and forth between both sets of speakers, and the headphones, in order to balance instrument levels and tones across all of these monitor sources. This will help to ensure that your remix sounds great over whatever sound system it's heard on.

Don't listen to your mix at high volumes for hours on end. Not only will this damage your hearing, over time, but your ears will become fatigued and your ability to recognize and interpret sounds accurately will be impaired. You should work mostly at low to medium volumes, with occasional listening tests at quiet or loud levels. Like different sets of speakers, different volumes will paint a different picture of your mix. For example, hi-hats that sound perfect at medium levels might be too loud and harsh sounding at high volumes, or a bass line that sounds great loud might disappear altogether at low volumes. The goal is to craft a mix that sounds excellent at all volumes. Remember to take breaks when you're mixing. Give your ears a rest every hour or two, because it's amazing how much more clearly you can hear everything with fresh ears.

The ability to burn reference audio CDs using standard CDRs is a tremendous advantage. There's nothing like listening to your remix outside of the studio to hear what's working and what's not. With a program such as Roxio's *Toast* (Mac), or *Easy CD Creator* (PC), and a standard CDR writer, you can create an audio CD that will play on most CD players. Listen to the mix through your car's sound system, on your friends' stereo, and try to find a club that will let you play your remix over their sound system before the doors open. During the mixing process, do this as often as possible, in order to get a clear picture of how your mix is sounding in the real world. And if you own a DJ setup that includes DJ CD players, try mixing your remix into a practice set to see how it stands up against commercially released tunes.

When your remix sounds nearly as good as your favorite label releases, with all of the instruments' levels and tones sitting just right in the mix, then it's time to bounce the track to disk and begin the mastering process (discussed in the next chapter).

When I finish a mix, I burn a CD. I think it's really important to sit on your mix for a while, play it around and see how it sounds, check it out in the car. I even go so far as to mix it in with records to see how it would fit in a DJ set. This way, I can not only look at it arrangement-wise, like was that drum intro long enough and was the outro easy to work with, but also sonically, to hear how the mix sounds when it's put up against records that are being released. A lot of times you might notice, for example, that all of your highs are gone compared to the other records. Then you know that your mix sounds dull and you can get back in the studio and re-EQ things. Your ears can really play tricks on you if you've been listening to the same mix for a long time. It's important to give your ears a break.

—Pablo La Rosa, Tune Inn Records

TUNE YOUR ROOM

Equally as important as good speakers is how your room is tuned. Major recording studios spend thousands of dollars tuning their studio control rooms, to make sure that when you sit in the "sweet spot" (between the speakers), the sound you hear is not adversely colored by the room. This is accomplished by lots of architectural considerations during the room's construction, as well as an array of acoustic tiles for affecting how sound is reflected off the room's surfaces and walls.

There's no need to go to such extremes to tune your listening environment, but fixing a few of the more common acoustic problems that plague most typical rooms is a must. For example, you can fix ping-pong echoes created by parallel surfaces (especially prevalent near where the walls meet the ceiling), or a room's inclination to boost a specific frequency (called a resonant frequency). Fortunately, companies such as Auralex offer room tuning kits that include an assortment of acoustic foam tiles and pieces for tuning most typical rooms. Though it might seem like you could save money by gluing egg cartons and packing foam to the walls, not only will these materials not be as effective because they are not designed for acoustic applications, but they are a very dangerous fire hazard.

CHAPTER 15

Mastering

The final phase of the remixing process is mastering. This is your last chance to make tonal and level changes to the stereo mixdown. During mastering, errant frequencies (such as too little bass, or too much mid-range) are corrected using pinpoint-accurate EQ. Multi-band compression is employed to make sure that the remix is as loud as possible.

Mastering should not to be taken lightly because a bad mastering job can completely ruin your final product. Good mastering engineers have spent years learning their craft. They work in finely tuned rooms, and are usually surrounded by expensive, high-end, analog outboard gear (such as Manley Compressors and Masenberg EQ). Though it's important to understand the basics of mastering so that you can create your own reference masters (home-authored audio CDs to listen to around town), for your remix to sound the best it possibly can, especially if you plan on releasing it commercially, consider hiring a dance-music-savvy mastering engineer for the final master (the copy you would use for commercial duplication). It never hurts to have somebody with lots of experience listen to your mix.

Having said that, there have been plenty of underground dance music releases that were mastered in home studios. (For example, the releases by Trance[ ]Control, the popular mp3.com electronica duo who master their own tracks using IK Multimedia's *T-Racks*, see figure 15.3.) Indeed, there is no shortage of amazing software available for mastering, and much of it is reasonably priced. You will need these tools to prepare your reference master, because the goal of the reference audio CD is to have the remix sound as close to the final product as possible (in terms of both EQ and loudness). Practice your mastering chops by creating reference masters—in this way, you'll get a good feel for whether you have the ears and the patience to do your own final mastering.

I highly recommend sending your first two or three finished recording projects out to a mastering engineer before having it pressed to vinyl. While there is great affordable software and hardware, the art of mastering a recording for vinyl is something that very few people understand, at first. A good mastering engineer can make your recording sound punchy and lively and achieve maximum loudness on vinyl (if it's well-recorded to begin with). They can also point out flaws in your mix and help make you a better mixer. You may spend a little more money, but it's worth it.

—Chris Gill (Gilla Monsta),
editor of *Remix* Magazine (1999–2002)

NEVER OVERWRITE

When you process your stereo mix, never overwrite the original file. Always save the processed file under a new name.

For example, "remix1_mix2_48k24bts.wav" would become "remix1_mast1_44k16bts.wav."

If you overwrite the original file, and later discover that your mastering job was less than perfect, you can't revert to your unprocessed mix without creating a completely new stereo mix from the remix's original multitrack session.

Bounce to Disk

Before you can begin mastering, you will need to create a stereo "mixdown" of the remix. In the past, this was done by recording the mix to a DAT recorder, or possibly a reel-to-reel tape machine. Thanks to computers and digital audio sequencers, it's now possible to "bounce" your mix directly to the computer's internal hard drive. This process is fast and much more convenient then mixing down to an external tape machine.

All good digital audio sequencers feature a bounce-to-disk function, but how the function is implemented varies from application to application. In general, it's a simple matter of selecting what you want to mix down and choosing the Bounce to Disk command, usually found in a main menu. All the audio that is going through your program's mixer will be captured (including effects returns and aux inputs). Some programs perform the mixdown in real-time, while others can bounce the mix to disk at speeds faster than real-time.

Be sure to mix down several variations of the mix. For example, if you're not sure about the bass level, make one pass with the bass a little louder (like +3 dB) and another with the bass a bit softer (like −3 dB). The mastering process may emphasize, or de-emphasize, particular instruments and tones, so having plenty of passes to work with is important. Since the changes from one mixdown pass to the next will likely be subtle, you will need to be very systematic in your naming of the versions. For example, "myremix_bass-3db_44k16bts.wav," or "myremix_kick-3db_48k24bts.aif" (that's remix name, a brief description of the mix variation, sample rate and bit depth, and the document's file type).

LEAVE THE FADE OUT FOR LAST

Don't bounce down with a fade out at the end of a mix. Instead, save the fade out for mastering. Compression during mastering will ruin a preexisting fade, causing the fade to lose its even slope as the compressor tries to boost the falling stereo level, adding noise to the mix in the process. By writing the fade post compressor, during mastering, you're putting the final fade exactly where it belongs: at the very end of the entire processing chain.

SKIP A STEP?

An alternative to bouncing your mixes to hard disk for mastering is to skip this step entirely and master right in your multitrack session. However, this is only possible if you have plenty of processing power to spare, since all of the plug-ins for the mix will likely be pushing your system to its limits, and mastering plug-ins will require even more DSP. Insert the mastering plug-ins directly in the mixer's master fader channel, making sure that they are pre fader. If you can't insert the plug-ins pre fader, then you will need to write the fade out after bouncing the mix to disk.

Mastering directly in the multitrack session is very convenient for creating reference masters, but not optimal for final mastering. This is because final mastering is best done using unprocessed stereo mixes. For example, when you are mastering several tunes for the same album, the goal is to make all of the tracks sound cohesive by processing them similarly (to give them equal frequency and amplitude levels). If just one of the album's tracks is overly compressed to begin with, then all of the album's other tracks would also require heavy compression in order to sound similar.

Since I mix everything in the computer, I often run a mastering plug-in right on my multitrack session, before bouncing it to 2-track. If I notice later that the mix isn't loud enough, I just go back into the session and make the changes.

—Pablo La Rosa, Tune Inn Records

CD 50

Master the Process

Though there are good standalone mastering applications and hardware devices, your digital audio sequencer in conjunction with select plug-ins is excellent for mastering. Begin by creating a new project just for mastering the remix (see figure 15.1). Import all of the mix passes and set them up on their own stereo tracks. Insert plug-ins on the individual tracks, not the master fader. Not only does this allow each mix to have its own settings, but the master fader can then be employed for the final fade, without affecting any of the levels going to the plug-ins. (Changing a level, post fader, that's feeding a compressor will affect when compression begins.) In general, the mastering process starts with EQ, followed by compression, multi-band compression, more EQ if necessary, and lastly, loudness maximization.

MASTERING EQ

If you've crafted a solid-sounding mix, then the amount of mastering EQ needed should be nominal. EQ fixes should be constrained to very narrow bandwidths and with only slight cuts or boosts (within about +/−3 dB). If you find yourself making big, sweeping EQ corrections, this is an indicator that you need to revisit the remix's multitrack session and make the appropriate changes to the mix from there.

When mastering, you generally want to employ parametric EQ that doesn't color the audio (such as Waves' Q series of plug-ins, see figure 15.2). However, if your goal is to give the remix a subtle analog flavor, then either an EQ plug-in from the Waves' Renaissance collection, or IK Multimedia's *T-Racks* plug-in bundle (see figure 15.3) can be effective.

> For vinyl, it's mainly in the high-end, around the 6 to 8 kHz range, that you need to watch out for. If a turntable has old cartridges, you can get a lot of sibilance in this range. We try to be really careful in this frequency range and even boost the mids up a bit more to compensate. We're also careful on the bass; we don't put a lot of subs in there. I'll roll some stuff off at 40 or 45 Hz; vinyl can take it, but when you play it in the club it's going to sound like total mud.
>
> —Chris Cox, Thunderpuss

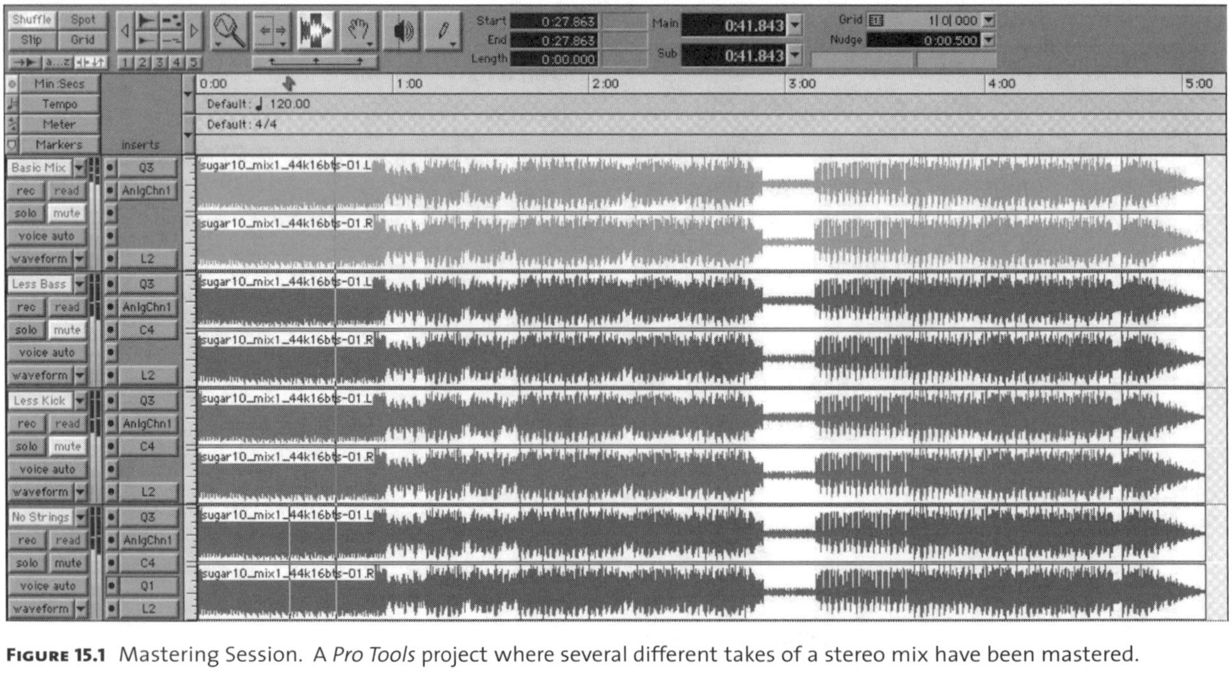

Figure 15.1 Mastering Session. A *Pro Tools* project where several different takes of a stereo mix have been mastered.

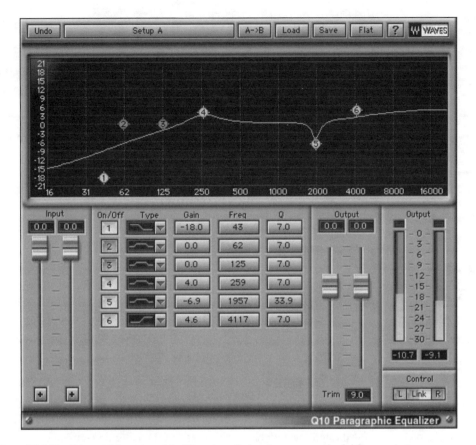

FIGURE 15.2 Waves' Q6. The Waves' Q6 parametric EQ series of plug-ins are wonderful for mastering.

MULTI-BAND COMPRESSION

Standard compression affects all frequencies equally, while multi-band compression allows you to target specific frequency ranges. For example, you could use a multi-band compressor to control a mid-range bump without squashing all of the surrounding frequencies. Examples of good multi-band compressor plug-ins include Waves' C4 and TC Electronic's MasterX (see figure 15.4).

> *I'll use a combination of Digidesign's Maxim and TC Electronic's MasterX. I like the 3-band over the 5-band for house music. I'll play around with the compression and limiting setting a bit, but don't compress it too much because you want to leave the mastering engineer room to fidget about with it.*

—(BT) Brian Transeau

LOUDNESS MAXIMIZER

Plug-ins that make stereo mixes sound as loud as possible are commonly called *loudness maximizers*. These programs are usually based on brick-wall limiting and automatic-gain makeup, and may also include noise shaping features. The brick-wall limiting allows you to set a threshold over which signals cannot pass, while the automatic-gain makeup intelligently keeps the material's peaks right at 0 dB. Noise shaping is used to optimize a signal for conversion to different bit depths through *dithering*, a process of adding "shaped" (to be less detectable to the human ear) noise to a signal in order to increase the digital signal's low-level sound resolution. Good loudness-maximizer plug-ins include Digidesign's Maxim, and Waves' L1 and L2 (see figure 15.5).

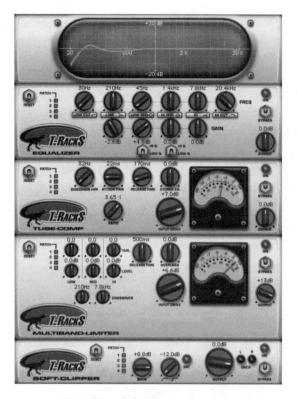

FIGURE 15.3 IK Multimedia's T-Racks. To give your mix an analog flavor, T-Racks, by IK Multimedia, is convenient because it bundles together several dedicated mastering, analog modeling plug-ins.

> *I use the L2 on stuff when the mixes go out for the A&R label guys to hear, when you want people to think you're the bomb. But if the mix is going to be mastered by a real mastering engineer, you can run into problems with too much L2 because there won't be any dynamic range to work with.*
>
> —Dave Audé

The Master CDR

If you plan on taking your remix to a mastering engineer, you need to burn a data CD, not an audio CD. This will allow the engineer to import the stereo mix audio files directly into his mastering program, without first converting them from an audio-CD track file type. The data CD should contain all of the different mix passes, to give the engineer plenty of versions to choose from.

Once the mastering is complete, if you plan on sending the remix out for professional duplication, you'll need to create a master audio CD. Be sure to burn this master CD using disk-at-once to ensure that there are no breaks in the data. Though it's okay to burn

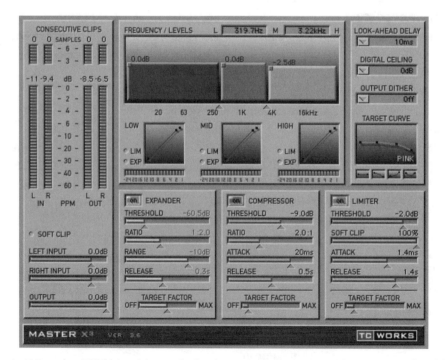

FIGURE 15.4 MasterX. Based on TC Electronic's popular hardware mastering unit, Finalizer, MasterX (available in 3- and 5-band configurations) is an excellent multi-band compressor with lots of handy presets.

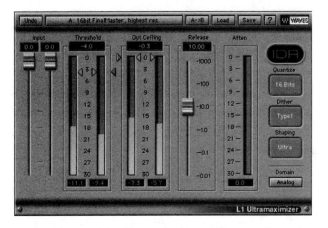

FIGURE 15.5 Waves' L1. The predecessor to the Waves' L2 is the L1, with less sophisticated parameters, but equally as capable, especially for dance music.

reference audio CDs at high speeds (such as 8x and higher), the final master CD should be done no faster than 2x speed; this helps to maintain data integrity. Check with the duplication house for any other requirements (such as whether they need a separate master audio CD for each side of the record).

> *When you burn the audio CD, make sure you burn it at 2x speed. This has the least amount of errors. Even if your CD recorder does 4x or 16x speeds, do 2x. It's okay to burn data CDs at higher speeds, but make sure you verify the data before sending off the CD. And try to use the best CDs possible. I would recommend the Mitsui Golds.*
>
> —Dave Audé

DIFFERENT ARRANGEMENTS

It's standard practice to include several different arrangements of a remix on a CD single or 12-inch release. These arrangements are called "versions," and are included to give DJs options. For example, one DJ may prefer the "Extended Vocal Mix," while another might choose to play the "Dub" version. Versions are usually produced after the main remix has been completed, as sort of a remix of the original remix. There are no rules when it comes to producing a new version, other than that it should

be of a different dance music style than the original, so that the single might appeal to the widest possible audience.

Edited versions of a remix are something entirely different, and are created by actually editing down the original remix. For example, a six-minute "Club" mix might be edited down to produce an under 4-minute "Radio" version, suitable for airplay on commercial radio stations. In fact, it's always a good idea to include at least one edited version of the full remix in order to satisfy radio programmers and, possibly, film and television music directors in search of a radio-length cue.

When you are concocting names for the different versions, be sure to include references to style, length, and the remixer. By clearly demarcating the versions, you are helping DJs, and others, identify your remixes. For example, "Hawk's Phenomenal Trance Mix," or "DJ Max's Tribal House Extended Mix." If you take your remix to a mastering engineer, make sure to include the stereo mixes for every version, because they all need to be mastered at the same time.

> *When people put too much program on one side of vinyl, it's painful; you lose the volume. Anything under twelve-and-a-half-minutes is optimum time for a side of vinyl, at 33 1/3 rpm. Over thirteen-minutes, and every fifteen to thirty-seconds thereafter, you lose a dB of volume. Labels that put eighteen to twenty minutes on a side, three full-length mixes—the vinyl just can't keep up. This can create a huge problem at clubs because if you're maxed out on the DJ-mixer, you have no more gain control, and you put on a record with a low pressing, that can kill the energy of the entire room.*
>
> —Chris Cox, Thunderpuss

Vinyl Versus CD

Homemade audio CDs can sound great and are a snap to create using your personal computer. "One-offs," as they are called, are perfect for handing out as demos. However, if you want to catch the eyes and ears of top DJs, especially those interested in underground remixes, you'll need spend the money and press the records. Though there are more and more serious DJs spinning CDs, a record release is still an important stepping stone to notoriety in the dance music movement. You should have CDs manufactured if you plan on distributing the mix to retail CD stores, and plan to shoot for airplay on commercial radio stations.

To locate a reputable record duplication company, check the ads in the back of music industry trade journals (like *Remix* or *Mixer* magazines). If you own a record that is particularly well manufactured, and sounds great, find out where it was mastered and duplicated. Always make sure that you receive—and *audition*—a test pressing before committing to the actual duplication run. The test pressing is your very last chance to make changes and hear how the final product will sound.

As with any duplication process, your per-unit price will be less expensive the more units you order at a time. Expect to spend a few bucks each on orders of 500 records or less, with the price falling below two dollars on orders over 1,000 units. More elaborate jacket and label designs (such as 4-color versus simple black-and-white, which is suitable for most independent releases) will also add to the per-unit cost.

All the same rules apply to record manufacturing that apply to CD duplication. Be sure to listen to a test pressing before committing to the manufacturing run, and your per-unit price will be cheaper the more units you order at once. Some companies offer CDR duplication services for runs under 100 units, but at around three dollars per unit, this can get expensive. For actual tin-stamped, shrink-wrapped, retail-ready CDs, expect to spend a couple bucks each on runs under 1,000 units. Above 1,000 units, the price usually falls below two dollars. However, be aware that multi-page CD booklets and 4-color graphics can add a lot to the price per unit. For an independent release, a two-page booklet and two-color graphics is usually plenty. With an innovative design and layout concept, you could get away with even less (like black and white with no booklet).

If you plan on releasing a single, it's important to start promoting several months before your product is manufactured. By the time your release-ready record is in your hands, press people and DJs should already be anticipating a copy, ensuring that they will listen to your release promptly. However, marketing and promoting a single, getting all of the infrastructure in place to support your release is no easy task. The next chapter discusses the process.

> One of the biggest benefits of using a local pressing plant is that it's easier to closely monitor and evaluate each step of the process, and you can learn a lot about the art of pressing a record to vinyl when you can actually see how a record is made. Choosing a local plant will also save you a significant amount of time and money. For example, you can save on postage by picking up your finished records directly from the plant, and you can shave days, or even weeks, off of your final delivery date by picking up your test pressings from the plant instead of waiting for them to be mailed to you.
>
> —Chris Gill (Gilla Monsta),
> editor of *Remix* Magazine (1999–2002)

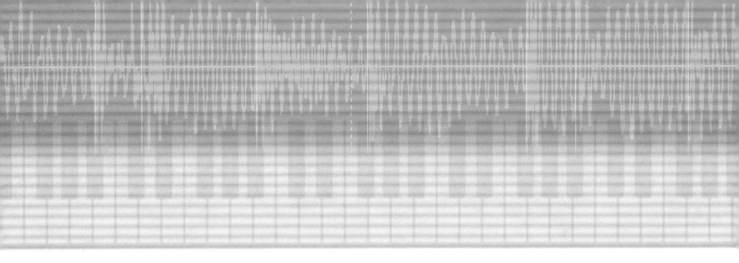

SECTION VII

Promote and Look Forward

CHAPTER 16:

Be Seen, Get Heard

Producing a great remix is a big accomplishment, and you may decide that playing it for your friends is recognition enough. On the other hand, perhaps you yearn for more recognition, and the chance to have your remix heard by a much wider audience. If this is the case, you will need to learn how promotion and distribution works in the music industry. This is a big subject and there is no way to cover it in detail in a single chapter. However, just to get you started, the most basic steps to getting your remix single heard and in record stores are presented here. But you should also read a few books dedicated to the subject (such as *Getting Signed!* by George Howard, Berklee Press 2003) in order to truly grasp the scope of this task.

Keep in mind that manufacturing a single, and promoting and distributing that single require a lot of time and money, and the chances are that you won't have a runaway hit. Less than one percent of artists in the music industry have a profitable single or album. Some say that the odds are worse than playing a state lottery. Having said this, it's possible that, with a good amount of effort, you will be able to generate some revenues and probably cover your manufacturing costs. If you begin the journey of self-releasing singles with your eyes open, as a vehicle for having fun and sharing your music with others, then you will not be disappointed. Running a small, independent label can be a blast, but don't quit your day job prematurely.

DOING BUSINESS AS

If you plan on running your own independent label, you will probably want to create a name for your business. You'll need to register this name with the county and city where your business is located in order to open a business checking account, to cash checks made out to your label. Your local post office or county court house can give you the details on registering a "fictitious business name," or D.B.A. (Doing Business As).

Unfortunately, registering a D.B.A. flags you for a lot of fees—money that you might not have when you're just getting started. For example, registering the fictitious business name costs money, banks charge at least ten dollars a month for business checking accounts (that fall below some minimum balance), and the city may come after you for business licenses and taxes. Though most of these individual fees are small, they add up. The alternative to a D.B.A. is to just use your own name, ensuring that every check is made out directly to you. Then you can use a personal checking account and avoid all the bureaucratic headaches.

Marketing

Some people have a talent for pushing their own material; others don't. Either way, it's a challenging task that can eat up a lot of time. Hiring an independent public relations (PR) firm to help market your remix single can be a wise business move. Though this will cost money (anywhere from $500 to $4,000, depending on the contract you negotiate), a good PR firm can save you valuable time because they know exactly how to generate publicity. And having a third party represent your material is always impressive.

The trick with hiring a PR firm, as with any independent contractor, is to thoroughly investigate the company's background. Talk to past clients, know the company's track record (their success stories), and be sure that they understand the dance music market. Lots of name artists and independent labels employ PR firms. Find out who is handling the PR for an artist or label that you respect, and give that company a call. Most PR firms are nonexclusive, so they'll work with just about anybody that can afford their services. When you discuss rates with them, be sure to let them know that you're an independent on a shoestring budget. Sometimes, they'll take this into account and give you a discount.

If you hire a PR firm, be certain that both of you are clear on what will be accomplished with the money you're spending. For example, many firms want to work on a contingency basis (a set fee for a set amount of time), but this is a bad idea for beginning artists because there's no real way to verify what's being done for you on a daily basis. Instead, hire the firm for very specific tasks, such as procuring magazine reviews (and be specific about which magazines will be targeted). By operating this way, you're paying to see tangible results. When you're satisfied that the first job has been handled professionally, contract the next job, and so on. Three of the most important avenues for promoting a single, in order of importance, are listed below.

CLICHÉ BUT TRUE

The number-one most important thing to remember about the music industry is that it's people driven. The cliché, "It's all about who you know," perfectly describes this industry. Making friends in all the right places by socializing, and always being humble and gracious, will help bolster your promotional efforts.

PRINT

Record reviews are very important because they help to expose your release. Knowing the people who actually write for the different magazines usually helps to expedite a review. Since it's difficult to know the writers and editors of every magazine, this is where a PR firm can lend a hand. Scope out the magazines that regularly run record reviews (like *Remix*, *Urb*, and *DJ Times*). Writers and editors who publish their e-mail addresses are generally open to some friendly correspondence. And don't forget about online publications, or zines. In fact, zines are often able to publish a review months in advance of traditional, hardcopy magazines because they don't have any printing delays.

RADIO

Most college radio stations and some progressive commercial stations host a mix or new music show. This is a timeslot reserved for new releases and is sometimes presented as a continuous DJ mix. It may be live, or it may be a syndicated program. Either way, debuting on one of these shows, and receiving a positive listener response, is a good way to get considered for "regular rotation" (being added to the station's normal playlist). (Of course, knowing a station's DJs and program director is helpful too.) *The American College Media Directory* (www.amercollegemedia.com) is a good way to find out about college stations in your area and around the nation.

RECORD POOLS

For DJs that are so busy gigging that they don't have the time to regularly browse record stores, there are record pools. These subscription services generally cater to a particular style of dance music, mailing out prescreened, new releases as they become available. However, it's usually a financial stretch for independents on a budget to service several record pools, since a lot of product must be thrown into the pools for free. The trick is to find a record pool with a few name DJs who you think will like your remix. This, again, is the type of information a good PR firm should know. Otherwise, you can research record pools on your own through the Internet (try www.recordpools.org and www.recordpoolcharts.com).

GETTING PLAY

Count on giving away about thirty percent of your records for promotions. Hand them out to your favorite DJs, clubs, and radio stations. Getting your remix played around town is essential for exposure, and ultimately, creating a fan base for your work.

Do some research before you hand your record to a DJ. Make sure that your remix sounds like a track they might play; otherwise, you're just wasting money. By matching your remix's style to that of the DJ, your actually doing them a favor, pre-screening new material.

Always follow up with the DJs that receive your records, because a new release from an unknown independent can get easily overlooked, and unintentionally forgotten. Check in every week or two to see if your record has been auditioned. If after three follow-ups, you're still getting a runaround, consider putting your energy elsewhere.

Distribution

A great promotional campaign doesn't mean anything if your record isn't available for people to purchase. Whether it's in local mom-and-pop record stores, online, or you're selling it on select street corners, people need to be able to find it after they've heard or read about it.

There are three key avenues (described below) through which an independent can distribute a record (or CD): online, a retail distributor, or the D.I.Y. approach (go store to store and distribute the record yourself). All three approaches are important—especially when you're just getting started. The Internet is an inexpensive way to bring your record to the global market, retail distributors can help you put the record into stores that are outside of your area, and you can support a regional promotional campaign by self-distributing. Indeed, focusing your efforts on promoting and distributing in a very specific region (like the cities of Miami or New York, or just Los Angeles county) can be a very effective way of stretching your budget. If you have a hit in one region, other markets generally tend to follow.

DO YOU NEED A BAR CODE?

All major label releases have a Universal Packing Code (UPC), more commonly known as a bar code. It allows stores and record companies to track sales, and these numbers are then reported to Sound Scan in order to calculate industry chart positions. Anybody can purchase their own bar code from the Universal Code Council (*www.uc-council.org*), but this is an extra expense that may not be necessary in the beginning. For example, most boutique record stores don't care whether your release has a bar code or not, nor do certain online stores (such as the indie-friendly CD Baby, *www.cdbaby.com*).

However, if you want to sell your CD release through normal retail outlets, you must have a bar code. Fortunately, many CD manufacturers (such as Disc Makers, *www.discmakers.com*) have taken to loaning out their bar codes in order to drum up business from cash-poor independents. The downside to this system is that, though you will be able to track your units sold, your label won't get credited for the sales because it's not your UPC code. But this is not that big of a deal in the beginning. When you're selling lots of records, that's when it's important, and at that point you should be able to afford your own UPC account.

RETAIL DISTRIBUTORS

These companies specialize in putting your product into "brick-and-mortar," retail outlets. In exchange for their distribution services, they take a percentage of sales. Most independent retail distributors, those that service small, mom-and-pop record stores, target specific regions (like the East Coast, or Italy and the South of France). This arrangement is helpful because it allows you to keep your promotional campaigns very focused, in order to get the best bang for your marketing bucks.

In general, the bigger the distributor, the more difficult it is to get your record or CD into their catalog. Independent distributors (such as Koch International or Navarre) are a bit easier to contact because they're always interested in a new source of revenue. If you can prove that you're launching an effective promotional campaign that will move units, and they like your music, chances are that they will agree to distribute your record.

D.I.Y. DISTRIBUTION

If you plan on launching a regional promotional campaign where you live, there's no reason why you can't distribute the records yourself. For example, in any major metropolitan city, there aren't usually that many boutique record stores. If there are five record stores in your area, drive to each store, find out who the buyers are, pass out promotional copies of the record, and make some new friends. Most independent record stores will take your record on consignment, and some, if they are really impressed by your music and promotional campaign, may buy a few records outright.

Using the D.I.Y. approach to distribute CDs is usually less fruitful. Major retail CD stores often sign exclusive purchasing deals with a major distributor. Moreover, few take CDs on consignment, and selling CDs outright can be a bookkeeping headache because CDs are subject to returns. When a CD is returned, the retailer will expect credit for that merchandise. With record sales, there are generally no returns because most record sales are final.

WORLD WIDE WEB

Selling online is something that's available to everybody, but that doesn't make it any less powerful of a tool. By having your remix single available through a variety of Internet retail outlets, you're greatly increasing your chances for sales around the globe. Be sure to give customers several point-of-purchase options, so that they can choose the method with which they feel the most comfortable. For example, from your Web site, provide a couple links to well known Web outlets (such as CD Baby or Amazon, www.amazon.com), and you can also encourage direct sales (and make more profit per unit) using services such as PayPal (www.paypal.com) and CD Street (www.cdstreet.com). The Internet is a distribution breakthrough for independent labels and artists. (A good book on this subject is *The Musician's Internet* by Peter Spellman, published by Berklee Press, 2002.)

Placements

If your sales generate enough revenues to meet your manufacturing costs, you're doing well. But you'll still need to cover your promotional expenses, and figuring out how to turn a small profit for all of your hard work is always nice too. Fortunately, even if you don't have a hit, there are ways to make extra money from your recordings besides retail sales. You can license your music for use in films, television shows, and mix compilation albums, and get paid.

FILM AND TV

Having your music selected for a film can earn you both up-front cash (called a sync fee—paying for the right to use your recording in a television show or film), and sometimes residuals for overseas distribution. Getting your music placed in a television show can garner residuals (a royalty) each time that show is broadcast. While the director has the final say on music selections for most film and television shows, a music director is generally in charge of selecting the preliminary cues. Music directors often depend heavily on music library services—companies that offer collections of music, ready for licensing, and organized into categories (such as music styles) for easy auditioning. You should maintain relationships with both music directors and music libraries, keeping them abreast of your releases, in order to increase the chances of having your music placed.

An organization called TAXI (www.taxi.com) offers a unique avenue for getting your tracks directly to music directors and music libraries. Though it costs several hundred dollars a year to join, the fee is a small price to pay for all of the industry leads posted each month, especially if you write and produce music in a variety of styles. The performing rights organization (see the sidebar, "Performing Rights Organizations") that you sign up with can also help place your material. If your material is good, they will go out of their way to provide leads because every time your music is broadcast, they make money.

MIX COMPILATIONS

Having your track chosen for a DJ's mix compilation CD, especially a name DJ, is a big compliment. It also has the potential to generate some decent cash. However, the only surefire way of being included on a mix CD is to have great tracks, and a solid relationship with the DJ who will be mixing the CD. Otherwise, just get the singles out there using the techniques discussed earlier in this chapter, and with a little luck, your tracks will be heard by the right DJs.

Each mix CD deal is different. You may be offered a onetime payment for the use of your track, or a percentage on each unit sold. What you settle for should depend on how well you think the mix CD will sell. If it looks like it's going to be a big hit, try to negotiate for a bit of cash up front, and a percentage on each unit sold.

Either way, don't sign anything until you have a qualified music attorney look over the proposed contract.

I always end up using a lot of independent labels' tracks in my mixes, because getting approval from major labels to use one of their artists' tracks is a pain, and expensive. Major labels that put out their own mix compilations take out the middleman by using their own artists, which is a smart business move.

—DJ Irene

PERFORMING RIGHTS ORGANIZATIONS

There are three main, competing organizations that keep track of songwriter's royalties. It's their job to make sure that every time a tune is broadcast, the writers of that tune get paid. The organizations are: American Society of Composers, Authors, and Publishers (ASCAP), *www.ascap.com*; Broadcast Music Incorporated (BMI), *www.bmi.com*; and Society of European Stage Authors and Composers (SESAC), *www.sesac.com*. If you want to get paid residuals for any of your tunes that are receiving airplay or have been placed, you must belong to one of these organizations. It's hard to argue that one is better than the others, because they all operate similarly. A separate organization, the Harry Fox Agency, *www.harryfox.com*, specializes in dealing with synchronization rights. Visit them all to find the one that fits your personality and needs.

Remixing Legalities

Remember that when you remix an artist's track, you're working from an original, copyright-protected piece of music. There was a writer, performer, and producer who all participated in the creation of that song, and they are all entitled to a percentage of any revenues generated by the song, in accordance with their original contracts. Remixing a song does not automatically entitle you to any songwriting rights. In fact, until recently, remixers have worked mostly on commission, for a straight fee, with little or no recognition for their creative input. Fortunately, this is changing and labels and artists have slowly begun to share the production credits, and percentages of sales with top remixers

Though it's illegal to release a remix of an artist's song without their express, written consent, "white label" records (remixes released without the consent of the artist) abound in the underground dance music world. However, despite the fact that this is clearly copyright infringement, savvy labels will look the other way for a time, if the remix is helping to promote their artist. But if the remix turns out to be a hit, and is selling thousands of units, the label and artist will come looking for their cut of the pie. In extreme cases, a "Cease and Desist" order will be served, revenues generated by the sale of the remix will be seized, and there may be an additional fine. The label may then turn around and officially release the remix, and maybe pay the remixer a commission (or just waive the fine).

Keep in mind that it's always easier to negotiate the right to release a remix of an independent artist seeking publicity, rather than trying to get approval to release a remix of a major label artist's song. Of course, you can remix a major label artist's tune for personal pleasure, as long as you don't profit from the remix. But if you want to put out quality, underground remix records, without the legal hassles, go after the independent artists. Working cooperatively, independents can help each other with promotions and exposure.

CHAPTER 17:
The Future of Remixing

DJ-style remixing began on stage with innovative DJs (such as Jam Master Jay, Kool Herc, and Francis Grasso) looking to extend beats and expand their creative boundaries. The techniques pioneered in the DJ booth have found their way into the recording studio, to become essential ingredients in the art of remix production. However, the exchange of ideas and techniques has not flowed only in one direction. As DJs have become more studio savvy, and as music producers have begun to DJ, studio production techniques have also found their way into the DJ booth.

Today's groundbreaking DJs (such as Richie Hawtin and Starcase) are now employing studio gear to program beats and write music as they DJ, working new sounds and musical ideas directly into their sets. Music producers and groups (such as BT and Deepsky) are hitting the stage with a host of DJ-inspired equipment, including DJ mixers and real-time effects boxes. Name DJs (such as DJ Sasha and Timo Maas) are producing their own artist albums, and some are even performing the material live, with a full band (such as Paul Oakenfold's tour to support his first artist album, *Bunkka*). A fundamental principle behind the international dance music movement is a world without borders—a global community—and the blurring of boundaries between stage, DJ booth, and the recording studio mirrors this idea beautifully.

DJ Hybrid

A popular way of incorporating studio gear into a live DJ set is to plug a "groove box" (such as Korg's ER-1) right into the DJ mixer. This allows a DJ to pre-cue cuts from the groove box just as they pre-cue their record selections. Music from the groove box can then be beat-matched to the current record before dropping it into the mix. This may be accomplished traditionally, by manually speeding up or slowing down the groove box's tempo, or by using a tap tempo feature (usually, a button on the groove box that you can tap to determine its tempo).

Taking advantage of a groove box's MIDI synchronization features, more studio gear can be added and locked to tempo (such as adding another groove box, a tempo-based effects unit, and a synthesizer workstation). The more complex such a system becomes, the more likely it is that the DJ will have a partner—another person to handle the "live" elements of the set (see figure 17.1).

CD 51

Live Sequencing

Another interesting twist in the conjoining of DJ and music producer is "live sequencing." This is the act of mixing sampled loops, pre-sequenced MIDI performances, and live playing all at the same time, on the fly, to create a continuous, DJ-like song set (see figure 17.2). Several manufacturers have implemented features in their products to enable live sequencing. Some of the most powerful live sequencing tools are software programs (such as *Live, Reason,* and *Logic*

FIGURE 17.1 Extended DJ Accompaniment System. One of the author's larger DJ accompaniment setups, featuring Korg's Karma workstation, Kaoss Pad 2, and Tascam's X-9 DJ mixer.

161

FIGURE 17.2 Live Sequencing. The author (left) and his partner (Maxwellhouse) playing live with a bevy of hardware and a laptop computer. (Photo by Wendy J. Wiencek)

Audio's Touch Tracks) that let you trigger complete sequences from MIDI notes. A few hardware units also sport similar features (such as the RPPR, short for Real-time Pattern Play/Recording, function of Korg's Triton and Karma workstations).

Working with a live-sequencing-capable application on a laptop can be an amazingly powerful and portable performance setup. For example, assign audio and virtual instrument tracks to a FireWire-based sound card's (such as the MOTU 828mkII) separate outputs, then connect these outputs to a DJ mixer for individual track cueing. (*Live* and *Reason* can both address multi-output sound cards.) Live sequencing with this type of system enables you to evolve remixes from a pool of individual loops and performances, constructing an extended mix from individual elements rather than fully arranged, pre-recorded songs.

It's easy to assume that there's a set formula to writing and remixing electronic music, but the simple fact is that when it comes to writing music, any type of music, there is no formula. There is no right or wrong way to get the job done, and different circumstances call for different methods. That's what makes this a creative process and not a mechanical one.

—Jason Blum, Deepsky

This Party Never Ends

Labels (such as Moonshine Records) are beginning to release DJ mix compilations in surround sound. It's only a matter of time before pioneering remixers begin producing remix's in surround sound. In fact, most of the top digital audio sequencers have extensive surround-sound capabilities, and a few even include impressive stock surround effect plug-ins (such as *Digital Performer's* Feedback Delay-Surround

Edition). Hook up a 5.1 surround sound speaker system to your multi-output sound card and you're ready to produce surround remixes. Someday, when dance clubs finally get serious about installing surround speaker systems, and DJ CD players and mixers feature surround sound connections, there will be many more speakers through which to swirl sound around the dance floor.

Until that time, and regardless of whether a remix is in stereo or surround, remixing has become a permanent part of the dance and electronic music movements. Whether you want to remix for fame and fortune, or simply as a pastime, remixing can be a rewarding enterprise. Reinterpreting a song, making it your own, and possibly sharing it with others who will appreciate your efforts is a lot of fun. As long as people want to dance, remixes will be an important tool for winning the hearts, minds, and feet of dance club patrons.

Today's dance-music movement is a powerhouse of creativity, and though it's hard to say exactly where the movement is headed, there's little doubt that the music it has produced will influence many forms of commercial music for years to come. The production techniques discussed in this book, when mastered, will help you in the production of many other forms of music. Whether you DJ, produce music in your bedroom or in a major recording studio, the technology to make great sounding remixes is available to almost everyone. Just keep in mind that learning an instrument and understanding basic music theory is equally as important as having a ton of cool studio gear, because these skills, combined with talent, is what can make a mediocre remixer a great remix producer.

Appendices

Appendix A

General MIDI (GM) Drum Note Assignments

A set of standard drum note assignments has been developed to facilitate the playback of General MIDI (GM) arrangements. In a GM song, the GM drum kit is always assigned to MIDI channel 10. Notes below note number 27, and above 88 are reserved for extended GM drum kits (such as GS and XG kits).

NOTE NUMBER	NOTE	DRUM SOUND
27	D#0	High Q
28	E 0	Slap
29	F 0	Scratch Push
30	F#0	Scratch Pull
31	G 0	Sticks
32	G#0	Square Click
33	A 0	Metronome-Click
34	A#0	Metronome Bell
35	B 0	Kick Drum 2
36	C 1	Kick Drum 1
37	C#1	Side Stick
38	D 1	Snare 1
39	D#1	Hand Clap
40	E 1	Snare 2
41	F 1	Low Tom 2
42	F#1	Closed Hi-Hat
43	G 1	Low Tom 1
44	G#1	Pedal Hi-Hat
45	A 1	Mid Tom 1
46	A#1	Open Hi-Hat
47	B 1	Mid Tom 1
48	C 2	High Tom 2
49	C#2	Crash 1
50	D 2	High Tom 1
51	D#2	Ride 1
52	E 2	Chinese Symbol
53	F 2	Ride Bell
54	F#2	Tambourine
55	G 2	Splash
56	G#2	Cowbell
57	A 2	Crash 2

NOTE NUMBER	NOTE	DRUM SOUND
58	A#2	Vibra Slap
59	B 2	Ride 2
60	C 3	Hi Bongo
61	C#3	Lo Bongo
62	D 3	Mute Conga
63	D#3	Hi Conga
64	E 3	Lo Conga
65	F 3	Hi Timbale
66	F#3	Lo Timbale
67	G 3	Hi Agogo
68	G#3	Lo Agogo
69	A 3	Cabasa
70	A#3	Maracas
71	B 3	Short Whistle
72	C 4	Long Whistle
73	C#4	Short Guiro
74	D 4	Long Guiro
75	D#4	Claves
76	E 4	Hi Wood Block
77	F 4	Lo Wood Block
78	F#4	Mute Cuica
79	G 4	Open Cuica
80	G#4	Mute Triangle
81	A 4	Open Triangle
82	A#4	Shaker
83	B 4	Jingle Bell
84	C 5	Bell Tree
85	C#5	Castanets
86	D 5	Mute Surdo
87	D#5	Open Surdo

Appendix B

MIDI Control Change Events

There are 128 (0–127) control change event numbers. Not all of the numbers have been assigned (these are listed below as "Not defined"), leaving manufacturers the ability to assign controls that are unique to their products to the unassigned numbers.

(A great example of a product that puts many of the unassigned numbers to good use is Propellerheads' Reason. The program's MIDI controller assignments are listed in the manual.)

NUMBER	CONTROLLER
0	Not defined
1	Modulation
2	Breath control
3	Not defined
4	Foot control
5	Portamento time
6	Data entry MSB
7	Volume
8	Balance
9	Not defined
10	Pan
11	Expression
12–15	Not defined
16	General purpose 1
17	General purpose 2
18	General purpose 3
19	General purpose 4
20–32	Not defined
33	Modulation LSB
34	Breath control LSB

NUMBER	CONTROLLER
35	Not defined
36	Foot control LSB
37	Portamento LSB
38	Data entry LSB
39	Main volume LSB
40	Balance LSB
41	Not defined
42	Pan LSB
43	Expression LSB
44–47	Not defined
48	General purpose 1 LSB
49	General purpose 2 LSB
50	General purpose 3 LSB
51	General purpose 4 LSB
52–63	Not defined
64	Damper pedal
65	Portamento pedal
66	Sostenuto
67	Soft pedal
68	Not defined
69	Hold 2

NUMBER	CONTROLLER
70–90	Not defined
91	Effect depth
92	Tremelo depth
93	Chorus depth
94	Celeste depth
95	Phaser depth
96	Data increase
97	Data decrease
98	Non regulation LSB
99	Non regulation MSB
100	Regulation LSB
101	Regulation MSB
102–120	Not defined
121	Reset control
122	Local control
123	All notes off
124	Omni mode off
125	Omni mode on
126	Mono mode on
127	Poly mode on

Appendix C

Suggested Listening

There are many rare 12-inch singles that would be excellent to study, but they can be extremely difficult to locate because they were limited vinyl pressings. Rather than frustrate you with a roster of impossible-to-find tracks, the list below includes only CD releases that you should be able to procure through most mainstream music stores.

"Blue Skies" (Tori Amos); *Ten Years in the Life*; BT, Rhino Records (September 10, 2002).

"Dooms Night" (Azzido Da Bass); *Music for the Maases*, Timo Maas, Kinetic records (October 3, 2000).

Fatboy's Slim's Greatest Remixes; Fatboy Slim, Brooklyn Music Limited (April 17, 2001).

"Girlfriend" (Neptunes Remix); *Gone Clubbin*, Import CD Single; N'Sync, Jive Internatiional (July 15, 2002).

"Heaven"; *Heaven*, DJ Sammy, Robbins (August 6, 2002).

"Hip Hop Phenomenon"; *R&R*; BT, Nettwerk Records (October 23, 2001).

In Silico; Deepsky, Kinetic Records (February 5, 2002).

Loud; Timo Maas, Kinetic Records (March 19, 2002).

J to tha L-O! The Remixes; Jennifer Lopez, Sony (February 5, 2002).

"Pop" (Produced by BT); Import CD single containing remixes by Pablo La Rosa and Deep Dish; N'Sync, BMG International (July 17, 2001).

"Rockafeller Skank"; *You've Come a Long Way, Baby*; Fatboy Slim, Astralworks/EMD (October 20, 1998).

"Sunset (Bird of Prey)" (The Doors, Jim Morrison); *Halfway Between the Gutter and the Stars*, Fatboy Slim, Astralworks/EMD (November 7, 2000).

"Tears From The Moon" (Conjure One); *Nyana*; DJ Tiësto, Nettwerk Records (May 6, 2003).

Touching Down; Roni Size, Full Cycle (November 5, 2002).

Thunderpuss, Thunderpuss, Tommy Boy (March 19, 2002).

Appendix D

Contributor Web Sites

Artemis	http://www.artemis.fm
BT	http://www.btmusic.com
Dave Audé	http://www.daveaude.com
Deepsky	http://www.deepsky.net
DJ Irene	http://www.djirene.net
Joe Solo	http://www.joesolo.com
Lygia Ferra	http://www.lygiaferra.com
Pablo La Rosa	http://www.djpablolarosa.com
Robbie Rivera	http://www.robbierivera.com
Sakai (Family Tree Productions)	http://www.familytreeproductions.com
Thunderpuss	http://www.thunderpuss.com

Appendix E
Manufacturer Web Sites

A

Ableton
http://www.ableton.com

Access
http://www.access-music.de

Advanced Micro Devices (AMD)
http://www.amd.com

Akai
http://www.akaipro.com

Alesis Studio Electronics Inc.
http://www.alesis.com

American DJ
http://www.americandj.com

AMG
http://www.amguk.co.uk

Antares Audio technologies
http://www.antarestech.com

Apple Computer Inc.
http://www.apple.com

AudioEase
http://www.audioease.com

Auralex Acoustics
http://www.auralex.com

B

Baltic Latvian Universal Electronics
(BLUE)
http://bluemic.com

BeatBoy
http://www.beatboy.com

BIAS Inc.
(Berkley Integrated Audio Software Inc.)
http://www.bias-inc.com

BitHeadz Inc.
http://www.bitheadz.com

Blue Chip
(Distributed by Music Industries Corp.)
http://www.musicindustries.com

Bomb Factory
http://www.bombfactory.com

C

CAD Professional Microphones
http://www.cadmics.com

Cakewalk
http://www.cakewalk.com

Carilon Audio Systems
http://www.carilonusa.com

CM Automation
http://cmautomation.com

Cycling '74
http://www.cycling74.com

D

Denon
http://www.denon.com

Digidesign
http://www.digidesign.com

Doepfer Musikelektronik
http://www.doepfer.de

Duy Research
http://www.duy.com

E

EastWest
http://www.soundsonline.com

Edirol Corporation North America
http://www.edirol.com

Emagic
http://www.emagic.de

E-MU/Ensoniq
http://www.emu-ensoniq.com

Event Electronics
http://www.event1.com

F

Focusrite Audio Engineering
(Distributed by Digidesign)
http://www.focusrite.com

Frontier Design Group
http://www.frontierdesign.com

Furman Sound Inc.
http://www.furmansound.com

FXpansion
http://www.fxpansion.com

G

Glyph Technologies Inc.
http://www.glyphtech.com

H

Hafler
http://www.hafler.com

HermanMiller
http://www.hermanmiller.com

I

IBM
http://www.ibm.com

IK Multimedia
http://www.ikmultimedia.com

Ilio
http://www.ilio.com

Ina-GRM
(*GRM-Tools TDM* distributed by Electronic Music Foundation)
(*GRM-Tools VST* distributed by Steinberg)
http://www.cdemusic.org/special/grm

J

J L Cooper Electronics
http://www.jlcooper.com

K

Keyfax Software
http://www.keyfax.com

Kid Nepro
http://www.kidnepro.com

Kind of Loud Technologies
http://www.kindofloud.com

Korg
http://www.korg.com

L

Line6
(*Amp Farm* TDM plug-in
distributed by Digidesign)
http://www.line6.com

La Cie
http://www.lacie.com

M

Mackie Designs, Inc.
http://www.mackie.com

Marathon Computer, Inc.
www.marathoncomputer.com

Microsoft
http://microsoft.com

Mixman http://www.mixman.com

M-Audio
http://www.m-audio.com

MindPrint
http://www.mindprint.com

MOTU
http://www.motu.com

N

Native Instruments
http://www.nativeinstruments.com

Numark
http://www.numark.com

O

Omnirax
http://www.omnirax.com

P

Pioneer
http://www.pioneerprodj.com

Propellerhead Software
http://www.propellerheads.se

R

Red Sound
http://www.redsound.com

Roland Corporation US
http://www.rolandus.com

S

Serato
http://www.serato.com

Smart Loops
http://www.smartloops.com

Sonic Foundry
http://www.sonicfoundry.com

Stanton Magnetics
http://www.stantonmagnetics.com

Steinberg North America
http://www.steinberg.net

Symantec
http://www.symantec.com

Symbolic Sound
http://www.symbolicsound.com

Synchro Arts
http://www.synchroarts.co.uk

T

TASCAM
http://www.tascam.com

TC Electronic
(Formerly known as, TC|Works)
http://www.tcworks.com

Technics (distributed by Panasonic)
http://www.panasonic.com/
consumer_electronics/technics_dj

W

Waves
http://www.waves.com

e Digital Systems

Wave Mechanics
http://www.wavemechanics.com

Wizoo
http://www.wizoo.com

Y

Yamaha Corporation of America
http://www.yamaha.com

About the Author

Erik Hawkins is a musician, producer, remixer, and author. His talents and technical expertise have earned him a reputation as a "tastemaker" among music industry leaders. More than one hundred of his articles have appeared in the industry's top publications, including *Remix, Mix, Electronic Musician, EQ,* and *Keyboard*. His first book, *Studio-in-a-Box* (published by ArtistPro, distributed by Hal Leonard) was a groundbreaking guide to assembling and effectively using computer-centered recording systems. For more remixing resources, tips on gear, and informative music industry articles, visit his personal Web site, www.erikhawkins.com.

Index

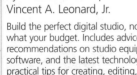